OCR GCSE History A Schools History Project

The American West, 1840–95

Allan Todd

www.heinemann.co.uk

✓ Free online support
✓ Useful weblinks
✓ 24 hour online ordering

01865 888080

Official Publisher Partnership

OCR AND HEINEMANN ARE WORKING TOGETHER TO PROVIDE BETTER SUPPORT FOR YOU

Heinemann is an imprint of Pearson Education Limited, a company incorporated in England and Wales, having its registered office at Edinburgh Gate, Harlow, Essex, CM20 2JE. Registered company number: 872828

www.heinemann.co.uk

Heinemann is a registered trademark of Pearson Education Limited

First published 2009

13 12 11 10 09
10 9 8 7 6 5 4 3 2 1

British Library Cataloguing in Publication Data
A catalogue record for this book is available from the British Library

ISBN 978 0 435 50143 3

Edited by Penny Rogers
Proofread by Carl Gillingham
Designed by Pearson Education Limited
Typeset by Wearset Limited, Boldon, Tyne and Wear
Produced by Wearset Limited, Boldon, Tyne and Wear
Original illustrations © Pearson Education Limited 2009
Illustrated by Wearset Limited, Boldon, Tyne and Wear
Cover design by Pearson Education Limited
Picture research by Q2AMedia
Cover photo/illustration © Getty Images/National Geographic
Printed in UK by Scotprint

Acknowledgements
The author and publisher would like to thank the following individuals and organisations for permission to reproduce copyright material:
Page 15 C University of Nebraska Press. Page 47 B University of Nebraska Press. Page 47 C University of Nebraska Press. Page 69 D By permission of Oxford University Press Inc. Page 97 A The New York Times.
The author and publisher would like to thank the following individuals and organisations for permission to reproduce photographs:
Page 3L Mary Evans Picture Library. Page 3TR Private Collection/The Bridgeman Art Library. Page 3BR Private Collection/Peter Newark American Pictures/The Bridgeman Art Library. Page 11L Private Collection/Peter Newark American Pictures/The Bridgeman Art Library. Page 11R Mary Evans Picture Library. Page 12 Private Collection/Peter Newark American Pictures/The Bridgeman Art Library. Page 13L Corbis. Page 13R National Anthropological Archives, Smithsonian Institution (GN00270b). Page 14 Bierstadt, Albert (1830–1902)/Private Collection/Photo © Christie's Images/The Bridgeman Art Library. Page 17 Mary Evans Picture Library. Page 18T Gift of William E. Weiss/Buffalo Bill Historical Center, Cody, Wyoming/23.62/The Art Archive. Page 18M Bibliotheque Nationale, Paris, France/Lauros/Giraudon/The Bridgeman Art Library. Page 18B Seth Eastman/Minnesota Historical Society Photograph Collection. Page 21 Seth Eastman/Minnesota Historical Society Photograph Collection. Page 23 Adrian J. Ebell/Minnesota Historical Society Photograph Collection. Page 25 Catlin, George (1794–1872)/Private Collection/Peter Newark American Pictures/The Bridgeman Art Library. Page 27 Private Collection/Photo © Christie's Images/The Bridgeman Art Library. Page 29 Mary Evans Picture Library/Photolibrary. Page 32 Photos 12/Alamy. Page 33TL Historical Standard/Corbis. Page 33TR Private Collection/Peter Newark Western Americana/The Bridgeman Art Library. Page 33B Private Collection/The Bridgeman Art Library. Page 37T Butler Institute of American Art, Youngstown, OH, USA/Gift of Joseph G. Butler III 1946/The Bridgeman Art Library. Page 37B American Photographer (19th century)/Private Collection/Peter Newark American Pictures/The Bridgeman Art Library. Page 39 Courtey Church History Library, Salt Lake City. Page 44 American School (19th century)/Private Collection/Peter Newark American Pictures/The Bridgeman Art Library. Page 45 Private Collection/Peter Newark Western Americana/The Bridgeman Art Library. Page 47 Bettmann/Corbis. Page 49 Library of Congress. Page 51 Private Collection/Peter Newark American Pictures/The Bridgeman Art Library. Page 52 Kansas Collection, University of Kansas Libraries. Page 53 Private Collection/Peter Newark American Pictures/The Bridgeman Art Library. Page 55T Historical Standard/Corbis. Page 55B Library of Congress. Page 59T Kansas Historical Society. Page 59B © Bettmann/Corbis. Page 61 John (fl.1872)/Private Collection/Photo © Christie's Images/The Bridgeman Art Library. Page 62 Denver Public Library; Western History Collection, F-29933. Page 64 Private Collection/The Bridgeman Art Library. Page 65T Private Collection/Peter Newark American Pictures/The Bridgeman Art Library. Page 65M Underwood & Underwood/Corbis. Page 65B Bettmann/Corbis. Page 67 North Wind Picture Archives/Alamy. Page 71 Used by permission of The Iliff School of Theology. Page 72 American School/The Bridgeman Art Library/Getty Images. Page 75 Bettmann/Corbis. Page 77 Bettmann/Corbis. Page 79 Private Collection/Peter Newark American Pictures/The Bridgeman Art Library. Page 83 University of Oregon Library. Page 85L Bettmann/Corbis. Page 85R Bettmann/Corbis. Page 87R Private Collection/Peter Newark American Pictures/The Bridgeman Art Library. Page 87L Private Collection/Peter Newark American Pictures/The Bridgeman Art Library. Page 88 Private Collection/Peter Newark American Pictures/The Bridgeman Art Library. Page 89 Private Collection/Peter Newark American Pictures/The Bridgeman Art Library. Page 91 Bettmann/Corbis. Page 95TL Avco Embassy/The Kobal Collection. Page 95BL Denver Public Library; Western History Collection, X-33615. Page 95TR Library of Congress. Page 95BR Nebraska State Historical Society. Page 97 Mary Evans Picture Library. Page 98 Charles Ferdinand (1829–63)/University of Michigan Museum of Art, USA/The Bridgeman Art Library. Page 101 Private Collection/Photo © Christie's Images/The Bridgeman Art Library. Page 103 Bettmann/Corbis. Page 105B Courtesey Colorado Historical Society (# 10025492). Page 105T Private Collection/Peter Newark American Pictures/The Bridgeman Art Library. Page 107T Bettmann/Corbis. Page 107B The Burton Historical Collection/Detroit Public Library. Page 109B Library of Congress. Page 109T Private Collection/Peter Newark Western Americana/The Bridgeman Art Library. Page 112 American Photographer (19th century)/Private Collection/Peter Newark American Pictures/The Bridgeman Art Library. Page 117T Gertrude Vanderbilt Whitney Trust Fund Purchase/Buffalo Bill Historical Center, Cody, Wyoming/48.61/The Art Archive. Page 117B Southwest Museum of the American Indian, Autry National Center of the American West, Los Angeles; 1026.G.1. Page 119 Private Collection/The Stapleton Collection/The Bridgeman Art Library. Page 122 Frenzeny, Paul (1840–1902)/Private Collection/Peter Newark American Pictures/The Bridgeman Art Library. Page 128 Private Collection/Peter Newark American Pictures/The Bridgeman Art Library. Page 131 Private Collection/© Look and Learn/The Bridgeman Art Library.

Every effort has been made to contact copyright holders of material reproduced in this book. Any omissions will be rectified in subsequent printings if notice is given to the publishers.

Websites
There are links to relevant websites in this book. In order to ensure that the links are up to date, that the links work, and that the sites are not inadvertently linked to sites that could be considered offensive, we have made the links available on the Heinemann website at www.heinemann.co.uk/hotlinks. When you access the site, the express code is 1433P

For Cyn – for her encouragement and support

Contents

Get ready for your Study in Depth: The American West, 1840–95

How this book can help

This book is designed to prepare you in two ways for your Depth Study of The American West, 1840–95:

1 It provides you with all the important information you will need in order to answer the questions you will face in the exam.
2 It explains the different types of questions you have to answer AND gives you tips and practice to help you improve your performance so that you can reach the highest levels.

Understanding the mark scheme

When you try to answer the questions in this book – and in your exam – it is useful to know how your teachers and examiners will mark your answers. There is a mark scheme for each question – the marks are divided into bands or levels, with each level representing a level of skill or understanding. The more marks available for the question, the more levels there will usually be. Some of the questions you will answer in this OCR A GCSE History exam have six levels. The examiner marking your answer has to decide which level it fits – the higher levels will be given to those answers that answer the question set AND display the specific skills needed for that question. So if the question is a Why? question which asks you to explain something (that is, give reasons why), it's no good just describing what happened and leaving it up to the examiner to pick out the bits that are relevant! In such a case, they will have to award a low level – no matter how plentiful and accurate the facts – as the answer would NOT be doing what the question has asked.

Four essential exam skills

One common misunderstanding among students taking GCSE History is that you need to know massive amounts of detailed information, dates, facts, and so on. This is NOT true! Remember – examiners don't award levels according to how much you write! Candidates who carefully read the questions, and so focus on what they are being asked to do, will often reach the top levels WITHOUT writing as much as candidates who misread the questions and/or just write down everything they know. Quality and relevance are what matter, not quantity. For instance, if asked to give reasons why something happened, a candidate who explains several reasons – with a few precise and relevant bits of own knowledge for each one – will score much more highly than a candidate who simply writes pages of accurate facts that just describe what happened.

To do well in History GCSE, you will need a combination of these four skills:

1 Sufficient knowledge to show the examiner that you have followed a course – and paid attention! – AND done some serious revision.
2 The ability to *use* the information you've remembered to answer the different types of questions you will be asked – such as those that ask you to *explain* something.

3 The ability to *select* from what you have remembered in order to address the specific question you are answering. Your answer needs to be relevant.
4 The ability to *understand* sources and *explain* what they do and do not tell us about a particular event or topic; how they are and are not useful; why they might have different views or attitudes; and how to add your own knowledge to what is and is not given by the source or sources.

This book will help you with all four of these skills and abilities – providing you with the necessary knowledge AND giving you practice with typical questions that will improve your exam technique. Every year, examiners mark papers of History students who show good knowledge but fail to use it effectively when answering the questions.

Top revision tips

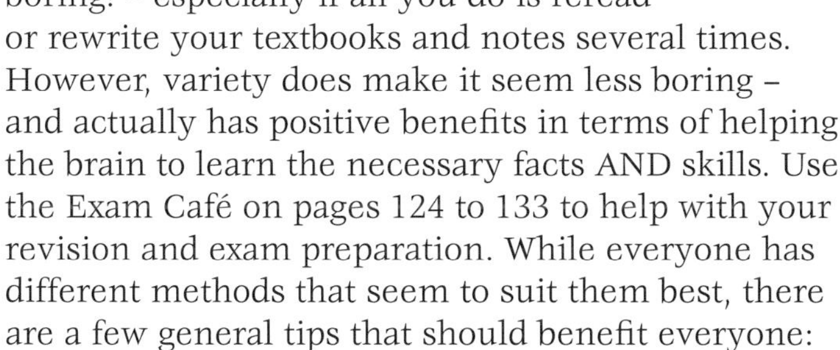

The final part of preparing yourself for this exam is, of course, revision. This IS boring! – especially if all you do is reread or rewrite your textbooks and notes several times. However, variety does make it seem less boring – and actually has positive benefits in terms of helping the brain to learn the necessary facts AND skills. Use the Exam Café on pages 124 to 133 to help with your revision and exam preparation. While everyone has different methods that seem to suit them best, there are a few general tips that should benefit everyone:

- Don't try to revise for hours at a time – after a bit, your brain will stop absorbing information, you will then start to panic AND you will get bored and dispirited. Instead, work for about 30 minutes, then have a short break of five to ten minutes, before you start again – this will give your brain time to absorb and process the information.
- Keep your brain well supplied with water and food – when you're thinking, your brain will need at least 70 per cent of everything your body takes in if it is to function well.
- Try highlighting or underlining key facts, dates, names and terms in your notes.
- Make use of spider diagrams and ideas maps – colourful visual displays (for example, on A3 paper) are often an easier way to learn.
- Try writing out key facts and terms on index cards that you can then glance at while standing in a queue, waiting for a bus/train or during your lunch hour.
- Try recording these brief notes and points – then you can listen to them while you are going from one place to another, cleaning your teeth, or just before you go to sleep.
- Work with a – conscientious! – friend, and test each other on the various topics.

Good luck!

GradeStudio

Helping you to write better answers

Throughout each chapter, you will find Grade Studio activities, which include practice questions to help you develop the skills necessary to answer the six different types of questions in the exam. Each Grade Studio activity is accompanied by Examiner's tips. In the Grade Studio at the end of each chapter, you will find an exam-style question. This explains the mark schemes the examiners have to apply to each type of question, and then gives you a typical sample answer with Examiner comments that include precise tips and advice on how the candidate could have pushed their answer into the top levels. You will then have the chance to produce your own – better! – answer.

By the time you have worked your way through this book, you will have had plenty of practice at all the different types of questions you will meet – and plenty of tips and advice to make sure that when you meet them in the exam, you will know exactly how to answer them in ways that will get you full marks.

Chapter 1

How did the Plains' Indians live on the Great Plains?

This chapter focuses on the lives and beliefs of the **Native Americans** – or American Indians – who were living on the Great Plains of the USA during the 19th century. These Native Americans are usually referred to as the 'Plains' Indians'. Today, many Native Americans still live and work on **reservations**. These are mostly situated on the old tribal lands, and vary considerably in size – some are very small, while about ten have over 400,000 hectares each. Source A shows the reservations belonging to the Sioux in the mid-1990s.

GETTING STARTED

What do you know about the Plains' Indians? In groups of four, take a blank piece of paper and write down:

- the names of all the American Indian 'tribes' familiar to you – for instance, those you may have seen in 'western' films about the 'Wild West'
- the names of any famous American Indian chiefs or war leaders.

At the end of five minutes, share these with the rest of the class to see which names occur most frequently.

SOURCE A

Native Sioux reservations in the USA.

In 1924, US citizenship was extended to all Native Americans, but serious problems of poverty remained, as the land on many reservations was poor. During the 1960s, some Native Americans began to campaign for better treatment. As a result, acts passed by US federal governments in 1975, 1978 and 1990 gave compensation, and new rights and powers of self-government, to these reservations.

Many Native Americans live off-reservation, and are successfully employed in various occupations, while on the reservations, some tribes have had success in industries such as timber, stock-raising and organised gambling. But many problems still remain.

There are many myths about the Plains' Indians and how they lived on the Great Plains. Sources B, C and D are common examples of the ways in which many people view the Plains' Indians. This chapter will try to separate myth from reality.

KEY WORDS

Native Americans – *the modern term for American Indians who lived – and still live – in North America. The Native Americans were usually referred to by early Europeans settlers as 'Indians' or 'Red Indians' – this is because Columbus thought he had landed in the Indies in 1492 when, in fact, it was the Americas.*

Reservations – *areas of land set aside for Native Americans by the US government. In the 19th century, US governments tried to force Indians to live on these areas, which were much smaller than their traditional hunting grounds on the Great Plains.*

Scalp – *the hair and skin, removed from the head of the dead or dying enemy, as a trophy of war/indication of bravery in warfare. Both Native Americans and Europeans engaged in this practice.*

SOURCE B

An engraving from 1892, showing an Indian **scalping** a dead US cavalryman.

HISTORY DETECTIVE

Find out more about the Plains' Indians by visiting www.heinemann.co.uk/hotlinks and enter the code 1433P, or try to watch films such as *Dances with Wolves* or *Little Big Man*; also useful, but violent, is *Soldier Blue.*

SOURCE C

A sketch showing Comanche Indians attacking a wagon train.

SOURCE D

A painting by Baldwin Mollhausen showing a Kiowa village.

1.1 How did the US expand in the early nineteenth century?

LEARNING OBJECTIVES

In this lesson you will:

- find out how the USA expanded its territory between 1783 and 1840
- learn how to understand a source and get information from it.

Fact file

The first Europeans to settle in what they called the 'New World' were Spanish; later came the French, the Dutch and the English.

The birth of the USA

The first European settlements in what eventually became the United States of America (USA) were on the eastern coast. As the white European populations there increased because of immigration, conflicts developed with the Native Americans who were already living in the area.

During the 17th and 18th centuries, lands were taken by force from the various Native American **nations and tribes**. Many were deliberately infected with European diseases to which the Indians had no resistance.

As a result, many nations (such as the Huron, Mohawk, Mohican and Delaware) were greatly reduced in numbers, or were even wiped out completely. The Europeans then formed new states in these areas. During the 18th century, Britain came to control most of North America.

In 1775, 13 east-coast states began a war of independence against British rule. In 1783, the states won the war, and then formed the new republic of the USA.

The boundary of the new USA to the west in 1783 was the Appalachian Mountains, but from 1783, this new country wanted to expand further westwards, from the Atlantic in the east to the Pacific in the west. This brought further clashes and conflict with Native Americans – first, in the region between the Appalachian Mountains and the land to the east of the Mississippi River.

KEY WORDS

Congress – *the governing and law-making body of the USA.*

Nations and tribes – *American Indians lived in bands and tribes, which were subdivisions of separate 'nations' with their own, often quite different, languages, beliefs, customs and ways of life. In the east of America, they included the Hurons, the Mohicans and the Iroquois.*

US expansion in the early 19th century

By 1800, the USA had expanded westwards as far as the Mississippi River. Then, over the next 50 years, the size of the USA increased even further as the result of various purchases, wars and deals.

There were two main expansions in the early 1800s:

- In 1803, the USA bought the area known as Louisiana from France, for $15 million – this stretched west from the Mississippi River as far as the Rocky Mountains, and was known as the Great Plains. Many Europeans were keen to explore the new region, and the US government also wanted it explored. So, in 1804, US President Thomas Jefferson employed Meriwether Lewis and William Clark to carry out a survey.
- In 1819, the USA bought Florida from Spain. As a result, the USA now owned all of the land east of the Mississippi as well.

The pressure was now on to move even further west.

Conflict with Native Americans

The expansion of the USA from 1803 to 1819 led to increasing conflicts with the Native American tribes who had lived in these areas for many centuries.

Several treaties were made – and broken. Many Indians moved – or were forced to move – west beyond the Mississippi.

For instance, when gold was discovered in the Appalachian Mountains in 1838 – in what had been declared by the US government in 1830 to be 'Indian country' – members of the Cherokee nation were rounded up by the US army and forced west during the winter, on what became known as their 'Trail of Tears'. One in four Cherokees died on that journey.

This was despite the fact that, in 1 834, the US **Congress** itself had approved the 1830 decision on what was to be 'Indian country'.

Eventually, by 1840, tensions became focused on the Great Plains in the West, beyond the Mississippi River.

SOURCE A

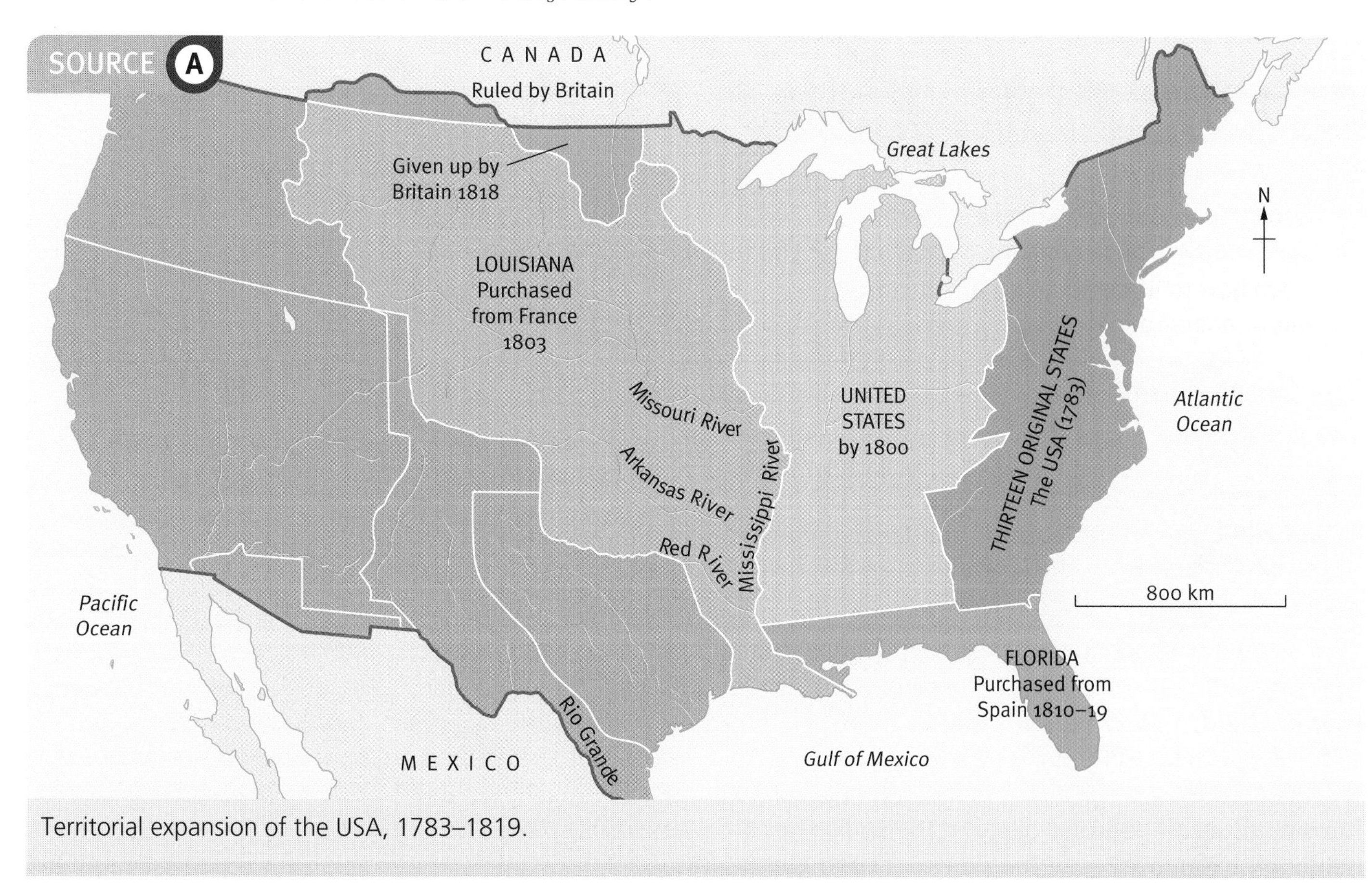

Territorial expansion of the USA, 1783–1819.

GradeStudio

Analysis of sources

Study Source A. What does this source tell you about the *nature* of US expansion westwards in the period before 1840? Use the source and your knowledge to explain your answer.

Examiner's tip

- As well as extracting the relevant information from a source, try also to comment – using the information/ knowledge you have picked up from this lesson – on what the source does NOT tell you.
- Try to make a general comment about the source, or make an informed/sensible inference about it from the information provided by the source.

1.2 Why were the Great Plains seen as 'The Great American Desert'?

LEARNING OBJECTIVES

In this lesson you will:

- find out about the Great Plains
- get practice in answering questions that ask you to assess the usefulness of a source.

KEY WORDS

Great American Desert – *this was what many whites at first called the Great Plains – its hot summers, cold winters and lack of water and trees made them think it was worthless, so they were prepared to let the Plains Indians keep the land.*

Manifest Destiny – *after 1845 used to justify what came to be seen as the USA's 'God-given mission' to settle and control all lands in the west, including those that had previously been promised to the Native Americans.*

Permanent Indian Frontier (PIF) – *the frontier between the USA and American Indian lands, agreed by the US government with Indian chiefs: all land west of the Mississippi River was to be given to the Indians. This was to be 'permanent', and the government said that non-Indians would not be allowed to settle there.*

West of the 95th meridian – *the PIF was later moved west, along the 95th meridian, the line of longitude running north–south.*

The Great Plains

The Great Plains are in the centre of North America – they were once a vast expanse of grasslands, often known as the Prairies. They extend from the Canadian border in the north to the Mexican border in the south, and from the Mississippi in the east to the Rocky Mountains in the west.

The eastern part is known as the Low Plains. It is flat, with long prairie grass. The western part rises towards the Rocky Mountains and is known as the High Plains – the grass here is short.

As Source B shows, the Great Plains are crossed by a number of rivers; despite this, the Plains further south are even drier than the Low and High Plains, and more desert-like.

The weather on the Great Plains is often severe, and makes farming there difficult, even today. There are rain shadows near the Appalachian Mountains in the east and the Rocky Mountains in the west. Many parts of the Great Plains experience drought in the summers, and heavy snow, blizzards and extremely low temperatures in the winters. Strong, drying winds are a feature all year round.

In 1840, this was a region of gentle grassland and slow-flowing rivers – some of the river valleys were wooded. Despite these problems, a wide range of animals and birds lived there, including rabbits, deer, antelope and huge herds of buffalo or bison.

SOURCE A

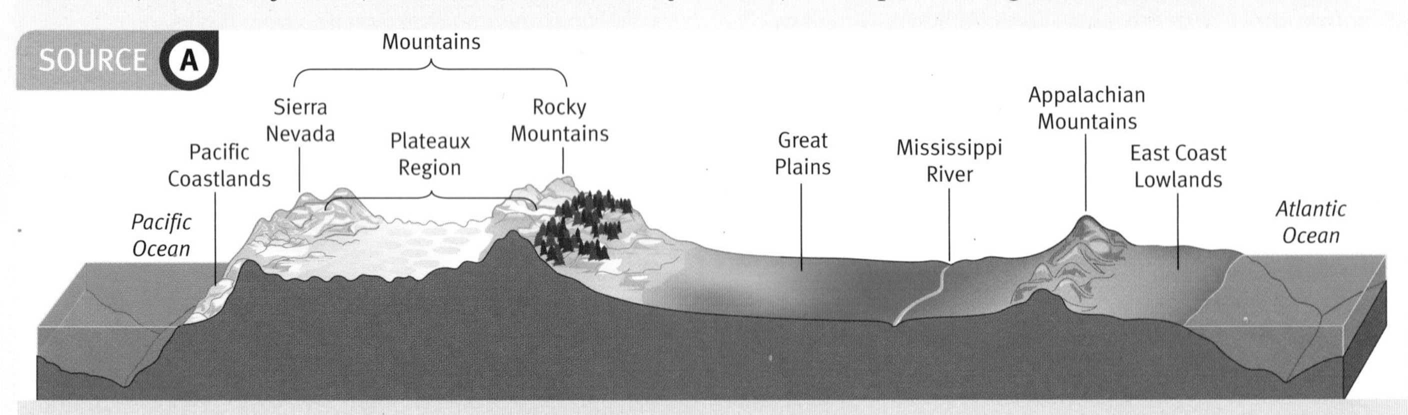

The main physical features of the USA, and the location of the Great Plains.

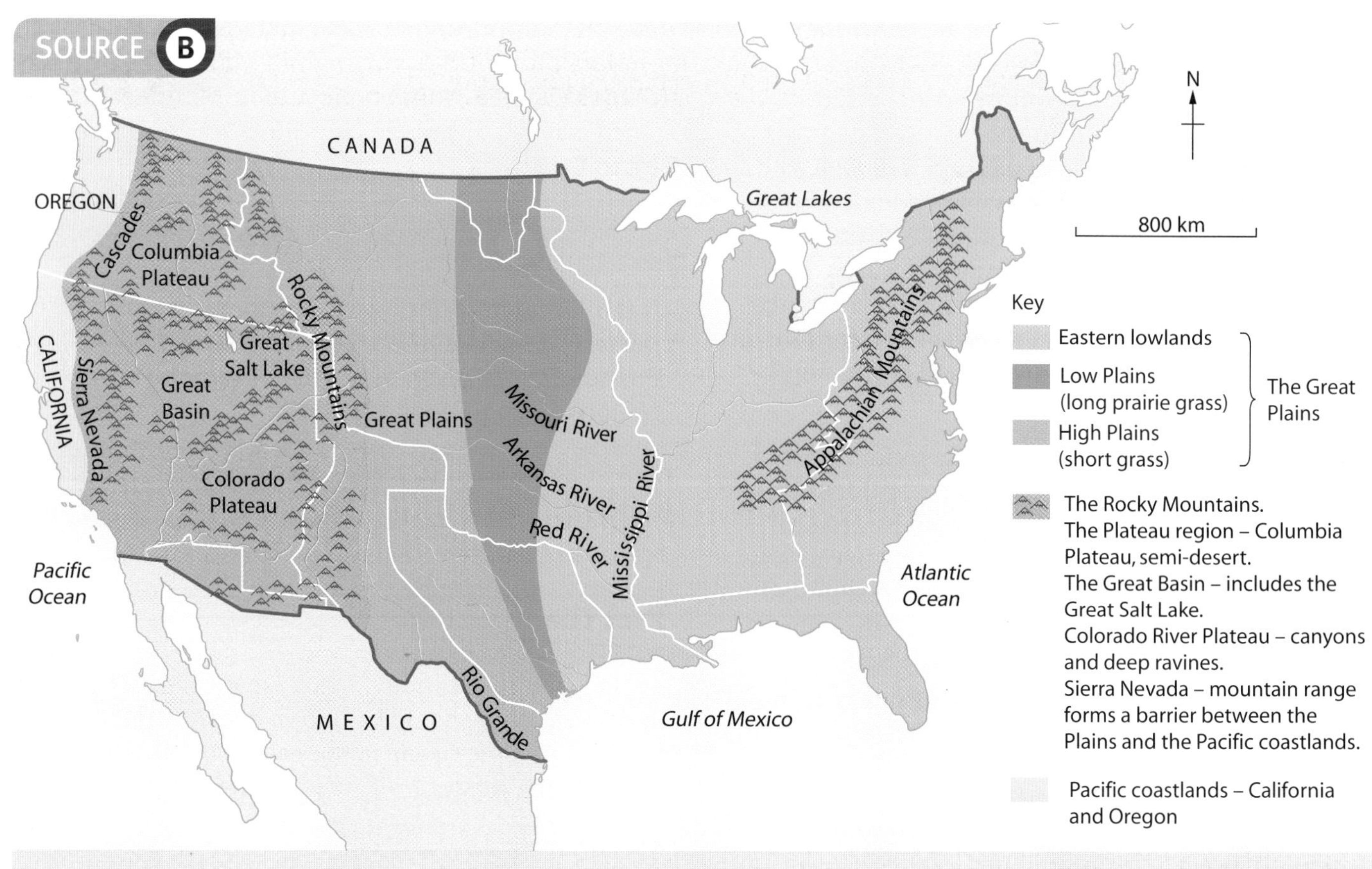

Geographical regions of the USA, and position of the Great Plains.

The 'Great American Desert'

At first, the early US expeditions west of the Mississippi reported that most of the Great Plains was a 'vast inhospitable wilderness'. In fact, it was often called the '**Great American Desert**' – not just by explorers, but even in 19th-century American school textbooks. As such, it was seen as a mostly barren land with an extremely hostile climate which was unsuitable for farming and therefore useless (see Source C).

US expansion, 1840–53

In 1830, the US government had agreed that all land west of the Mississippi would be 'Indian country', with no white persons allowed to settle there. In 1834, this was ratified by the US Congress. The US government agreed to a new **Permanent Indian Frontier (PIF)** – all this largely unwanted land west of the Mississippi could be kept by the Indians who lived on it.

However, shortly afterwards, the US federal government persuaded the Plains' Indians' leaders to agree to move the Permanent Indian Frontier further west, beyond the Mississippi River.

Now all land **west of the 95th meridian** would be 'Indian Territory'. A series of forts was set up running south from Fort Snelling on the Mississippi River, to prevent unauthorised whites from crossing this new PIF.

In 1846, however, the US army crossed this land on its way to fight the Mexicans; then, in 1848, gold was discovered in California.

SOURCE C

In regard to this extensive section of country, I do not hesitate in giving the opinion, that it is almost wholly unfit for cultivation, and of course uninhabitable by a people depending upon agriculture for their subsistence. Large areas of fertile ground are occasionally to be found, but the scarcity of wood and water will prove an insuperable [impossible] obstacle in the way of settling in the West.

A description of the Great Plains, by Major S. Long, 1819–20.

During the 1840s and 1850s, the US government gained other territories – Texas in 1845, and Oregon from Britain in 1846. Many more were added following Mexico's defeat in the US–Mexican war of 1846–48. By the Treaty of Guadalupe Hidalgo, the USA got California, present-day New Mexico, Nevada, Utah and areas of Colorado, Arizona and Wyoming in exchange for $15 million. Later, in 1853, Southern Arizona and southern New Mexico were bought from Mexico at a cost of $10 million. This meant that the USA now owned all the land west of the Mississippi.

Much of this new land, which lay beyond the Great Plains, was more desirable, as it had a milder climate and more fertile soil – this was especially true of California and Oregon. Some Americans began now to talk of the USA's **Manifest Destiny** to settle all the land west of the Mississippi, and 'civilise' the Native Americans who lived there (see Source E). The idea of Manifest Destiny was based on the belief that white Americans had a 'God-given natural right' to expand westwards, and to use the new lands as they saw fit. This was seen as sufficient justification for forcing Native Americans off their traditional lands, so that the 'superior' white civilisation could advance, 'improve' the land, and spread Christianity.

However, many Americans – including several members of the US government – did not at first support this idea. Some believers in Manifest Destiny saw such people as traitors to the US, and even to God.

SOURCE E

It is our manifest destiny to overspread and to possess the whole of the continent which Providence has given us for the development of the great experiment of liberty.

Extract from an article by John L. O'Sullivan, editor of the *Morning Post*, 1845.

Fact file

By the early 19th century, many Americans had come to believe there should be one vast USA, stretching from the Atlantic Ocean in the east to the Pacific Ocean in the west.

SOURCE D

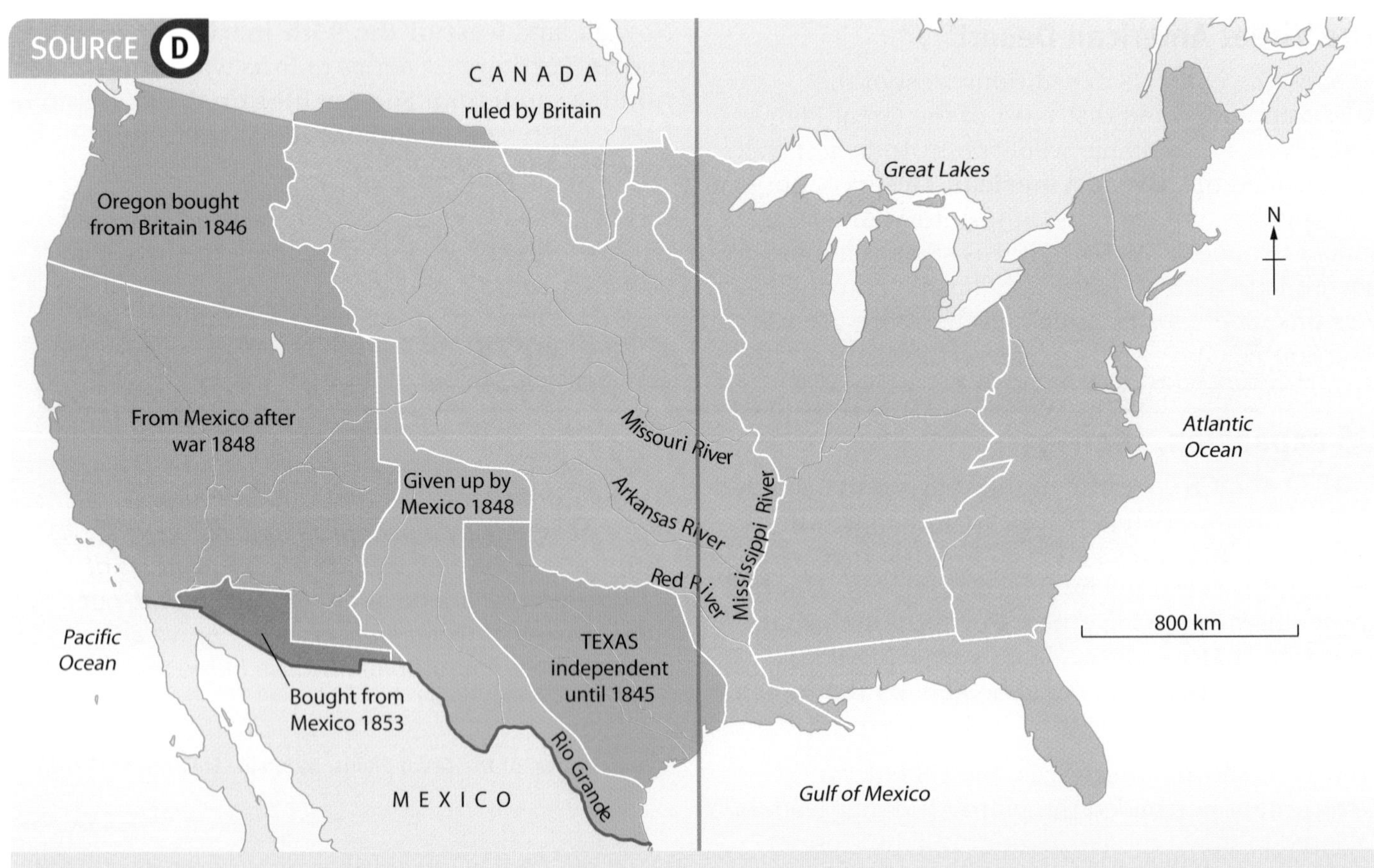

How the USA expanded, 1845–53 (the 95th meridian is shown as an orange vertical line).

Fact file

The lands west of the Rocky Mountains and the Sierra Nevada, on the Pacific coastlands, are much more fertile and have a gentler climate. Soon after these had been obtained by the USA by war and purchase, many white Americans were attracted by the idea of a better future in these new lands – but to get there, they had to cross the Great Plains.

ACTIVITIES

Copy and complete the table using Source B and pages 4–8.

Expansion of USA 1783–1853		
Date	**Territory**	**Method**

GradeStudio

Analysis of sources

Study Source E

Why was the 'Permanent Indian Frontier' breached after 1840?

Use the source and your own knowledge to explain your answer. **[7 marks]**

Examiner's tip

- As well as extracting the relevant information from a source, try also to comment – using the information/knowledge you have picked up in the lesson – on what the source does not tell you.
- Make sure you do more than just describe what the source shows – describing is NOT the same as explaining.

Simplified mark scheme

Using your own knowledge to explain usefulness of this source or using your own knowledge to explain other reasons.

Level	Skill	Mark
Level 1	Vague or general answer/identifies reasons	1
Level 3	Identifies reasons in the source OR gives other reasons from own knowledge, but doesn't explain them	2
Level 4	Explains one reason from the source or from own knowledge	5–6
Level 5	Explains one reason from the source and one reason from own knowledge	7

VOICE YOUR OPINION!

Manifest Destiny – do you think a 'more advanced' society or culture has the right to impose its way of life on 'less advanced' ones?

1.3 How were the Plains' Indians able to live on the Great Plains?

LEARNING OBJECTIVES

In this lesson you will:

- find out which were the main groups of Plains' Indians
- get practice in extracting information from sources.

KEY WORDS

Refugees – *people fleeing/escaping from areas of bad/violent situations to new areas, in search of safety/peace.*

Who were the Plains' Indians?

By 1840, the Great Plains was the main area left to Native Americans in North America. It was home to the Plains' Indians, who were mostly hunter-gatherers. Many of them had originally lived in areas in the east, but a combination of 'push' and 'pull' factors had led many of them to move west during the early 18th century. The 'push' factors were associated with growing pressures from and problems with the increasing numbers of European settlers, while the 'pull' factors included the large numbers of bison on the Great Plains, and the availability of horses, which made hunting easier.

Their way of life developed quite differently from that of the Native American nations who continued to live in other areas, such as in the eastern or south-eastern parts of the USA. For instance, the Cherokee nation, who before 1838 had lived in the fertile woodland areas of the east, had been farmers who grew maize, beans and squashes.

Those who lived on the Great Plains had heard how white Americans had taken lands from the American Indians living in the east – many had accepted **refugees** (rather like asylum seekers), such as the Cherokees, when they were forcibly removed from their lands in 1838. The stories they heard made many of these Plains' Indians determined to resist any white settlements on their traditional hunting lands. But, during 1836–40, over 17,000 Plains' Indians had died in a smallpox epidemic which had been spread by white traders; a cholera epidemic in 1849 killed thousands more. These epidemics weakened many of the nations of the Plains' Indians.

SOURCE A

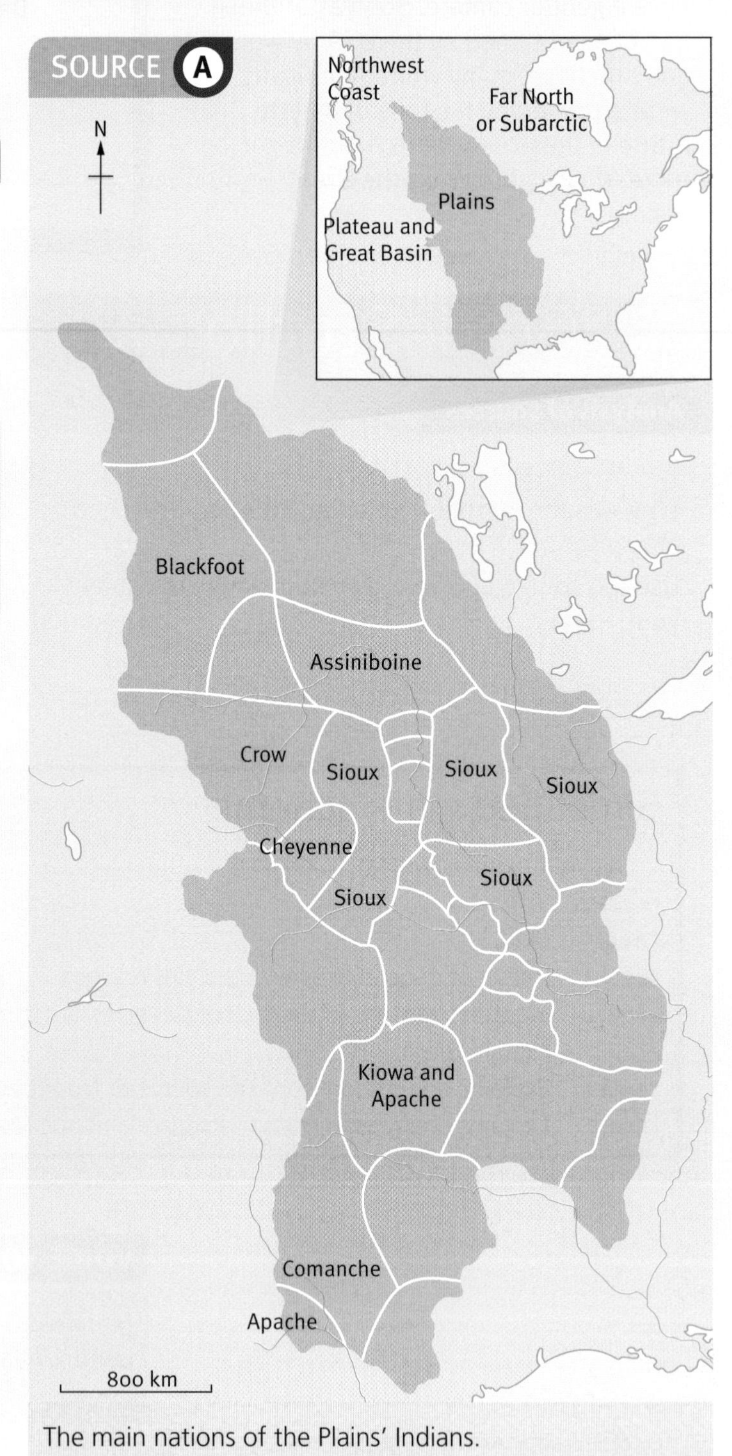

The main nations of the Plains' Indians.

SOURCE B

A Crow Chief on Horseback, a painting by George Catlin.

The nations of the Plains' Indians

There were as many as 30 different nations of Plains' Indians. Although they were often organised in a similar way and had many things in common, there were also many differences. Each of the different nations spoke a different language. While, within each nation, different tribes had different dialects. For instance, the Sioux spoke Siouan, but the three tribes or divisions – Lakota, Nakota and Dakota – spoke their own versions of it.

Each nation had its own history, customs, myths and religious beliefs; and members of the different nations could be identified by the different clothing and decorations they wore.

The five most important nations of the Great Plains were the Sioux, the Cheyenne, the Comanche, the Crow and the Apache. Also important were the Kiowa and the Arapaho. The largest and most powerful of these nations were the Sioux, the Cheyenne and the Comanche.

By 1840, the Crow, dominated the northern Great Plains, the Sioux and Cheyenne the central Plains, and the Comanche, Kiowa, Arapaho and Apache the southern Plains (see Source A). However, there were no clearly marked divisions between their traditional hunting grounds.

Political organisation and alliances

In order to survive on the Great Plains, the members of an Indian band had to cooperate with each other as closely as possible. At times, this was also important for the larger tribes and even the nation. Hence they needed an organisation that would allow this to happen.

Each of the nations of the Plains' Indians was usually divided into many different tribes – each tribe being made up of several bands, which consisted of different families, containing between 100 and 500 people. Each band had a chief and a council of elders, but all important decisions – such as going to war – had to be agreed by all the men.

The Sioux

The Sioux nation was itself divided into three main groups: the Lakota in the west, the Nakota in the centre and the Dakota in the east. Each of these three groups was divided into smaller tribes – for instance, the Lakota Sioux were made up of the Brule, the Hunkpapa, the Oglala, the Blackfeet, the Minneconjou and the Sans Arc tribes (see Source E on page 13).

The Sioux nation's organisation and decision-making were broadly similar to that of other Plains' Indians. For instance, though each band had a chief, these were neither elected nor did they inherit the role from their fathers.

SOURCE C

Comanche Meeting the Dragoons, a painting by George Catlin, 1834–35.

Fact file

The Sioux sub-groups were usually referred to by names given to them by white Americans – Teton, Yankton and Santee; however, the Sioux called themselves the Lakota, the Nakota and the Dakota. The word 'Cheyenne' comes from a Sioux word, meaning 'people speaking language not understood'.

SOURCE D

Sioux Indians Moving Camp Using a Travois, a painting by Charles M. Russell, 1898.

BRAIN BOOST

Using this Lesson and Lesson 1.1, copy and complete the ideas map to show and describe the main American Indian nations in the east and west of the USA.

- American Indian Nations
  - West
    - Sioux
    - Apache
  - East
    - Cherokee
    - Mohawk

Instead, men became chiefs for a number of different reasons – their skill as hunters or warriors, their wisdom and knowledge, or their spiritual powers. Chiefs very often had limited powers, and did not retain the job for life; if they made decisions which many bands disliked, the bands often chose to follow other leaders. Also, chiefs could not order their bands or tribes to do something. Even after a council meeting where a decision was taken (for example to go to war or make peace), individual bands were allowed to follow their own course of action (see Source F).

Normally, the whole tribe or nation met only in the summer in a huge gathering. For the rest of the time, they operated in bands. This helped to ensure that large numbers of Indians were not all hunting the same herd of buffalo at the same time.

The Cheyenne

The Cheyenne called themselves 'the people' or 'the human beings'; they usually got on well with the Sioux, and were also often allied to the Arapaho. They were led by a council of 44 peace chiefs – these were older men chosen to serve for ten years, and were considered to be more important than the war chiefs. They tended to decide when and where to move camp, and the formation of alliances.

The Comanche

The Comanche were often described by white people as 'Lords of the South Plains' because of their excellent horse-riding skills and their great bravery in combat. They were often closely allied to the Kiowa and the Kiowa-Apache.

Several of these nations were often allies: for example, the Sioux, Cheyenne and Arapaho (in what was sometimes known as the 'Great Sioux

Fact file

George Catlin (1796–1872) was an artist who travelled widely among the Plains' Indians during the 1830s. He wanted to make a collection of paintings and drawings to record the life and culture of the Plains' Indians which he believed would soon disappear. In all, he produced over 600 pictures. He also wrote a book, *Manners, Customs and Conditions of the North American Indians*, published in 1841. His main studies were done among the Lakota, Crow and Blackfoot Indians – they seem to have trusted him, as he was allowed to observe their buffalo hunts and their religious ceremonies and rituals.

ACTIVITIES

1. Look carefully at Sources B, C and D. What *similarities* and what *differences* can you see between members of the three Plains' Indian nations?
2. Make a chart, titled 'The Plains' Indians', with the following headings: Area, Language, Clothing. Use the information from the sources and lesson 1.3 to complete the chart.

(Later in this book, you will be covering other aspects of the lives of the Plains' Indians which show further similarities and differences, so make sure you leave sufficient space to add extra information as you complete this course. *And make sure you don't lose this chart!*)

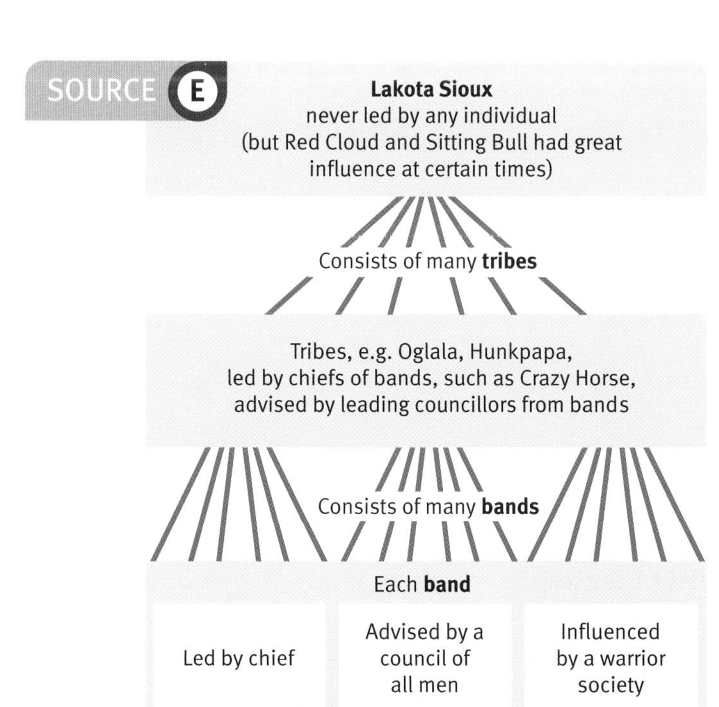

How the Lakota Sioux Nation was organised.

Alliance'), and the Comanche, Kiowa and Kiowa-Apache. However, many nations often had traditional enemies as well, such as the Sioux and the Crow who often fought each other. These divisions would make effective resistance to increased white American pressures on the Great Plains much harder to organise.

Punishment

The Plains' Indians did not have written laws to control their behaviour, but they did have long-established customs. Punishment for breaking these was not usually physical – because of the importance of cooperation in bands for survival on the Plains, public humiliation (for example, for boasting or cowardice, or for deserting a leader or band at a time of danger) was considered far worse, as it injured personal pride and status within the band. Murderers were very often forced to look after the family of their victim, or, at worst, expelled from the band.

Fact file

By 1840, there were about 30,000 Sioux living on the Great Plains, and probably 250,000 other Plains' Indians. The US population at the same time was more than 20 million.

SOURCE 

The chief has no control over the limbs, or liberty of his subjects, nor no other power whatever, excepting that of influence. [This] he gains by his virtues and his exploits in war. In fact, he is no more than a leader whom every young warrior may follow, or ... go back from ...

An extract from George Catlin's book of 1841, describing the government of the Plains' Indians.

HISTORY DETECTIVE

Using appropriate history textbooks or websites, see what you can find out about any three of the following Plains' Indian leaders or warriors:

- Sitting Bull (see Source G)
- Red Cloud
- Crazy Horse
- Dull Knife (see Source H)
- Cochise
- Geronimo
- Quanah Parker.

Display this information in a table, title it 'Plains' Indians' leaders' and use the following headings: Nation/Tribe, Dates, Main actions.

Sitting Bull, a Lakota Sioux leader, 1885.

Dull Knife, a Northern Cheyenne leader.

1.4 Land and hunting

LEARNING OBJECTIVES

In this lesson you will:

- find out about some of the Plains' Indians' beliefs about the land and hunting
- learn how to produce high-scoring answers to questions that ask you to use sources and your own knowledge – *in combination* – in order to explain an aspect of your course.

KEY WORDS

Dog Soldiers – *a special hunter/warrior society of the Cheyenne nation. Most native American nations had these special warrior societies.*

SOURCE A

Whoever crossed the Plains at that period, notwithstanding its herds of buffalo and flocks of antelope, its wild horses, deer and fleet rabbits, could hardly fail to be impressed with its vastness and silence and the appearance everywhere of an innocent primitive existence.

An extract from the *Autobiography of Worthington Whitteredge*, published in the *Brooklyn Museum Journal* in 1842.

The Plains' Indians did not see the Plains – as many Europeans did – as the 'Great American Desert'. Instead, they saw it as their home – the land and all the animals on the Plains were seen as a gift from their god or gods. As some early European travellers commented, a great variety of wildlife was to be found on the Plains (see Source A).

Although Source B was painted by a European, it shows what the Plains' Indians thought about the Plains – a vast, limitless landscape, in which animals and people were free to move as they wished. The idea of fences and restrictions on travel was alien to them, which was why, at first, European settlers were allowed to cross the Plains.

Attitudes to the land

Each Plains' Indian nation and tribe had its own complex culture and social structure. But, for the vast majority, hunting – especially of buffalo – was central to their way of life and existence, and they often had great respect for the environment, though some historians have questioned the extent of this.

The Plains' Indians did not believe areas of land could be owned by individuals or families. Instead, they believed that the tribal homelands belonged to the people as a whole – and to future generations. This attitude was very different from that held by many other people, who viewed land from an individual perspective. Most made little effort to understand the views of the Indians, and often dismissed their religious views about the land as primitive superstitions that could be ignored. This often led to conflicts, especially after 1840 as more and more white Americans began to cross and settle on the Plains. The Plains' Indians saw the land as part of the circle of nature, life and death, and often believed that the land not only belonged to all people, but also to the animals and plants too, and so should be respected (see Sources C, D, E and F).

Hunting

As hunting was vital for their survival, the Plains' Indians saw their hunting lands as vitally important – no one could buy, sell or fence it off. The Sioux, for instance, believed they were part of the land, and that such land could not be owned by anyone – not even

SOURCE B

Buffalo on the Plains, a painting by Albert Bierstadt.

by a whole nation. This was often closely connected to their religious beliefs (see Lesson 1.9, pp. 26–29).

To make sure the hunt was as successful as possible, it was organised and controlled by members of the tribe so that the herd was not frightened off before everyone was ready to start. For example, the Cheyenne had the **Dog Soldiers** who supervised the hunts and also helped to act as police to keep the peace in camps (see Source G).

Limits on the number of buffalo that could be killed were sometimes imposed so that the herds were not overhunted, although some historians have suggested that not all hunts were so carefully managed and often ended with some waste.

SOURCE C

We did not think of the great open plains, the beautiful rolling hills, and winding streams with tangled growth, as 'wild'... To us it was tame. Earth was bountiful and we were surrounded with the blessings of the Great Mystery.

An extract from Luther Standing Bear's *My People the Sioux*, published in 1975.

SOURCE D

The soil you see is not ordinary soil – it is the dust of the blood, the flesh, and the bones of our ancestors... The land, as it is, is my blood and my dead; it is holy.

The views of a Crow Indian.

SOURCE E

Our land is more valuable than your money. It will last forever. As long as the sun shines and the waters flow, this land will be here to give life to men and animals. We cannot sell the lives of men and animals. It was put here by the Great Spirit and we cannot sell it because it does not belong to us.

The view of Crowfoot, a Blackfoot Indian.

SOURCE F

The great chief [the US president] sends word that he wishes to buy our land... How can you buy or sell the sky, the warmth of the land? The idea is strange to us. If we do not own the freshness of the air and the sparkle of the water, how can you buy them?

Chief Seath's reply to the US president, 1854.

SOURCE

Whatever the power of the chief and the council there is another power to which both have to yield. This power is the hunters of the tribe, who form a sort of guild. Among the Cheyenne these men are called 'dog soldiers'. This 'guild' comprises the whole working force of the band... They supply the guards for the camp and choose the hunting parties. One of the most important functions of the dog soldiers is the protection of the game [animals to be hunted]. Except when laying in the supply of meat for winter, only enough buffalo are killed for the current needs of the camp.

An extract from *Hunting Grounds of the Great West*, by Colonel Richard I. Dodge, published in 1877.

ACTIVITIES

1. How do Sources A–F reflect the different reasons or factors that led to conflict between the Plains' Indians and white settlers over the land of the Great Plains after 1840?
2. Identify those sources in this lesson that share the same viewpoint about the plains being large and full of animals that could be hunted by the Plains' Indians.
3. Which source conflicts with the European settlers' view of the plains as 'wild' or a 'desert'?

GradeStudio

Examiner's tip

- Use the activities and sources in this lesson to practice answering A952 style questions.
- Before starting your answers, look carefully at the sources to see who produced them and when – if they came from people who were alive at the time and were in a position to know, then you should be able to use them in your answer. Also, if views from different 'viewpoints' are given, this could also add to their value.
- Try to link sources to different reasons or factors that relate to the outbreak of conflict.

  It is not necessary to refer to all the sources – but do make sure you refer to several. If you fail to use any sources, and just write an essay, you will not get high marks.

1.5 Case study: Why were horses and buffalo so important to the Plains' Indians?

LEARNING OBJECTIVES

In this case study you will:

- find out why the horse and the buffalo were so important to the Plains' Indians
- get practice in answering questions about the usefulness of a source.

KEY WORDS

Chips – *the dried dung of buffalo, which is then used as fuel, for cooking and heating.*

Nomadic – *a way of life which, instead of being settled in one place (like a farmer), is based on hunting and therefore the need to move so that herds of animals can be followed.*

Tipi – *(also known as tepees or lodges) – large conical tents made from 10 to 20 buffalo hides sewn together in a semicircular cover and spread over about 25 wooden lodge poles, depending on the size of tipi required.*

Travois – *a Native American transportation sledge, made from tipi poles and hides, used to carry goods/possessions from one camp to the next.*

The life of many Plains' Indians – the Lakota in particular – revolved around the hunting of buffalo (or bison) which provided them with almost all they needed. Although they hunted other creatures, such as antelope, elk, beaver and rabbit, their life centred on the buffalo and the horses they rode during the hunts.

Horses

Horses were first introduced into America by the Spanish invaders in the 16th century. After some Indians in Mexico had captured horses from the Spaniards in the mid-17th century, Indians had begun to breed and trade horses among themselves.

It was the possession of horses that had encouraged Indian nations such as the Sioux and the Cheyenne to move far into the Plains during the early 18th century. This allowed them to give up farming in the river valleys and woodlands bordering the eastern Plains, move away from the growing numbers of European settlers and instead rely on hunting on the Great Plains (see Source A).

SOURCE A

My grandmother told me that when she was young ... the people themselves had to walk. In those times they did not travel far nor often, but when they got horses, they could move more easily from place to place. Then they could kill more of the buffalo and other animals, and so they got more meat for food and gathered more skins for lodges and clothing.

An extract from an account by Iron Teeth, a Cheyenne woman.

The use of horses not only allowed the Plains' Indians to kill more buffalo, it also allowed them to travel longer distances. This led to a change in their way of life – from being fairly static hunters, food-gatherers and farmers, to being **nomadic** hunters on the Plains.

Horses were also important as they allowed the Plains' Indians to move camp easily and travel quickly from place to place in pursuit of the buffalo herds. The lodge poles of the **tipis** were tied together to form a sledge known as a **travois** – this carried all a family's belongings. In fact, horses became so important to their way of life that wealth and status was often counted in horses – the more horses a man possessed, the more important he was. For instance, giving horses to less well-off people earned extra status – it was also useful to give horses to more important people, and as part of a gift to secure marriage. The horse, for instance, allowed a man to have several wives (polygamy) – the more buffalo he killed, the more women were needed to prepare the skins and the meat (for more on the role of women, see Lesson 1.7 on pp. 22–23).

The buffalo hunt

The Plains' Indians did not farm the buffalo, they *hunted* them – normally, two or three hunts a year

SOURCE B

A painting by George Catlin, showing Sioux Indians wearing wolf skins, and approaching a buffalo herd.

were enough to feed, shelter and clothe a band. The buffalo was central to the way of life and culture of the Plains' Indians by 1840. At that time, there were about 60 million buffalo on the Great Plains. Forty years later, they were almost extinct, having been hunted for their hides and tongues by white Americans – in large part as a deliberate attempt to make it impossible for the Plains' Indians to continue their way of life.

The hunt itself was a communal activity, beginning with religious and magic rituals performed by shamans (or 'medicine men' – see Lesson 1.9, p. 26). This often took the form of a Buffalo Dance, which could last several days. Hunters would dress in buffalo skins and copy the movements of the animal. This was to ask for the help of the spirit world in the forthcoming hunt.

After the dancing, scouts would be sent out to find out where the buffalo herd was. Before the use of horses, the Plains' Indians would have to creep up as close as possible, and then try to kill them with their traditional hunting weapons, the lance and the bow and arrow. To do this, they would wear wolf skins, as buffalo herds allowed wolves to come quite close while they were grazing on the prairie grasses (see Source B). An alternative method was to stampede a buffalo herd, either to drive them over cliffs ('buffalo jumps') or to trap them in small valleys ('compounds'), where they could then be killed.

However, once horses were introduced, the main method was to stampede or surround the herd, force the buffalo into 'drive lanes', and then fire arrows at the running animals. The buffalo's poor eyesight gave the Indians an advantage, but such hunts were still dangerous because, in order to kill a buffalo with their traditional weapons, warriors had to get really close to the animals. Hunters could gain status and honour from the bravery or skill shown in a hunt (see Source C). To help divide the kill after a hunt, each hunter had their own personal and distinctive designs on their arrows.

SOURCE C

Then the head man went around picking out the best hunters with the fastest horses, and to these he said, 'Young warrior, your work I know is good; so today you will feed the helpless. You shall help the old and the young and whatever you kill shall be theirs.' This was great honour for young men.

Black Elk's account of the preparations for a buffalo hunt, taken from *Black Elk Speaks*.

Fact file

Black Elk was an Oglala Sioux, born in 1863, who later became a shaman for his tribe. He lived through the battle of the Little Big Horn in 1876, and survived the massacre of part of his tribe at Wounded Knee in 1890. He later wrote his memoirs, *Black Elk Speaks*.

SOURCE D

The Buffalo Hunt, painted by Frederick Remington, 1890.

Why was the buffalo so important?

The buffalo was so important to the Plains' Indians that it was seen as sacred (holy). Consequently, every part of the buffalo was used (for food, clothing, tipis, containers, tools, weapons, shields and religious ceremonies) – even their dung (**chips**) was burnt as fuel (see Source G).

SOURCE E

A Buffalo Hunt on the Plains, by George Catlin, 1840.

SOURCE F

A Dakota Hunting Buffalo on the Prairie near the Mouth of the Minnesota River, by Seth Eastman, 1846–48.

Fact file

By 1840, there were about 60 million buffalo on the Great Plains. Forty years later, they were almost extinct, having been hunted for their hides and tongues by white Americans, largely as a deliberate attempt to make it impossible for the Plains' Indians to continue their way of life.

SOURCE G

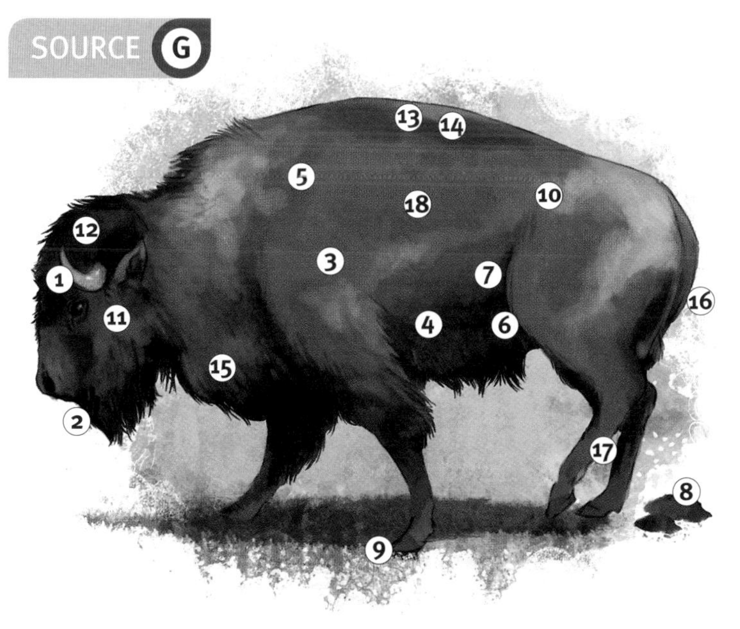

1 Horns – used for arrow straighteners and quill-flatteners; cups, spoons and ladles; fire-carriers and powder flasks; headress ornaments; toys.
2 Tongue – eaten raw as a delicacy; or used as a hairbrush.
3 Heart – eaten raw to help a hunter have the power and strength of the buffalo; or left on the ground to give new life to the herd which had just been hunted.
4 Fat – used for cooking; to make soap; used as hair grease.
5 Shoulder blades and Bones – used for arrowheads, knives, war clubs; needles, shovels and tools (e.g. hoes); saddle frames; sledge-runners; dice and game counters.
6 Bladder – used as food bags.
7 Intestines – used for cooking utensils and buckets.
8 Dung – used for fuel; or smoked by men in special religious ceremonies.
9 Hooves – used to make glue; tools; rattles.
10 Kidneys, Liver and Gall – the kidneys and liver were eaten raw as a delicacy; gall was used to make yellow paint.
11 Skull – decorated and used in religious ceremonies.
12 Brains – used to tan the hides.
13 Hide – used for bags, bedding, clothes (e.g. dresses, leggings, robes, moccasins, mittens); tipi covers; saddle covers; drums; pouches; and toys (e.g. dolls).
14 Rawhide – used for parfleches (bags for carrying belongings), sheaths, shields, snowshoes, horse harnesses, belts, containers, bags, masks, string and lashings for travois.
15 Fur – used as decoration on clothes, stuffing for saddles and pillow; to make rope and mittens.
16 Tail – used as fly swats, ornaments, and whips.
17 Sinews – used for bowstrings and thread.
18 Flesh – sometimes eaten raw, but usually cooked (boiled or roasted); or smoked, or dried (process known as 'jerking') in the sun and wind, and mixed with fat and wild berries and herbs to preserve it as pemmican. This could last for a long time, until another hunt was needed.

How the buffalo was important for the Plains' Indians.

BRAIN BOOST

Make an ideas map to summarise the different ways in which the buffalo was used by the Plains' Indians. Use the following four headings: Food, Clothing and shelter, Tools, and Warfare and religion.

Fact file

Many of the ancestors of the Plains' Indians had come from the east, where they had originally been farmers. They had been forced westwards by the expansion of the white settlers, and had had to become hunters.

ACTIVITIES

1 Make a chart or ideas map to show the ways in which horses were important, using the information and the sources you have just looked at.

Analysis of sources

Study Source D.

How useful is this source in helping us understand about buffalo hunts?

Use the source and your own knowledge to explain your answer.

Examiner's tip

- Remember – you have to do TWO things in source questions for the exam – extract points from the source AND use your own knowledge to explain what the source says/shows AND add extra information about other aspects not shown by the source.

1.6 What was family life like for the Plains' Indians?

LEARNING OBJECTIVES

In this lesson you will:

- find out about aspects of everyday life for the Plains' Indians
- get practice in answering questions that ask you to explain why different sources give different views.

KEY WORDS

Exposure – *the Native American practice/custom where elderly/infirm members of a band left their family and village to go off and die, so that they were not a hindrance/burden to the band or tribe.*

Monogamous – *marriage based on having just one husband/wife at a time.*

Family life was based on the fact that the Plains' Indians were nomadic hunters. This meant they spent most of the year travelling, hunting and camping with their band. Each band was made up of 10 to 50 families, many of whom were related to each other. As they moved frequently throughout the year in search of game, their homes had to be easy and quick to erect, dismantle and transport.

Tipis

Each family lived in tipis (see Sources A and B). The lodge poles were arranged in a circle, and the tipis of other families in the band's village were placed in a circle as well, as the circle was considered to have special spiritual properties. It was also an ideal shape to withstand the strong winds that swept the prairies of the Great Plains (see Source C).

In summer, the sides of the tipi could be rolled up to let in cooling breezes, in winter, the sides were banked up with earth to keep as much heat in as possible. Tipis were often decorated: for example, Sioux men would paint geometric patterns on them, or draw scenes from hunts or battles, and the Blackfeet usually had brightly coloured paintings of important animals and birds. However, the tipis of the Crows were usually undecorated. Also, scalps could be hung from the lodge poles, to indicate the skill and bravery of the warrior within.

The tipi could be taken down and packed ready for transport in about ten minutes. When dismantled, the lodge poles and coverings acted as a sledge known as a travois, on which the family's entire belongings could be carried; it was pulled by a horse – though it was often light enough to be pulled by hand or by dogs. Hence the tipi was ideally suited for people who depended on following the migrating herds of animals they hunted.

Marriage

Family life for most Plains' Indians was largely male-dominated. Most marriages were **monogamous** (one man, one wife), and in some Indian nations – such as the Cheyenne – they were usually arranged by the families concerned.

However, in most cases, marriages were love-matches. Often, in order to marry, a young man would have to impress the young woman and her parents with his ability to protect and provide for a wife and family. This would mean reciting poems and playing tunes on flutes; showing skill and bravery in hunting and warfare; and presenting gifts to the woman's parents – such as horses and buffalo skins. However, wives could not be bought, and a woman was free to decline the offer of marriage, even if her parents approved of the man.

In Plains' Indian nations, family descent was through the female line (matrilineal) so, when they married, men went to live with their wife's family. Divorce was also possible, with each partner declaring that the marriage was over – but, because of the matrilineal aspect of Indian society and culture, the woman kept the tipi.

Some tribes allowed a man to have more than one wife – usually to marry widows, so that they and their children were looked after, or in situations where there were more women than men. This was often the case, as hunting and especially warfare were dangerous activities.

Within the family, there were different roles for men and women (you will find out about women's roles in Lesson 1.7), and for children and old people.

The role of men

Men were expected to hunt, fight in wars to protect the band or hunting grounds, look after the horses, participate in decision-making, and some played important roles in religious ceremonies (you will find out more about religion in Lesson 1.9).

Children in society

Children were considered very important because they carried the future of their family and the band. They were corrected but not physically punished. They did not go to formal schools but were certainly taught the skills they would need to survive on the Great Plains, and play their role in the band. This was done mostly by their parents and relatives.

Boys often went on their first hunt at the age of 14. Girls were also taught to ride, but they did not spend as much time on this as the boys. Girls played with toy tipis and cradles and deerskin dolls, and learned how to perform household tasks (such as collecting wood, water, nuts, fruits and berries, and cooking), and especially the various tasks they would perform as women following the buffalo hunts – for example, in preparing the skins and preserving the meat.

Both boys and girls played with balls and hoops, and also often acted as unofficial lookouts as they played on the outskirts of their village – they could give warnings about the approach of strangers or unwelcome visitors.

The role of old people

Old people had an important role to play in the daily life of a Plains' Indians band. As 'story tellers', they passed on the history of the band, tribe or nation, and used their experience of life to give valuable advice when important decisions had to be made – for example, about preparing for a hunt, or whether to get involved in fighting. Old people were thus respected for their wisdom, and were cared for.

In return, however, they made sure they were not a burden on the tribe when they became too old or infirm to travel with the band. When this happened, they often stayed behind to face death on their own, or wandered off into the Plains to die – this practice or custom was known as '**exposure**'. For the Plains' Indians, as life by hunting was often precarious, the continued survival of the band was seen as of greater importance than that of an individual.

SOURCE A

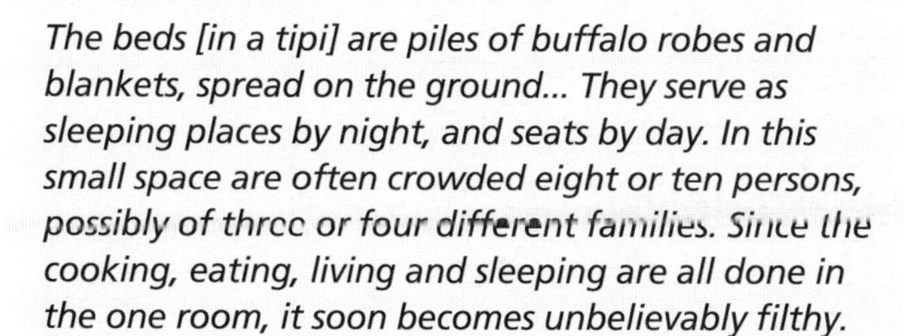
The beds [in a tipi] are piles of buffalo robes and blankets, spread on the ground... They serve as sleeping places by night, and seats by day. In this small space are often crowded eight or ten persons, possibly of three or four different families. Since the cooking, eating, living and sleeping are all done in the one room, it soon becomes unbelievably filthy.

An extract from Colonel Dodge's description of a tipi, from *Hunting Grounds of the Great West*, 1877.

SOURCE B

The white man builds big house, cost much money, like big cage, shut out sun, can never move. The Tipi is much better to live in: always clean, warm in winter, cool in summer, easy to move.

Remarks made by Flying Hawk, a Sioux chief; published in a history textbook in 1947.

SOURCE C

An engraving of a Dakota encampment with tipis, by Seth Eastman, 1852.

ACTIVITIES

Using the chart you compiled in Lesson 1.3 showing the similarities and differences between Plains' Indian nations, add with appropriate headings, what you have found out in this lesson.

1.7 What were the roles of women?

LEARNING OBJECTIVES

In this lesson you will:

- find out about the roles and position of women in Plains' Indian society
- get practice in expressing your opinion about a topic.

Among the main nations of the Plains' Indians, there were clearly defined roles for women, who generally took charge of all domestic matters and moving camp. Also, Plains' Indian women made most of the finished goods and owned them, including the tipi: this gave them some power. However, the position of women was not the same in all American Indian cultures.

Women's roles

As far as the Sioux and several other Plains' Indians were concerned, gender roles were not determined exclusively by biology or sexuality. As a result, there was some flexibility among the sexes in carrying out so-called 'women's' tasks. In other words, although gender roles and tasks were clearly marked, they were not closely tied to biological differences.

The four main areas to examine are work, domestic relations, decision-making and ritual/religious life.

Work

In Sioux society, there were clear differences between the roles of men and women. Women's tasks were essentially domestic, though sometimes very strenuous – gathering (and sometimes growing) food, water and fuel; keeping 'house'; the very important task of processing buffalo hides and meat; and bearing and caring for children.

It was women who prepared and then decorated the buffalo skins – this was highly skilled work which took months to complete. Women often formed themselves into societies, which gave them a higher status in the band. The Cheyenne women, for instance, had their 'Quiller Society' – named after the porcupine or bird quills used to paint the coloured dyes on to the buffalo skins.

The job of taking down the tipis was women's work. They also had to carry their babies when on the move and had to teach them from an early age to be quiet, in case they frightened a herd of buffalo, or gave away their presence to enemies.

Men were often away for long periods hunting, trading or fighting. However, when men and women were together, routine domestic chores were sometimes carried out together.

Because all work was essential to the family or band, marriage did not always mean women had a lesser position or were totally subject to their husbands – their work roles were seen as just as important as the men's. Women were judged for their skills at crafts and as homemakers, and especially as the bearers of children because these ensured the future of the family or band.

At times, women accompanied war parties as cooks and horse-holders, and there are even a few recorded cases of women warriors (see Sources A and B). When the men were away from the village, it was the role of women to defend it.

Domestic relations

Within marriage, although he usually had the last word on important decisions, it was wise for a man to listen seriously to his wife's views. As both boys and girls were taught to be polite, generous and cooperative, relations between husbands and wives were usually friendly.

Decision-making

When it came to public political decisions, such as going to war, making peace or moving camp, women were unequal to men, and could exert influence only through their husbands, their personal status or by gossip. Women had no official status as band or tribe decision-makers (see Source C).

Ritual/religious life

Once again, in the areas of rituals and religion, there was inequality between men and women. While some women could be 'dreamers' or have other ceremonial roles, in many nations they did not usually have leading roles in these. For instance, they could not participate directly in the major annual ritual of the Sun Dance (see Lesson 1.9 on pp. 26–29).

Some historians think the move to nomadic hunting on the Great Plains resulted in a worsening of the position of Indian women. They argue that the differences came as the result of changes brought about by the introduction of horses, nomadic hunting and Plains warfare by the Lakota, and were a deterioration in the position of women, when compared to that of the Dakota. Once Indians were forced on to reservations, it is argued that the position of women generally worsened in relation to men – particularly as the men lost their traditional hunting and warfare roles and so played an even greater part in general decision-making.

SOURCE A

Now I shall have to tell you about the fighting, because it was a woman's fight. A woman won it. The men never tell about it... I saw Strikes Two, a woman sixty years old... She carried her root digger... She rode straight out at the Sioux...

An extract from the account of Pretty Shield, a Crow woman, describing how a woman of her band drove off a Sioux raiding party.

VOICE YOUR OPINION!

How similar do you think the position of Plains' Indian women in the second half of the 19th century is to that of most women in Britain today?

Fact file

While 19th-century Europeans tended to think in terms of only 'male' and 'female', many Native American nations recognised three gender categories – male, female and transgender. The last category was seen in Sioux society, for instance, as a 'Two Spirits' person. Such a person was usually a man who wore female clothing, adopted female behaviour and engaged in traditional female roles such as pottery or basket-making. They were sometimes seen as having special spiritual or mystical powers.

SOURCE B

Chief-Comes-In-Sight was the bravest of all [the Cheyennes], but as he was swinging his horse about after a charge into the soldiers' flank the animal was shot down in front of a Bluecoats infantry line. Suddenly another horse and rider galloped out from the Cheyennes' position and swerved to shield Chief-Comes-In-Sight from the soldiers' fire. In a moment Chief-Comes-In-Sight was up behind the rider. The rescuer was his sister Buffalo-Calf-Road-Woman, who had come along to help with the horse herds. That was why the Cheyennes always remembered this fight as the Battle Where the Girl Saved her Brother. The white men called it the Battle of the Rosebud.

An extra from D. Brown, *Bury My Heart at Wounded Knee* (Barrie & Jenkins, 1970), in which a Cheyenne woman describes how a young woman rescued her brother at the Battle of the Rosebud.

SOURCE C

Women... are always held in a rank inferior to that of the men, in relation to whom in many respects they stand rather in the light of menials and slaves than otherwise...

An extract from George Catlin's book, 1841, about the position of women in Plains' Indian society.

SOURCE D

Dakota women and children protecting corn from blackbirds, 1862.

1.8 What were the beliefs of the Plains' Indians concerning warfare?

LEARNING OBJECTIVES

In this lesson you will:

- find out about aspects of warfare amongst the Plains' Indians
- get practice in answering questions that ask you to extract information from sources.

KEY WORDS

Counting coup – *the act where Indian warriors struck an enemy with a coup stick – it usually brought more honour or status than killing him.*

Why did the Plains' Indians fight each other?

Although some of the nations of the Plains' Indians were allied to each other, war between nations was also common. These wars were mainly fought to steal horses or captives (who were kept as family slaves for a time). They were also fought as revenge for a previous raid or attack by another tribe or, very occasionally, to destroy a particularly hated or troublesome enemy.

However, because they were nomadic hunters, the main aims of war were not to conquer tribes or land, in the way that white settlers on the Plains later attempted. There was rivalry from time to time over hunting grounds and, as pressures from the white Americans in the east increased, for living space.

Some modern historians have suggested another possible reason for warfare amongst the Plains' Indians – the need to keep different bands or tribes united, by giving them a 'common enemy'. This was often difficult, as separate bands often went their own way for much of the summer. By 1840, for instance, the Comanche and Apache had become traditional enemies.

Wars were also fought to give young warriors practice in the skills of war, and the chance to gain glory and honour, which would give them extra status in the band or tribe. Also, by capturing horses and weapons, they became wealthy – this could help them marry the girl of their choice. Later, of course, wars were fought against settlers and the US army, as the Plains' Indians tried to protect their way of life.

Warfare amongst the Plains' Indians

Indian wars were not fought in the winter, as the Plains were covered in snow. So, instead, campaigns were fought in the summer, when movement was easy, and supplies of food had been built up by buffalo hunting.

Success in war was of particular importance to each tribe, as well as to individual warriors. For Indian chiefs, success was judged by the number of horses or captives brought back, and keeping their own losses small. If successful, it increased their authority within the band or tribe; if unsuccessful, warriors would stop following them. In the main, wars consisted of short, fierce battles or raids fought by relatively small groups of warriors – often just for honour which was achieved by proving courage and bravery.

Counting coup

There were strict codes of honour in warfare. Especially prized was '**counting coup**' – this involved running or galloping up to the enemy and touching him with the end of a coup stick (about 2.5–3 metres long, and usually decorated with feathers). This was considered braver than killing your enemy, and gave a warrior higher status in the band. This warfare ritual meant that, even when Plains' Indians began to possess guns, warfare was not particularly destructive between tribes.

Unlike Europeans, they did not see death on the battlefield as particularly honourable – the important thing was to survive, so they could continue to look after their family and band. So, if outnumbered, Plains' Indians would retreat – white people saw this as cowardice. Similarly, the Plains' Indians considered it sensible to 'creep up' on an enemy in a surprise attack – in this way, deaths on both sides would be kept to a minimum. So, before the coming of white people, warfare on the Great Plains was low-intensity, 'sustainable' warfare – that is, with not much emphasis on killing.

Treatment of prisoners of war varied greatly from tribe to tribe, with atrocities sometimes committed – the Comanche had the most terrifying reputation. Women and children, though, were usually treated mercifully, and accepted into the conquering tribe or band.

Warrior societies

Most warriors were usually members of a warrior society, such as the Fox Soldiers of the Cheyenne, the Kaitsenko (the ten bravest) of the Kiowa, or the Kit Foxes of the Lakota Sioux. Their role within a band was usually to help the chief and council of elders. In order to belong, a man had to distinguish himself in some way.

The decision to go to war was a very serious one. The Cheyenne, for instance, usually made decisions about war in a special council of war chiefs.

Weapons

Another reason why warfare on the Great Plains did not result in heavy casualties amongst the American Indian tribes was because of the type of weapons they used – tomahawks, war clubs, lances, and the bow and arrow, which were also used for hunting. Weapons were made of good-quality wood (mainly yew or ash), with sharpened flint or bone used for arrow or lance heads, or for cutting edges (see Source A).

Horses

Not only did horses change the nature of hunting, they also affected Plains' Indians warfare. They allowed warriors to range further afield – as well as giving an extra reason for raids. They also meant warriors had to learn new fighting skills – these soon became part of the ways in which warriors could increase their status within the band (see Sources B and C). Horses became highly prized – and an important goal of warfare. The Comanche called the horse a 'god dog' while the Sioux referred to it as a 'medicine dog'. The theft of horses from an enemy was seen as an act of bravery.

SOURCE A

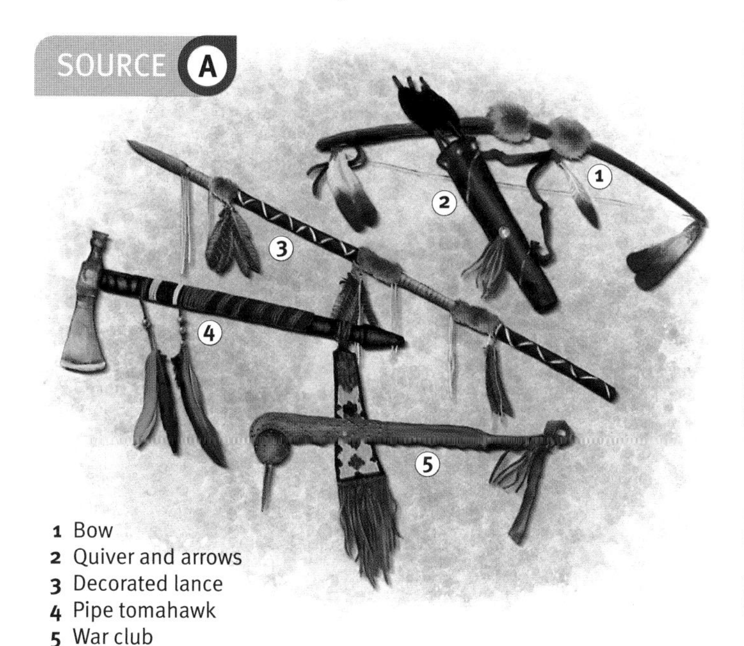

1 Bow
2 Quiver and arrows
3 Decorated lance
4 Pipe tomahawk
5 War club

Weapons used by the Plains' Indians.

SOURCE B

Amongst their feats of riding, there is one that astonished me more than anything of the kind I have seen, or expect to see, in my life, a stratagem of war learned and practised by every young man in the tribe. By this he is able to drop his body upon the side of his horse and he is screened from his enemies' weapons... In this wonderful condition, he will hang whilst his horse is at full speed, carrying with him his bow and shield, and also his long lance of fourteen feet in length, all of which he will use against his enemy as he passes, rising and firing his arrows over his horse's back, or with equal ease and equal success under the horse's neck.

An extract from George Catlin's book, 1841, describing the Comanches' horse-riding skills.

SOURCE C

Comanche Feats of Horsemanship, a painting by George Catlin, 1834.

ACTIVITIES

Add information on warfare to the chart you first compiled in Lesson 1.3.

1.9 What were the main beliefs of the Plains' Indians concerning religion and health?

LEARNING OBJECTIVES

In this lesson you will:

- find out what Plains' Indians thought about religion and medicine
- get practice in answering questions that ask you to give factual information about a topic.

KEY WORDS

Shaman – *a holy man with special powers, known to the Europeans as a medicine man. Each tribe had a shaman. They also gave advice to chiefs and the councils of elders. They often had strong personalities and great wisdom.*

Sweat lodge – *a low hide-covered hut, used by Native Americans in religious/health rituals. Water was thrown onto fires to produce steam – this was meant to 'purify' someone (perhaps so they could receive a 'vision') or to cure an illness.*

Religious beliefs

The Plains' Indians had strong religious beliefs, and religious ceremonies played an important part in everyday life.

The various nations had different creation beliefs – some believed in one 'Father of Life' or 'The Great Spirit'. The Lakota Sioux, for example, worshipped one 'Great God' known as 'Wakan Tanka'. They shared a sense of unity with nature, based on their belief that humans were one part – but only one part – of all the other elements of the natural world.

However, some tribes did not believe there was just one supreme being. They believed that even trees, rivers and rocks had spirits, which could influence their lives and so had to be respected. But all believed that each creature had a place in nature. Therefore, it was wrong to kill more than you needed, or to pollute the environment. On death, they believed the spirits of all went to the Happy Hunting Ground – they did not believe in a separate heaven and hell.

The importance of circles

Plains' Indians also believed that nature worked in circles – the sun and moon, the seasons, and life itself. So circles became important symbols – shields were round, tipis were round, villages were built in circles, councils sat in circles, and even dances took the form of a circle (see Source A).

Sacred land

As well as their general belief that the land could not be bought or sold, the Plains' Indians considered some areas to be sacred – especially high places, which were seen as being closer to the spirit world (see Source B). For the Lakota Sioux, for example, the Black Hills were sacred. They also believed that their ancestors' bodies had become dust on the Plains, thus making their tribal lands sacred. This was to cause great problems after 1840, as more and more people wanted to cross and then settle on the Plains.

Visions

Plains' Indians believed that the spirit world was the real world, while the world people lived in was only a shadow of the real world. The spirit world could be contacted through dreaming and having a vision. Everyone wanted to have a vision – young boys would go to a **sweat lodge** to cleanse their body, then go without food and pray, waiting for an animal or bird to appear to them in a vision as their guardian spirit.

The visions would also be interpreted by a **shaman** – this would give the young boy his adult name. This was how, for instance, Sitting Bull of the Lakota Sioux received his name. Women also had visions. As puberty and menstruation began, a medicine woman would help them make contact with the spirit world – as with boys, this gave them their adult name.

Visions were often believed to be important in battles – both Sitting Bull and Crazy Horse had had visions before the Battles of the Rosebud and the Little Big

Horn (see Source C). Sitting Bull had bled himself, then danced the Sun Dance until he fell into a trance and had a vision – he believed Wakan Tanka was giving the soldiers to the Indians to be killed.

Dances and ceremonies

Shamans played an important part in many aspects of the lives of the Plains' Indians, and they usually conducted the many important ceremonial and religious dances. Sometimes, these involved painful ceremonies. The rituals and dances – and worship in general – were intended to keep the tribe in harmony with the spirits of the natural world important to their life – such as buffalo, bear and antelope.

Women often played a part in these dances and rituals – if not the main roles. Amongst the Cheyenne and the Comanche, when they performed their Massaum (or animal) dance, which was to ask the spirits to help them have a successful buffalo hunt, it was the women who carried the sacred buffalo skull into a special lodge.

Some ceremonial dances were especially important and were intended to protect the tribe. They were used when the whole tribe needed to contact the spirit world, such as before a buffalo hunt or before a battle or raid. Dances also took place after a successful hunt or battle, to give thanks to the spirits for their help – for example, the Scalp Dance. For the small number of tribes who grew crops, there were also corn dances.

SOURCE A

Everything an Indian does is a circle, and that is because the power of the world works in circles, even the seasons form a great circle, and come back to where they were before. Our tipis are round, like birds' nests, and they are set in a circle, the nation's hoop, a nest of many nests, where the Great Spirit meant us to raise our children.

Black Elk (a holy man of the Oglala Sioux) comments on circles – from his book, *Black Elk Speaks*.

SOURCE B

Funeral Scaffold of a Sioux Chief near Fort Pierre, a painting by Karl Bodmer, 1834. After the body had been dried by wind and sun, the bones were buried on sacred land.

SOURCE C

For a long time Crazy Horse had been waiting for a chance to test himself in battle with the Bluecoats... Each time he went into the Black Hills to seek visions, he had asked Wakantanka to give him secret powers so that he would know how to lead the Oglalas to victory if the white men ever came again to make war upon his people... On this day, 17 June 1876, Crazy Horse dreamed himself in to the real world, and he showed the Sioux how to do many things they had never done before while fighting the white man's soldiers.

An extract from D. Brown, *Bury My Heart at Wounded Knee*, 1970, p. 289, about a vision seen by Crazy Horse of the Oglala tribe.

ACTIVITIES

Add information on religion to your chart first compiled in Lesson 1.3.

Sun Dance

Some dances, such as the Sun Dance, which was common to most Plains' Indian tribes, were often more of a ritual than a dance, as it often challenged young warriors to undergo pain (see Sources D and E). They sometimes took place on a dancing area surrounded by a circle of tipis or, with the Cheyenne, in a specially built New Life lodge, with a large central post. The pain they endured as they were hauled off their feet, facing the sun, was believed to set their spirits free to contact the spirit world – for instance, to ask for their help if a family member were ill. In another version, Lakota men danced, pulling against the ropes, until their skin ripped free. In some tribes, they then sometimes had one or two fingers or toes cut off. Such rituals were overseen by shamans who decided when enough pain had been suffered. However, not all Plains' Indians had this painful aspect to their Sun Dances – for instance, the Cree and Assiniboine concentrated instead on prayer and meditation.

Medicine and health

Because of their physically active way of life, most Indians were fairly fit. They lived in small groups and frequently moved camp, so they did not suffer from some public health problems such as sewage waste polluting water supplies. The main causes of death for Plains' Indians were warfare, hunting accidents, food shortages and old age. However, when they came into contact with Europeans, they became exposed to a range of new illnesses for which they had no immunity, such as cholera and smallpox.

Shamans played an important role in the life of Plains' Indians as curers of illnesses and injuries, often believed to result from possession by 'evil spirits'. If someone was ill, the evil spirits needed to be driven out. This was connected to the general belief that there was a link between the human world and the 'real' world of the spirits. 'Cures' were attempted by the use of medicine chants and dances.

They also used traditional practical cures and remedies, using herbs, animal fats, bark and mosses as ointments and potions. Plains' Indians knew the medicinal properties of over 2000 plants and herbs.

For their help and advice, shamans charged high fees – often payments were made in ponies. But they had to return these gifts if their treatments were unsuccessful.

GradeStudio

Analysis of sources

Study Sources A and C.

How useful are these sources in telling you about the religious beliefs of the Plains' Indians? Use the sources and your own knowledge to explain your answer.

Examiner's tip

- For this type of question make sure you explain both ways in which the sources are useful AND the ways in which they are not useful/or their usefulness is limited, for example by explaining other aspects of religious beliefs. Your answer must reach a judgement about the usefulness of the sources.

SOURCE D

The Sun Dance Ceremony of the Mandan Indians, a painting by George Catlin, 1835.

SOURCE E

The medicine men would lift the young man and lay him under the pole. An old man would then come forward with a very sharp pointed knife. He would take hold of the breast of the young brave, pull the skin forward and pierce it through with the knife. Then he would insert a wooden pin… through the slit and tie a strong buckskin thong to this pin.

From the pole two rawhide ropes were suspended. The candidate would now be lifted up … and was hanging from his breast.

Description of the Sun Dance, taken from *My Family the Sioux*, by Luther Standing Bear.

Fact file

Other tribe members often undertook fasting and prayer (and even self-torture) to receive 'visions' from the spirits – these were then interpreted by the shamans.

ACTIVITIES

1. Explain what is meant by the term 'shaman'.
2. Why was the buffalo so important to the Plains' Indians?
3. What was the purpose of the Sun Dance?
4. Add information to your similarities and differences chart first compiled in Lesson 1.3.

GradeStudio

You have now completed this unit which has focused on various aspects of the life of the Plains' Indians in the years before 1840. You have also had practice in answering questions designed to prepare you for your exam. Below is an example of one type of exam question, with some hints to help you write a top-scoring answer.

Fact file

In the exam, you will be asked to answer two questions from Section B, the Depth Study: a source-based question and a structured question. The structured question is divided into three parts – **a**, **b** and **c**.

b Explain why the warfare practised by Plains' Indians before 1840 usually resulted in relatively low casualty rates. **[7 marks]**

Examiner's tip

- Remember, in questions that ask you to explain something, the examiners are expecting you to show both knowledge of AND understanding of a particular topic or aspect of your course. This means more than just 'listing' two or three factors – you need to use your knowledge to show or explain why/how they are important.
- It is also important to make sure you identify AND explain two different points. While one explained factor will get you into Level 3, it will not get you the highest mark.
- To get to the top level, you will need to explain TWO or more reasons.

Before you write your answer, below are two things to help you start on the right lines.

First, look at the simplified mark scheme below. This should help you write your answer in a way that will allow you to get the full 7 marks available for such questions.

Simplified mark scheme

Level	Skill	Mark
Level 0	No answer or irrelevant answer	0
Level 1	Vague or general answer/no precise own knowledge	1
Level 2	Identifies 1–2 specific reasons, but doesn't explain them	2–3
Level 3	Identifies AND explains one reason	4–5
	Identifies AND explains one reason, AND identifies another	6
Level 4	Identifies AND explains two reasons	7

Second, look at the sample answer below, noting especially the examiner's comments.

Candidate's answer

The reason why the warfare of the Plains' Indians resulted in low casualties was **because of the types of weapons they mostly used**.

Their main weapons were the bow and arrow, the lance, the tomahawk, the knife and the war club. In the early years of their time on the Great Plains, guns were not widely used. Such low-tech weapons did not usually produce high death-rates, as they were mainly used in close-combat situations.

Examiner's comment

The first highlighted part of the answer (**green**) gets the candidate into Level 2, as one reason is identified. The candidate has also begun wisely by starting with a quote from the question – this is a good habit to get into, as it should help make sure that you answer the question set!

The second highlighted part of the answer (**red**) is providing useful and precise information supporting own knowledge and so is EXPLAINING how the weapons used helped to keep casualty rates low. This gets the candidate – who clearly understands the topic – into Level 3.

Look again at the mark scheme, and you should be able to see what the candidate could have done to push this good answer from Level 3 into Level 4 and score the full 7 marks.

You will see that in order to get to the top of Level 3, and score 6 marks, all the candidate needed to do was just mention one more reason or factor. To get full marks in Level 4, the candidate would then need to explain this second reason, using some precise knowledge to support the point being made.

Once you think you have fully understood what was needed to improve this candidate's answer, write your own answer – BUT don't use the reason given above in the sample answer! There are at least two other reasons you can use – and remember to explain them, using precise own knowledge.

Before you start, look back at Lesson 1.8 and focus on the main aspects of the nature of the Plains' Indians' warfare. Then try to write your answer without looking at the relevant pages.

Chapter 2

Why did people settle and stay in the West?

KEY WORDS

Cattle rustling – *stealing other people's cattle. Rustlers were sometimes known as Jayhawks.*

Vigilantes – *ordinary people who deal with suspected lawbreakers themselves, without waiting for official law-enforcement officers or agencies to take action. They were quite common in the West, especially in the early days.*

SOURCE A

A still from the film *Young Guns*, 1988, which is about the life of the outlaw known as Billy the Kid.

GETTING STARTED

In the 21st century, many of those who have a huge desire to explore and travel to new places are increasingly drawn to the idea of space travel. At the moment, though, only the select few have a chance of this – but it's likely that it won't be too long before the curious – and the rich! – will be booking flights in space.

Space is often referred to as 'The New Frontier', and there are many books, television programmes and films – fictional and non-fictional – that deal with the topic of space travel. Some studies have stated that it might be possible – with the appropriate technology – to sustain human life on some of the other planets in our Solar System.

In groups of four, take a blank piece of paper and write down:

- the 'push' factors that might make you keen to move to a new planet – the things you don't like about life on Earth
- the 'pull' factors that would excite you to try a new life elsewhere.

At the end of five minutes, share these with the rest of the class to see which negative and positive factors occur most frequently.

This chapter focuses on the lives and experiences of those people who began to move to and settle in the West after 1840 – in particular, those who came to the Great Plains, which were already inhabited by the various nations of the Plains' Indians. You will find out what drew these people to the West – even though the journeys they made, and the conditions they found on arrival, were hard and often dangerous.

There are many myths about the 'Wild West' – in particular, images of gunfights, **cattle rustling**, **vigilantes** and Native American attacks on wagon trains readily come to mind when talking about the West. These are often drawn from films and comic books. But how true as these commonly held views?

Sources A, B, C and D are common examples of the ways in which many people view the 'Wild West'. This chapter will try to separate myth from reality.

HISTORY DETECTIVE

Find out more about the 'Wild West' by visiting www.heinemann.co.uk/hotlinks and enter the code 1433P or try to watch at least one Western film.

SOURCE B

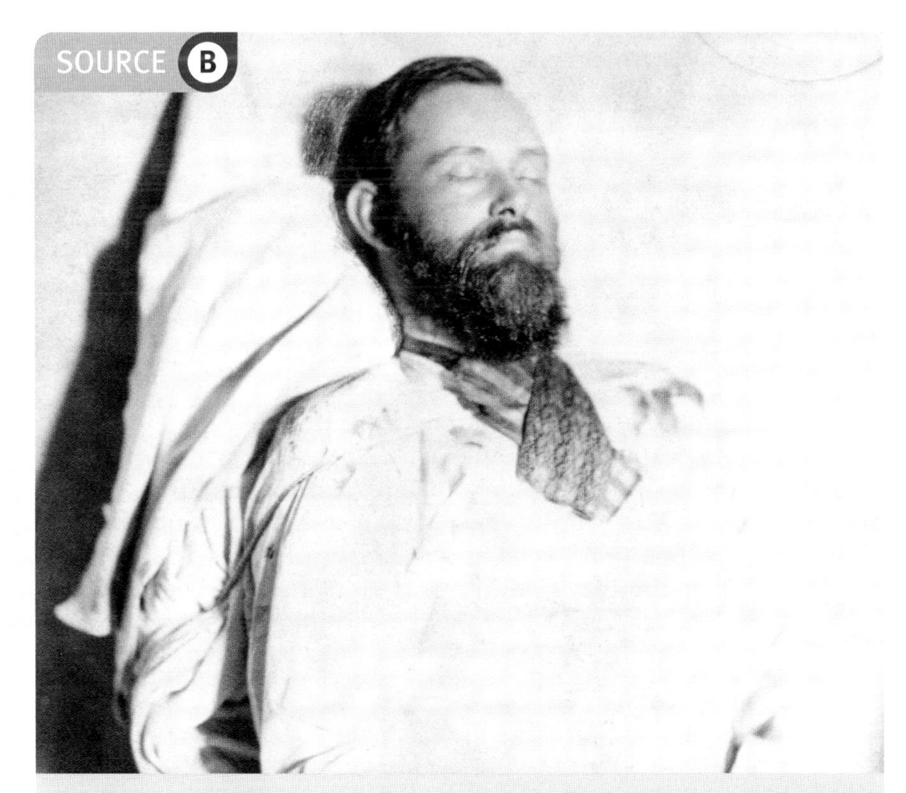

A photograph of the outlaw Jesse James, taken in 1882, after he had been shot by Bob Ford.

SOURCE C

A victim of a vigilante lynching.

SOURCE D

Smoke of a .45, a painting by Charles M. Russell, 1908, showing a typical view of the lawlessness of the 'Wild West'.

2.1 The early trailblazers to the West

LEARNING OBJECTIVES

In this lesson you will:

- find out about how the first routes – or trails – to the West were discovered
- get practice in answering questions that ask you to describe and explain something.

KEY WORDS

Mountain men – *the first European men who hunted in the Plains and beyond, before the great move West. Many of them later helped establish ('blaze') trails for the wagon trains of early pioneers.*

Trailblazers – *the first people to find and set up the best routes or trails for the early pioneers/settlers moving West (often in wagon trains) – many of these 'trailblazers' had previously been 'mountain men'.*

After 1840, many people wanted to 'go West' – first across and then on to what for many years had been seen as the 'Great American Desert' (see Lesson 1.2 on pp. 6–9). There are many reasons why this move West took place after 1840 – for adventure, for a better life, for gold and for land, to name just a few of the more important ones.

However, in order for large numbers of people to travel across – and eventually settle on – the Great Plains, there needed to be reasonably safe trails or routes. These were the work of the first Europeans who travelled to and explored the West.

Mountain men

Before 1840, the first steps in opening up the West to Europeans were taken by those involved in the fur trade as trappers, hunters and traders – mostly of beavers. The skins of beavers were sold back in the East, where they were used to make luxury hats and clothes which were in great demand in US cities and in Europe. From the 1820s to the 1840s, the fur trade experienced a boom.

The fur trappers and traders were often known as '**mountain men**' as many spent most of their time in the mountains. The more famous ones included Jim Bridger, Kit Carson and James P. Beckwourth.

Many of these mountain men were also adventurers and explorers, and built up considerable knowledge of the Great Plains and the mountains and lands beyond them to the West. When they went back to the East, they told stories about their experiences and discoveries – some of these then appeared in newspapers and magazines. Another way stories and information about the West reached people in the East was by the yearly 'rendezvous' or gathering, which took place annually from 1825 to 1840. Here the mountain men, fur traders and merchants met and traded. The trappers sold their furs, and then bought new supplies of hunting weapons, traps, food supplies and clothing.

The big fur companies also built trading posts – or forts – where trappers and merchants could meet in order to trade. Such stories began to excite some people about the idea of moving West themselves. Many of these mountain men later helped 'blaze' trails which were then used by the early pioneers or settlers.

Relations with Native Americans

The early mountain men faced many hazards – as well as severe weather, there were wild animals such as bears and wolves. But, although there was sometimes conflict with Native Americans – for instance, the Blackfoot Indians were usually hostile – relations with most Plains' Indians in the years before 1840 were usually good.

This was because the activities of the mountain men did not disrupt or threaten the Native Americans' way of life. By the early 1830s, however, there were few independent trappers and hunters. Most of the mountain men were by then working for one of two large fur companies – the American Fur Company or the Hudson's Bay Company.

And yet, by 1840, the fur trade was beginning to decline – this was the result of changing fashions and over-hunting of beavers which resulted in a sharp drop in numbers. Smaller fur companies went out of business. Soon, the number of mountain men acting as fur trappers and traders declined rapidly.

Trailblazing

After the collapse of the fur trade, many mountain men who wanted to stay in the West decided to act as scouts, guides or miners. Many of them helped 'blaze' the first trails (routes) across the Great Plains to new areas in the West (see Source A).

The first – and most important – trails were the Oregon Trail, which developed after Jedediah Smith found the South Pass through the Rocky Mountains in 1823, and the Sante Fe Trail, which owed much to the work of Joseph Walker.

In the early 1840s, further work on developing trails was done by John Charles Fremont – another adventurer and pathfinder. Using information provided by mountain men – and backed by funds from the US government – he carried out a survey of the Rockies, using the South Pass. During 1843–44, aided by the US Army Corps of Topographical Engineers, Fremont made a detailed map of the Oregon Trail. This map was published by the US government as part of its encouragement of the move West. These **trailblazers** thus opened up the West for the huge wave of settlers who, after 1840, began to follow them westwards (see Source B).

SOURCE 

Not a hole or corner of the vast wilderness of the 'far West' but has been ransacked by these hardy men. From the Mississippi to the mouth of the Colorado in the West, from the frozen regions of the North to Mexico in the South, the beaver-hunter has set his traps in every creek and stream. All this vast country, but for the daring enterprise of these man, would even now be an unknown land to geographers, as indeed a great portion still is in 1849.

An extract from an account by George Ruxton, an Englishman who in 1847 had lived for a time with some of the last mountain men.

GradeStudio

Recall and select knowledge; write a multi-causal explanation

Explain why the mountain men were important in opening up the West.

Examiner's tip

- Do not just state or describe reasons. Make sure you explain two or three reasons why they were important.

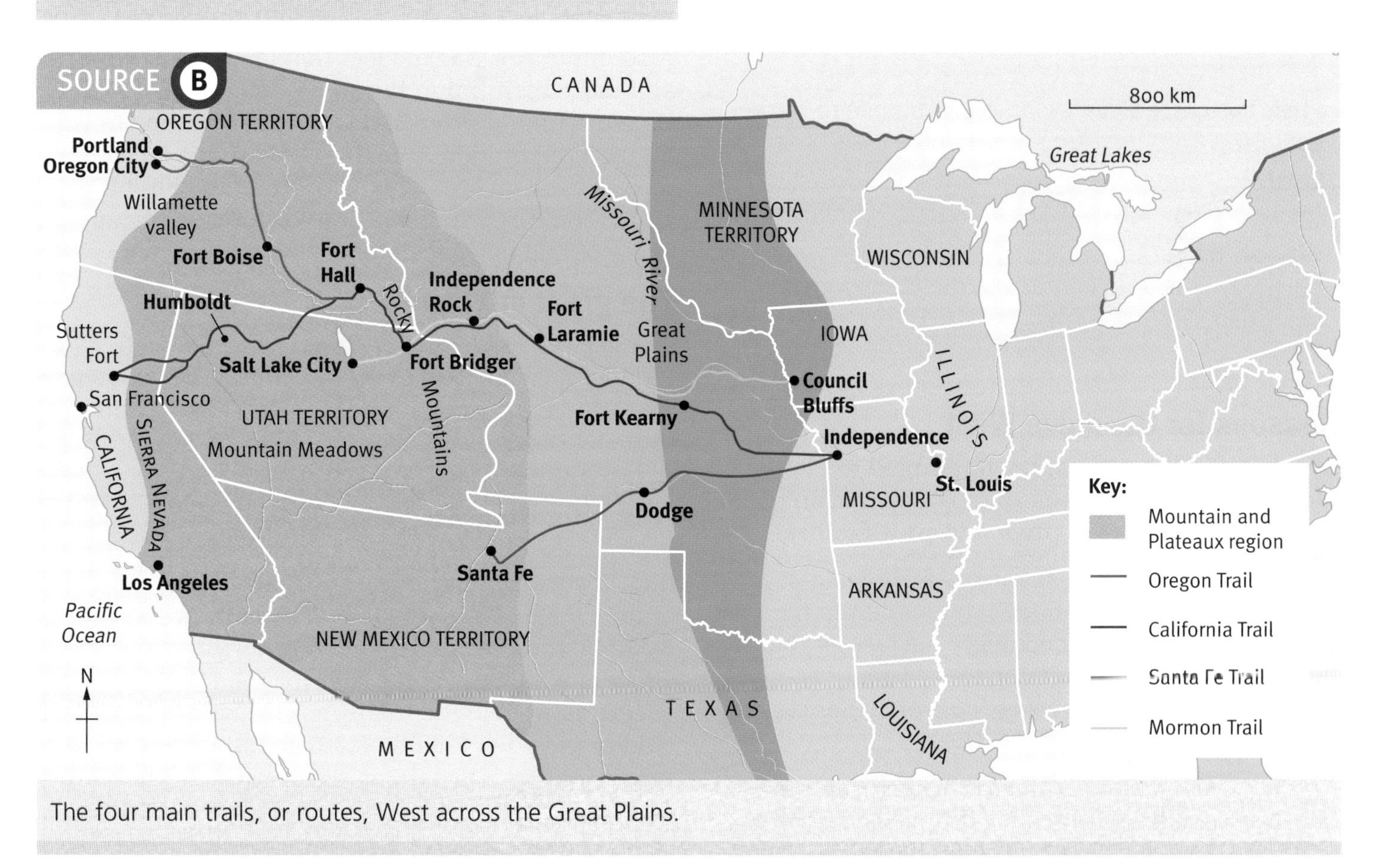

The four main trails, or routes, West across the Great Plains.

2.2 Why did early pioneers want to move West?

LEARNING OBJECTIVES

In this lesson you will:

- find out why people moved West, and what the journeys were like
- get practice in answering questions that ask you to describe and explain something.

KEY WORDS

Migration – *the act of moving (migrating) from one area to another to make a new and hopefully better life. A migrant is a person who migrates.*

Pioneers – *the name given to the early migrants/settlers who moved West to the Great Plains and beyond.*

Pull factors – *factors that had a positive attraction, leading people e.g. to move West.*

Push factors – *factors that forced people to move e.g. away from the East.*

Settlers – *people who travelled West to settle on the land of the Great Plains and establish farms.*

Wagon train – *a number of pioneer/settler wagons travelling West into and across the Plains together, for added safety/security.*

Reasons for the move West

By 1840, there were many who wanted to move West, for a number of reasons. The five main ones were a combination of **push** and **pull factors**.

The most important push factors included a financial crisis and economic depression in the East in 1837, which had ruined many businesses; led to the collapse of banks and the loss of many people's savings; and resulted in wage cuts of 40 per cent and increased unemployment by 1839.

Another push factor was a farming crisis in the Mid-West resulting from a big drop in the price of grain. Also, there was a land shortage in the East and Mid-West, as a result of population growth: some **settlers** in the Mississippi–Missouri areas began to feel 'overcrowded'.

Fact file

In 1842, Oregon was territory owned jointly by the USA and Britain.

There was further encouragement to move later in the 1840s when the USA gained new lands by purchase and war – especially important were Oregon in 1846 and California in 1848 (see Lesson 1.2 on pages 6–9). As part of the growing belief in Manifest Destiny, the US government now wanted to encourage even more people to move West in order to settle these new areas.

The main pull factors included the information which had been travelling back East from the early **pioneers** and mountain men, saying how wonderful things were in the West for hunting and trapping, with good farming land and gentle climates.

Also important was the fact that land was cheaper and more plentiful in the West. As early as 1842, the US government promised land to settlers in Oregon by the Pre-emption Act which said that a farmer who cleared an area of land of trees and built a house could buy the land at a low price without being outbid by speculators.

The great migration

In 1843, the first group of would-be settlers left Independence, Missouri, to travel 3200 km to Oregon (see Source A). At this time, people did not want to settle on the Great Plains (see Lesson 1.2 on pp. 6–9).

In all, 913 people left on what became known as the great **migration**. The following year, in 1844, in order to encourage even more settlers to go West, the US government printed 10,000 copies of the map of the Oregon Trail, made by Fremont in 1843–44. By 1845, there were over 6000 Americans in Oregon, which made it easier for the US government to argue that Britain should sell this land to the USA. Finally, in 1846, following an agreement with Britain, it became part of the USA.

As a result, thousands more crossed the Great Plains in the 1840s to make a new life in Oregon and, after 1848, in California, which became part of the USA after a war against Mexico. By 1848, nearly 15,000 settlers had journeyed West, across the Great Plains.

Wagon trains and the journey West

To travel West across the Great Plains, the early settlers used the trails that had been blazed earlier by the mountain men. The main starting points were Independence or St Joseph – both in Missouri.

The best chance of a safe and successful crossing was to be part of a **wagon train** led by a pilot and his scout. But some people tried to go on their own or in smaller groups, using just a map.

Most travelled in covered wagons, pulled by oxen, mules or horses (see Source B). These wagons were loaded with the equipment and supplies likely to be needed for their new life, plus their own treasured possessions. However, very often such items had to be thrown off, in order to cross the deep and swift rivers and to climb the mountain passes. Even so, because the wagons were so loaded, people very often had to walk beside them.

There were many hazards, such as severe weather, disease, buffalo stampedes, shortages of food and water. To avoid winter blizzards, most journeys began in late April/early May. Progress was slow – about 25 km a day – so journeys usually took about four-and-a-half months.

At first, most Plains' Indian tribes traded with these early white migrants because they were only crossing their lands on the Great Plains to get to Oregon or California. But when the numbers of settlers later increased, tensions grew. The US government then sent troops to protect the settlers, and built forts along the trails on Indian lands.

SOURCE A

The Oregon Trail, a painting by Albert Bierstadt, 1869.

SOURCE B

Emigrants resting on the Oregon Trail, showing the type of wagons used.

GradeStudio

Recall and select knowledge

The early pioneers faced many problems on their journeys to the Great Plains.

a) Briefly describe the main difficulties faced by the early pioneers.

b) Explain, using your own knowledge, why most of these journeys began in late April/early May.

Examiner's tip

- Remember – you need to do more than merely identify the problems: they need to be explained, using your own precise knowledge.
- Also – remember to give AND explain at least TWO reasons.

BRAIN BOOST

Copy and complete this ideas map by adding extra details about the main reasons for moving West after 1840.

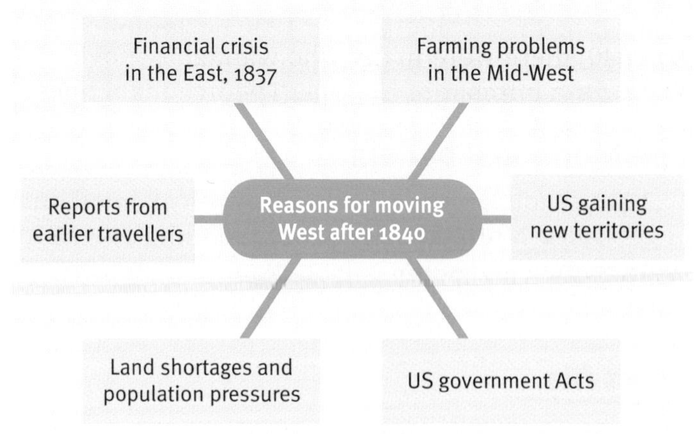

When you have done this, shade the boxes in one of two colours – one for 'push' factors, and one for 'pull' factors. Remember to add a key to explain this.

2.3 Case study: Who were the Mormons, and why did they move West?

LEARNING OBJECTIVES

In this case study you will:

- find out about the Mormons and why they moved West
- get practice in answering questions that ask you to explain why a source is and is not useful.

KEY WORDS

Mormons – *members of the Church of Jesus Christ of Latter-Day Saints, founded by Joseph Smith in 1830.*

Polygamy – *a system of marriage based on having two or more wives/husbands at the same time.*

Saloon – *a place selling alcohol, with added attractions such as music, dancing and gambling.*

Who were the Mormons?

The **Mormons** were another group of white Americans who decided to move West in the 1840s. In many ways, they were very different from the other migrants travelling West. In particular, they were a religious group who lived a communal life, sharing everything, and owning nothing themselves. Their religion was founded in 1830 by Joseph Smith, and in 1831 it was officially named the Church of Jesus Christ of the Latter Day Saints.

The Mormons' beliefs

In 1823, when he was 17, Joseph Smith claimed an angel called Moroni had appeared to him in a vision, telling him about some golden plates which were hidden in a hillside near his father's farm in Palmyra in New York State, and which, once he had found them, were to be kept secret for four years. He found the plates and translated the text on them, and dictated the translations to his wife – he published them in 1830 as the Book of Mormon.

He later allowed 11 witnesses to see the plates and verify their contents. He then founded his church, and believed it was his duty to spread the word. At first, he had only five followers, but this soon grew to several hundreds. Their main beliefs and practices are shown in Source A.

Early history, 1831–44

Many non-Mormons were hostile to their beliefs and, in 1831, Smith decided to set up a 'holy city' in Kirtland, Ohio. Despite some violent opposition, the Mormon population continued to grow and, in 1833, Smith built the first Mormon temple. Members of the Mormon community also set up businesses and a bank, which prospered. However, non-Mormons (referred to as 'gentiles' by the Mormons) began to fear they would be outnumbered and began to resent the Mormons' prosperity. When the financial crisis of 1837 caused their bank (along with many others) to collapse, hostility increased as many non-Mormons had savings in the Mormon bank. Violent gangs began to attack Mormon houses and they were driven out of Kirtland.

They then moved to Missouri – but their anti-slavery beliefs made them particularly unpopular there, as many landowners owned slaves. Partly as a result of violent attacks, the Mormons set up their own police force – the Sons of Dan (often known as the Danites). This only increased opposition to them, and a situation close to a small-scale civil war broke out. Eventually, Smith and other Mormon leaders were imprisoned.

Fact file

The Book of Mormon describes the migration to America, in 600 BCE, of the tribes of Israel, and said that Jesus came to America after his resurrection. There was constant warfare between these tribes until only a tribesman called Mormon and his son, Moroni, survived. Mormon then wrote down this history on the golden plates. When he died, Moroni hid them. Hence believers were often called 'Mormons'.

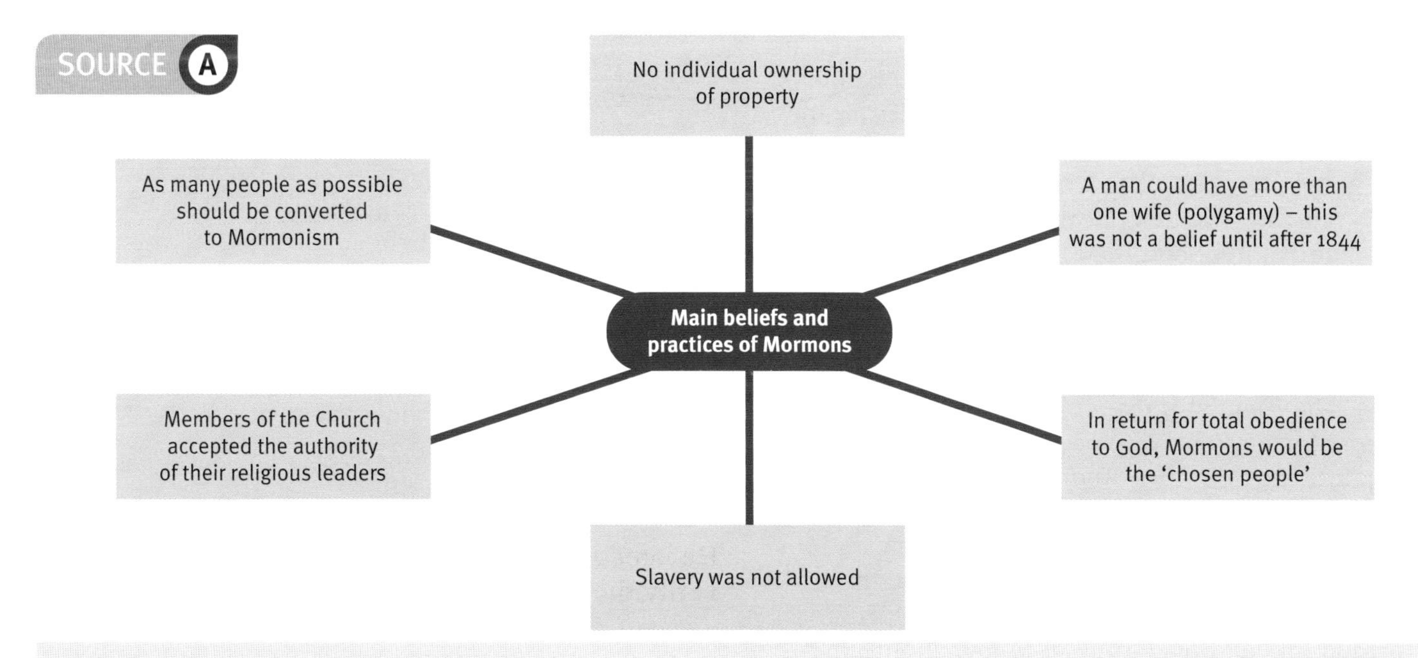

The main beliefs and practices of the Mormons.

On his release at the end of 1838, Smith went to the village of Commerce in Illinois, where another Mormon leader, Brigham Young (who had not been imprisoned), had led the persecuted Mormons. Smith then renamed this place Nauvoo.

For greater protection – and in return for their votes in an election in 1840 – Smith persuaded the state government of Illinois to grant the Mormons the right to have their own army and make their own laws. By 1842, their army – the Nauvoo Legion – was over 3000 strong. Nauvoo became prosperous and, by 1844, was the largest city in the state.

Reasons for moving West

Many non-Mormons resented this 'state-within-a-state' and the fact that Mormons often ignored the laws of Illinois. They thought Joseph Smith was trying to get non-Mormons to live the Mormon way; and their fears were increased in 1844 when Smith announced his intention to stand for election as president of the USA.

The banner of the Nauvoo Legion, which by 1844 had over 3000 members.

Fact file

In 1843, Smith's 'holy city' of Nauvoo was described as being carefully planned, with straight, tree-lined roads and well-built houses. It was dominated by the Mormon Temple. It was prosperous, with many shops and businesses – there were no **saloons** or gambling places, and smoking was forbidden.

The resentment against the Mormons increased in 1844, when Smith told people that he had had a revelation from God in which he said that certain Mormons could have more than one wife; this is **polygamy**. By then, Smith already had several wives (some estimates put the figure at ten); his bodyguard, John Scott, had five.

This angered some Mormons and a breakaway group attacked Smith's idea in their newspaper. He retaliated by destroying the newspaper's printing press. The issue of polygamy soon became known to non-Mormons in Nauvoo who were angry as they thought it was immoral and against the Bible, and would lead to chaos and confusion in society. Mobs began to roam the streets, so Joseph Smith and his brother, Hyrum, fled to Carthage and sought protection in the jail. But a mob of non-Mormons stormed the jail on 27 June 1844 and shot them dead.

HISTORY DETECTIVE

Try to discover more about why the Mormons were often very successful in business.

The decision to journey West

After the murder of Smith in 1844, the Mormons split – mainly over the issue of polygamy. Eventually, most accepted Brigham Young as their new leader. As the violent hostility against Mormons in Nauvoo continued through 1845, he decided that the Mormons should move again – but this time to a remote place in the West. He made an agreement with the Illinois authorities that the Mormons would leave in 1846, in return for the ending of attacks on them.

Young decided that the Mormons should settle by the side of Great Salt Lake (now in the state of Utah), as it was barren but had mountain streams which could be used for irrigation. It was also controlled by Mexico at that time, and so out of the control of the US government. Some Mormons thought this was a bad choice, but Young said if there was a place on earth that no one else wanted, then that was the place for the Mormons.

Fact file

Brigham Young converted to the Mormons in 1832, and was a good organiser. He soon became one of the Twelve Apostles who governed the Mormon Church. After leading them out of Missouri when the other leaders were imprisoned, his influence increased. He was not in Nauvoo when Smith was murdered, but returned quickly, and remained the leader of the Mormons until his death in 1877. Like most of the main Mormon leaders, he practised polygamy: in all, he had 27 wives.

GradeStudio

Analysis of sources

Study Source B.

How useful is this source in telling you why the mormons experienced hostility in Nauvoo. Use the source and your own knowledge to explain your answer.

Examiner's tip

- Remember to use BOTH the source AND your own knowledge to explain your answer.
- Try to give at least TWO reasons – and make sure you explain these, don't just identify them.

The move West

The main migration began in the spring of 1846, and involved 16,000 people (see Source C). Earlier, Young had sent out a smaller group to establish a way-station in Iowa, which they called Garden Grove. The main group had to leave earlier than planned, as mobs began attacking their houses. Once they got to Garden Grove, Young split them up into separate groups of wagon trains of 100 wagons each, under the control of a captain selected by him. Each wagon train was then divided into groups of ten, each of which had a lieutenant. Young left in the first one, setting up further way-stations or rest camps as they went for those who would be following. By June they had reached the Missouri River where they set up camp and stayed for the winter months. It was called Winter Quarters. Bad weather and food shortages, and then a plague, resulted in the deaths of over 700 people. In April 1847, they set off again, crossing the Rocky Mountains by the Smith Pass. They reached Great Salt Lake on 24 July 1847, and founded Salt Lake City.

VOICE YOUR OPINION!

Do you think that the polygamy practised by the Mormons was just for the benefit of the men?

SOURCE C

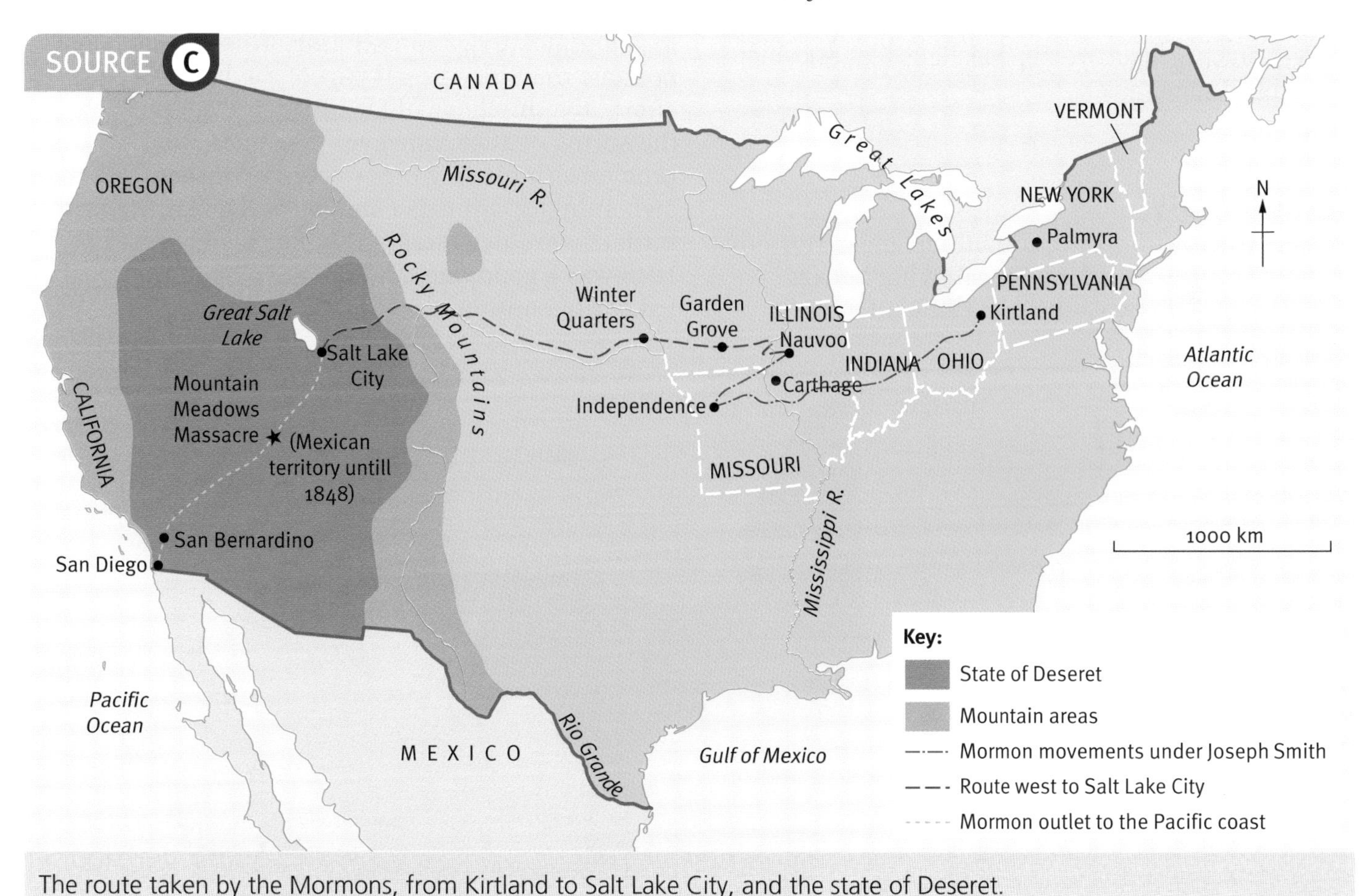

The route taken by the Mormons, from Kirtland to Salt Lake City, and the state of Deseret.

2.4 Case study: How did the Mormons live in Salt Lake City?

LEARNING OBJECTIVES

In this case study you will:

- find out what the Mormons did in Salt Lake City in order to survive
- get practice in answering questions that ask you to explain something.

Salt Lake City

Despite the unpromising conditions, most Mormons accepted Young's leadership, believing he was inspired directly by God – some saw him as a modern version of Moses. In line with Mormon beliefs, Young announced that there would be no private ownership of land or water. Instead, the land would be shared out to families according to need.

To 'make the desert bloom', the Mormons invested in a complex irrigation scheme. This proved possible only for a small part of the land – so alternative methods of farming were adopted. By the spring of 1848, however, a combination of problems (including crops eaten by insects and their own animals, animals eaten by wolves), the first settlers were near starvation. But the harvest in 1848 was a good one, and the development of Salt Lake City continued.

SOURCE A

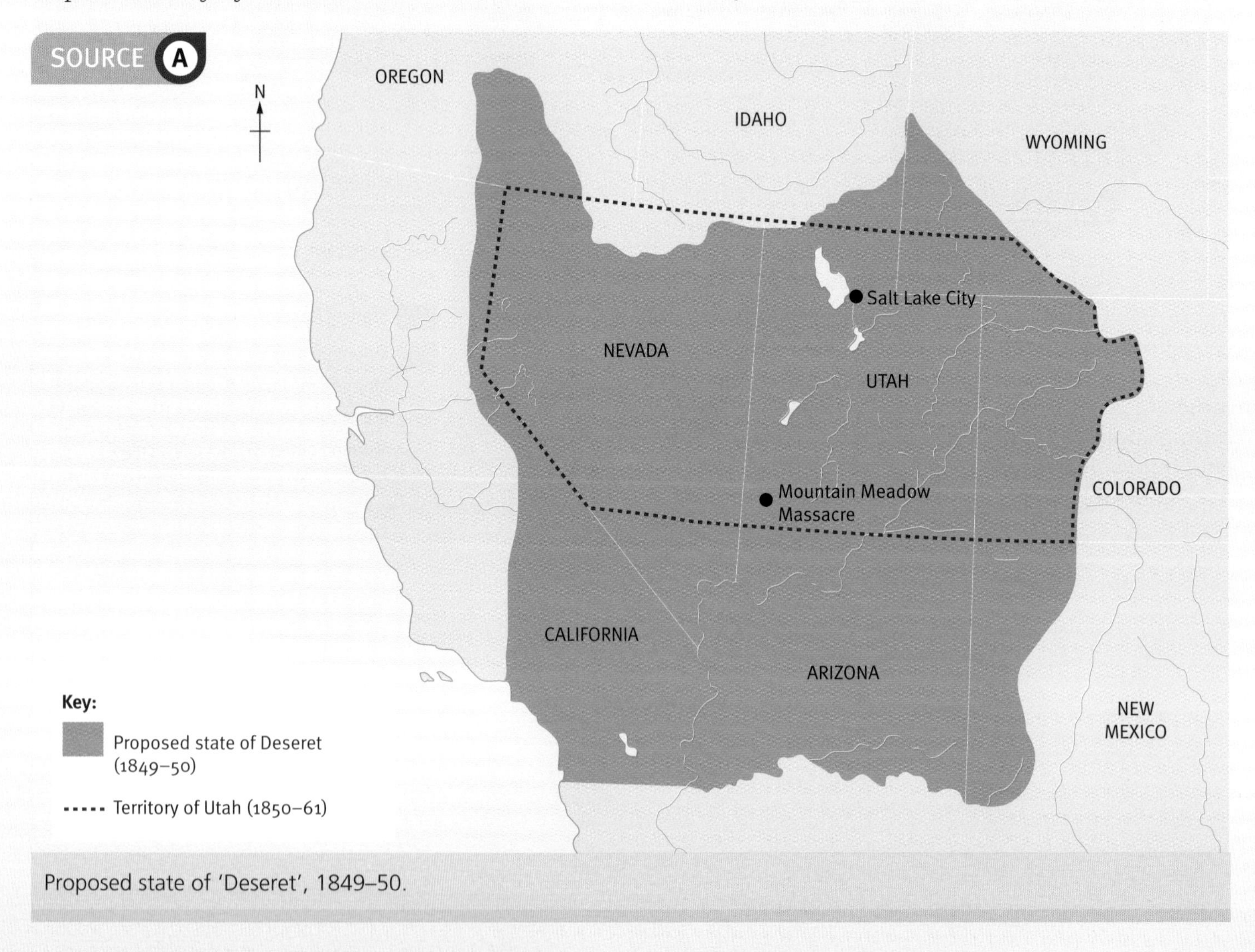

Proposed state of 'Deseret', 1849–50.

Young encouraged people to come from abroad – especially if they had manufacturing skills – setting up a Perpetual Emigrating Fund in 1849, which granted money and livestock to new emigrants, which had to be repaid once they were settled. During the 1850s, thousands of new converts arrived. But not all ventures were successful, and education was often poor or inadequate.

Although some animals were stolen by Native Americans, relations with most of the tribes were good. As Mormons believed Native Americans were one of the tribes of Israel who had come to America, Young instructed the Mormons to treat them kindly. This did not please the US government or non-Mormon settlers.

From desert to Utah

Young not only wanted the Mormons to be self-sufficient in food, he also wanted them to be self-governing, in order to avoid the persecution they had suffered previously. So, in 1848, when the USA declared war on Mexico, Young thought it would be wise to send a Mormon battalion to fight for the USA. In return, he received not only funds but, eventually, approval of his plans to set up a Mormon state. However, his first suggestion in 1849 for a Mormon-run territory to be called Deseret ('land of the honey bee') was turned down by the US government (Source A). In 1850, he was granted a smaller area to be called Utah, with himself as its governor. Although there were non-Mormons appointed to help run Utah, Young was still in overall control and many US laws were ignored.

Young then began plans to settle more and more of the territory of Utah with farms and businesses. After gold was discovered in California in 1848, Mormon farmers and business people made money selling supplies to those going west to California's gold mines. However, as the numbers increased, many began to complain that the Mormons were charging too much, and resentment against them began to grow. Rumours began to circulate that the Mormons were plotting with Native Americans to kill non-Mormon settlers.

The US government decided to intervene, and in 1857 sent an army to control the Mormons. This led to the so-called Mormon War, in which Mormons fought to protect their lands and way of life.

More US troops were sent and thousands of Mormons began to leave Utah. The newspapers took the side of the Mormons, and in 1858 the US government offered a compromise – there would be a non-Mormon governor, but the Mormons would be allowed to develop in peace. Disputes still continued over polygamy, with an anti-polygamy law of 1862 being ignored by the Mormons. But as the Mormons wanted Utah to be part of the USA, they eventually had to agree to abandon polygamy. Utah became a US state in 1896.

HISTORY DETECTIVE

During the Mormon War, an incident took place at Mountain Meadows – see what you can find out about this.

Explanation and analysis

Explain why the Mormons still faced problems after the move to Salt Lake City.

Examiner's tip

- Remember – you need to do more than just identify the problems: you must try to use your own knowledge to explain why they were problems.
- Also – make sure you explain TWO different reasons.

2.5 How important was gold mining in the opening up of the West?

LEARNING OBJECTIVES

In this lesson you will:

- find out about the start of gold mining in the West and its impact on the West
- learn how to produce high-scoring answers to questions that ask you to analyse sources for usefulness. You will find below some helpful tips about how to do this, and activities which give you practice at answering such questions.

KEY WORDS

Forty-Niners – *those miners who took part in the Great California Gold Rush of 1849.*

The California Gold Rush

The next important factor in opening up the West was the California Gold Rush in 1849. This soon led to large new settlements which needed a wide range of services. The people in these areas also wanted faster transport; this eventually led to the coming of the railroads (see Lessons 2.7 and 2.8).

The Gold Rush and its impact

The discovery of gold by Henry Bigler and James Marshall in January 1848 at Sutter's Mill, California, was kept secret at first. But when news leaked out, it led to thousands flocking there in what became one of the biggest migrations in the history of the West. By the end of 1848, over 10,000 were in California digging for gold – by 1849, there were over 90,000. They became known as the '**Forty-Niners**'. These were mostly men, under the age of 30, from many different countries – in the first wave about 25,000 came from China, and thousands from Mexico. They were attracted by the possibilities of adventure, a better life and, of course, the chance to become very rich.

The California Gold Rush was followed by discoveries (of gold or silver) from the 1850s to 1890s, in places such as Colorado, Montana, Wyoming, Idaho, Dakota and Nevada. These discoveries further encouraged the move West.

A few miners became rich, but most were unsuccessful. Finding small quantities of gold might earn an average of $20 a day – but the costs of food and equipment could be as much as $18 a day. In poorer sites, miners made only $3 a day.

Mining towns

Because of the great numbers of people, mining towns grew up rapidly anywhere that mining lasted more than a couple of months. Most were dirty and unhealthy places, with diseases such as cholera being quite common. Often, such a settlement was shortlived – once the deposits were exhausted, the miners moved on – and many soon became 'ghost towns'. However, in some towns, big business moved in and many miners later brought their families out West to join them.

The thousands of migrants rushing to the gold mining camps and towns in the West needed a wide range of services, such as food, wood and equipment and tools. This demand stimulated the development of the West, as it increased profits for logging companies, farmers, shopkeepers and merchants. It also added to the wealth and expansion of the USA itself, as increased investment led to industrial growth, and provided the wealth with which to buy essential materials such as steel for the railway lines. Between 1851 and 1855, the USA produced almost 45 per cent of the world's gold.

It also encouraged both the US government and entrepreneurs to expand and improve transport to the West, to connect up with the more permanent settlements. Roads were improved, and new towns grew up along the routes; later, railways were built. The seaport of San Francisco also benefited, and soon became an important financial centre.

SOURCE 

A newspaper extract about the discovery of gold in California in 1849.

GOLD MINE FOUND.—In the newly made raceway of the Saw Mill recently erected by Captain Sutter, on the American Fork, gold has been found in considerable quantities. One person brought thirty dollars worth to New Helvetia, gathered there in a short time. California, no doubt, is rich in mineral wealth; great chances here for scientific capitalists. Gold has been found in almost every part of the country.

The impact of mining

Much of the mining took place on Native American lands, and the influx of travellers and the expansion of transport increasingly disrupted the way of life of the Plains' Indians, as thousands of migrants crossed their hunting grounds. This became more of a problem for the Plains' Indians when gold was discovered on their lands: for example, the discovery of gold in the Black Hills in Dakota was on ground sacred to the Sioux. The tension increased when the US government began to build forts to protect the miners and their settlements.

SOURCE B

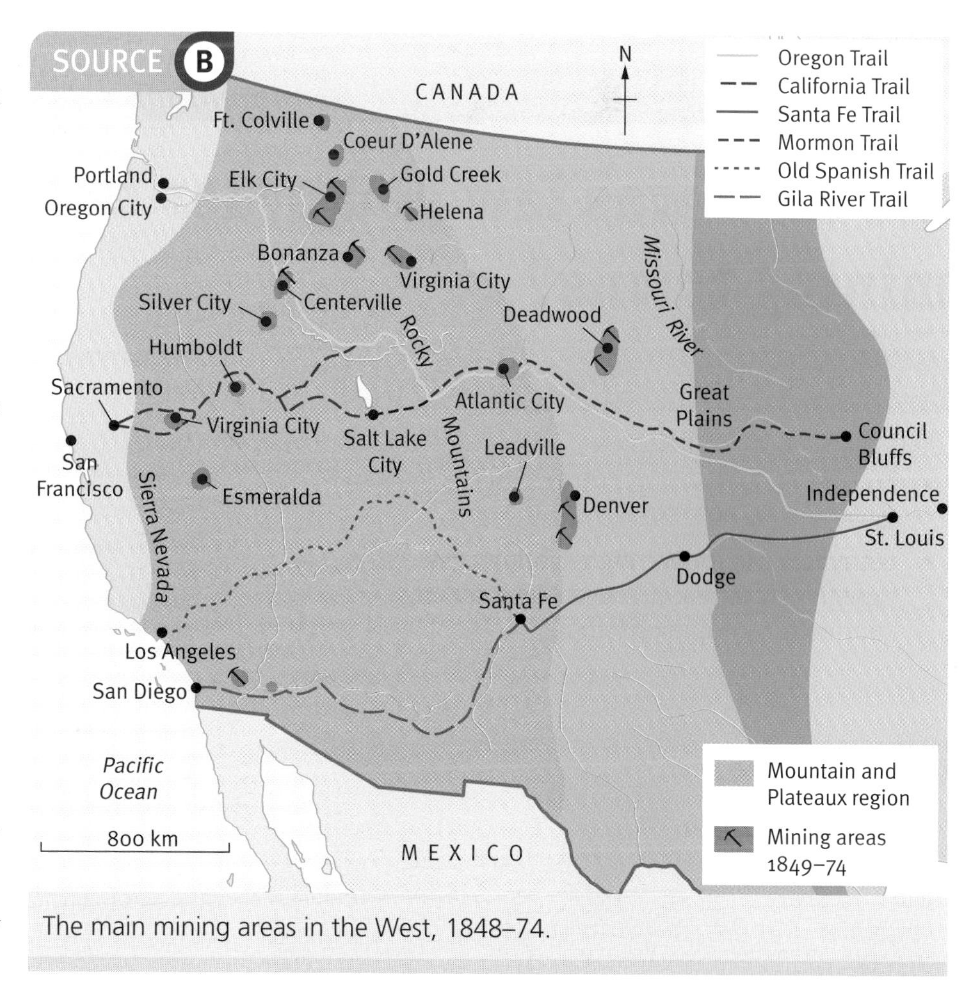

The main mining areas in the West, 1848–74.

Later developments

As the deposits of gold and silver near the surface began to run out, mining became an increasingly expensive operation. Often, it was necessary to tunnel or quarry into the sides of mountains – this required a great amount of money, beyond the reach of most individuals. So large mining companies and corporations began to take over. Individual miners often found they had no choice but to become the paid employees of these large, powerful organisations.

Working underground often meant more unpleasant conditions and greater danger than working on the surface. In addition, pay was often poor and the hours were long.

SOURCE C

Miners 'panning' for gold in 1849.

GradeStudio

Analysis of sources

Study Sources A, B and C.

How useful are Sources A, B and C in telling you about the impact of gold mining on the Great Plains in the second half of the nineteenth century?

Use the sources and your own knowledge to explain your answer.

Examiner's tip

- Before you start to write your answer, look carefully at the sources to see what they say about gold mining and the various areas affected.
- In order to properly assess the usefulness of these sources, you will now need to use factual information from this lesson to show the actual impact of gold mining. How many of these reasons are shown/referred to by the sources?
- Now see if you can make an overall judgement about how useful the sources are AND which one is the *most* useful – if you fail to do this, you'll miss out on the top marks.

2.6 How was law and order organised in the mining towns?

LEARNING OBJECTIVES

In this lesson you will:

- find out about law and order problems in mining towns
- get practice in answering questions that ask you to explain why different sources give different information or opinions about a topic.

KEY WORDS

American Civil War – *this was the civil war fought from 1860–65, between the Northern states (Unionists) and the Southern states (Confederates) in large part over the issue of slavery.*

Claim-jumping – *the act of taking over another miner's claim or stake to a gold mine, or someone else's land.*

Lynching – *the unlawful hanging by a mob of an accused person, usually without a proper trial.*

Law and order in mining towns

Because mining took place in remote places, the federal and state governments at first found it difficult to enforce law and order. In particular, the distance and the difficulties of travel meant that decisions from the authorities often took a long time to reach these new centres. Mining towns, which often grew up very quickly, had no US government or state law officers such as marshals and sheriffs. Consequently, miners often took matters into their own hands. (To find out about law and order in the 'cow towns', see Lesson 3.6 on pp. 78–81.)

Main problems

One of the most frequent problems related to **claim-jumping**, so miners often held meetings to choose a chair and officers, and drew up their own 'mining code'. Claims to mines were recorded, and any disputes were meant to be settled by a committee of miners. They sometimes appointed their own sheriff and vigilante groups, and had their own 'miners' courts' which decided on punishments.

As there were no prisons in the early towns, the punishments were often brutal: they included flogging, cutting off ears, banishment and **lynching**. Justice was not always fair, witnesses were often intimidated and there was usually no appeal. However, this was not true of all mining towns. In many, conflicts were usually settled democratically, without violence.

Another cause of law and order problems was racial tension between different groups. This was still a time when slavery was common in many US states, and many white miners looked down on the Chinese, Indians, Mexicans and black miners who came in significant numbers. Many mining camps and towns banned ethnic minorities from mining in their area. Mobs often attacked such minorities, and tried to drive them off from any good claims – murder was not uncommon, especially of Native Americans. In California, the Native Americans were virtually wiped out by the spread of mining.

A further cause of problems was the number of saloons in most mining towns. In 1855, San Francisco had 537 saloons. These often led to gambling and alcohol-related problems, made worse by the poor conditions in most mining towns, and the large and frequently changing populations. Many turned to drunkenness and gambling as a way to relieve boredom and hard work. Prostitution was also an issue – with so few women in the mining towns, disputes over them were common.

How violent were mining towns?

One of the best known mining towns was Deadwood in South Dakota. In 1876, when gold was discovered in the Black Hills, over 7000 miners rushed to it. In 1877, it had 75 saloons, and many gambling places, and, for a brief period, built up a notorious reputation for lawlessness and violence (see Sources A and B). Probably its most famous crime took place on 2 August 1876, when a man shot Wild Bill Hickok in the back of the head, while he was playing poker – because, he claimed, Hickok had shot his brother.

However, like many other mining towns, law and order problems in Deadwood were much worse in the first few years of the mining boom following the 1876 discoveries. As the town began to settle down, the violence began to decline.

SOURCE A

Downtown Deadwood at the height of its fame, 1876.

SOURCE B

Full of crooks of all kinds – gamblers, confidence men, pickpockets, thieves, highwaymen, and murderers.

An extract from a description of Deadwood made by Nathan Butler, a citizen of Deadwood, in 1877.

SOURCE C

Deadwood is one of the most moral and best behaved mining towns in the west.

An extract from the *Deadwood Times*, 1883.

HISTORY DETECTIVE

In the early days, when a miner found gold, he staked his 'claim' to mine it by leaving a set of tools in a hole in the ground. As more and more miners arrived, 'claims-jumping' became common. Try to find out more about 'claims-jumping'.

Fact file

Wild Bill Hickok's real name was James Butler Hickok. He picked up his nickname during the **American Civil War** (1861–65) and, after the war, acted as an army scout. He was both a gunfighter and a law enforcement officer, and killed many men. In 1869, he was appointed town marshal of Hays, in Kansas, and then became a marshal in the cattle town of Abilene. He came to Deadwood in 1876, but disappointed many by gambling and focusing on gold mining when they hoped he would help to impose law and order in the town.

GradeStudio

Analysis of sources

The early mining towns in the West were often violent places, though this gradually changed over time.

1. Study Source A. What impressions of Deadwood does this source give you?
2. Study Sources B and C. Why do you think these two sources give different accounts of Deadwood? Use the sources and your knowledge.

Examiner's tip

Question 1
Do not simply describe what you can see in Source A. You need to make **inferences** from the source e.g. does it look a good place to live, does it look as if it was built quickly or had been developing over a long period, does it look large? However, make sure you support your inferences by using details from the source.

Question 2
Make sure you explain **why** Sources B and C give different accounts of Deadwood. Do not simply describe ways in which they differ.

Make sure you use what you have just learned about how, and why, mining towns changed over time. This will help you explain why the two sources give different accounts of Deadwood.

2.7 Why were railways constructed across the Great Plains to the West?

LEARNING OBJECTIVES

In this lesson you will:

- find out why the US government wanted to build railways connecting the East to the West
- get practice in answering questions that ask you to describe aspects of a topic.

KEY WORDS

Shanty towns – *settlements/towns of poorly built houses/shacks, normally used as temporary accommodation (e.g. the early mining camps, or for those building the railways).*

Transcontinental railroad – *the idea of a railway system going across the USA, to link the Atlantic coast in the East to the Pacific coast in the West.*

Problems of travel and communications

There were many reasons why the US government and other organisations wanted to build railways to the West. After purchasing Oregon from Britain in 1846, and then defeating Mexico and taking California in 1848, nationalism increased in the USA. In particular, it made sense to link up the East Coast with the new territories in the West. This was closely connected to the growing belief in 'Manifest Destiny', as improved routes would enable even more people to settle in the West.

This led the US government to finance mapping and surveying for new routes to the West. Also, the first settlers who had moved across the Great Plains to the new territories of Oregon and California wanted regular deliveries of post and goods from the East – but, at first, this took over four months. They also wanted good links to send their products back East.

In addition, the US government wanted to absorb and control the new territories coming into its possession – especially as there were often law and order problems in the mining towns and, later, in the cattle towns. The federal government was keen to benefit from the gold and wealth being created in the West, and to open seaports on the West coast, in order to trade with countries such as China.

At first, the government began to subsidise shipping and stage-coach lines. However, the first emphasis was on steamboats and sea travel, which were both slow and costly.

By the 1850s, there were also many US army forts in the West that needed to be supplied. The emphasis then shifted to stagecoaches and freight-wagons. The US government paid money to improve the roads. Most famous of the stagecoach companies was the Wells Fargo Express. In 1858, the Butterfield Overland Mail began regular services carrying passengers and post between East and West. Though this cut the journey to 25 days, it was still not fast enough.

The need for a railway network

After 1848, as the numbers of miners and settlers in the West increased, the US government began to see a **transcontinental railroad** as a way of uniting the country – and it soon gave strong support to such a scheme. As early as 1853, it paid $150,000 for a survey to be undertaken for possible routes from the Atlantic to the Pacific. The US army then began surveying possible routes, but the American Civil War, which began in 1861, closed off southern routes so a central one was chosen.

How the railways were built

In 1862, Congress passed the Pacific Railways Act, which set up two companies: the Central Pacific Railroad (starting in California) and the Union Pacific Railroad (starting in Omaha). The plan was for the Union Pacific to go as far as Missouri, and then branch out across the Great Plains (see Source A).

The government helped by giving generous loans, grants, and land next to the tracks, to last for 30 years (see Source B). However, the companies needed more money than this and, as private investment was slow to come, the railway companies used the land grants as security for getting loans from banks and, later, often then sold the land cheaply to settlers, to raise the extra money needed.

Routes through mountains were difficult. About 10,000 immigrant workers were brought in, including many Chinese, by the Central Pacific

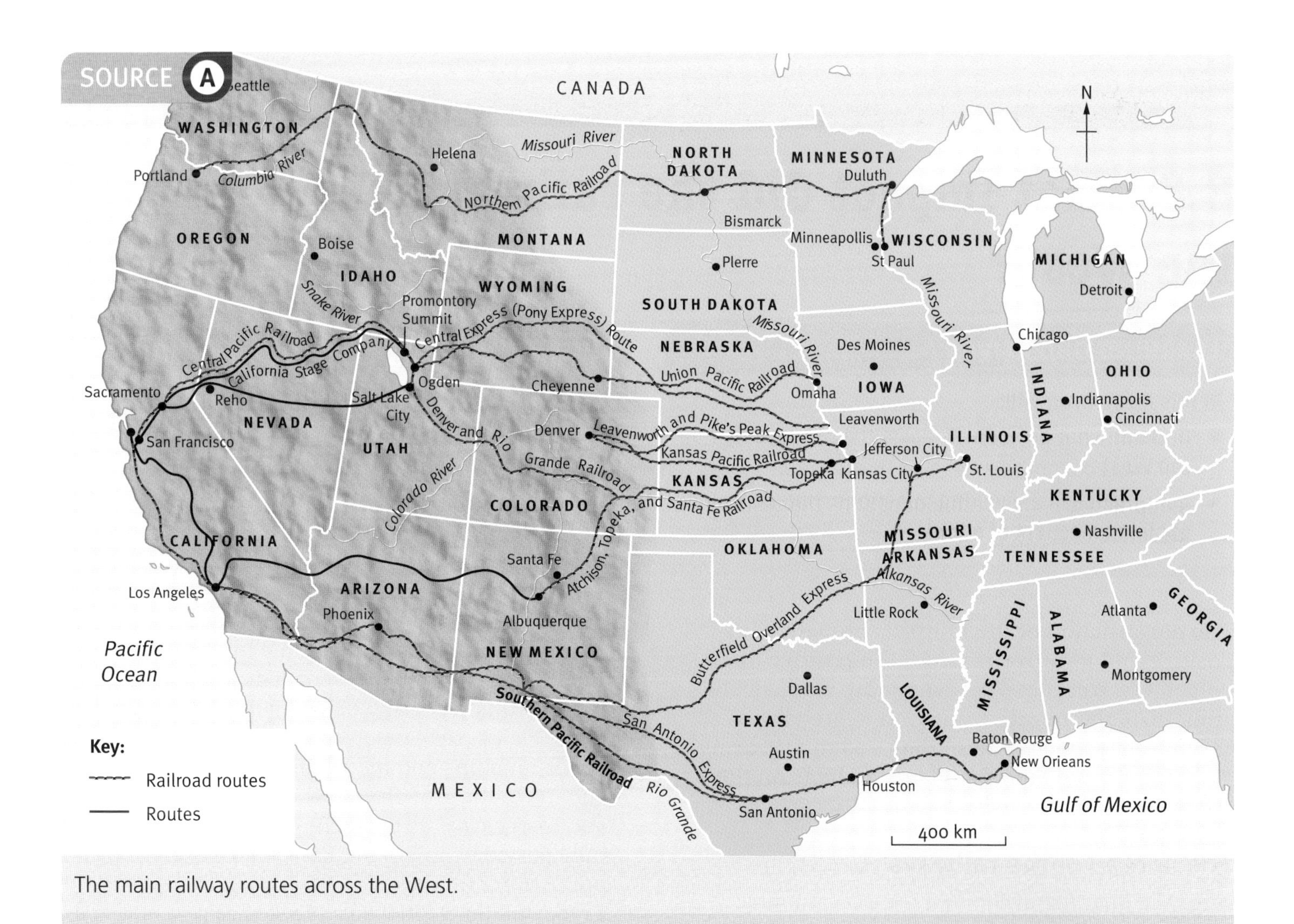

The main railway routes across the West.

Railway Company (see Source C). As in the mining camps and towns, these workers often suffered bad treatment and prejudice. Conditions were hard and dangerous – including severe weather and landslides. Then the government set 10 May 1869 as the completion date – so immigrant Irish labourers were recruited to speed things up. But the Civil War continued to slow progress.

Once the Civil War ended in 1865, however, even more workers were brought West. They often lived in **shanty towns**, which grew up alongside the tracks; these could be as unhealthy and violent as the mining towns. Finally, on 10 May 1869, at the Golden Spike Ceremony, the two lines met at Promontory Summit, Utah. The journey time from San Francisco to New York dropped to just ten days.

SOURCE B

How the US government helped finance the building of the railways.

Government and state land grants to railway companies (1856–71)
180,233,966 acres (at about $5 an acre)

Government loans to state railway companies (1861)
$16,000 per mile (flat land)
$32,000 per mile (mountain areas)
$48,000 per mile (mountains)

SOURCE C

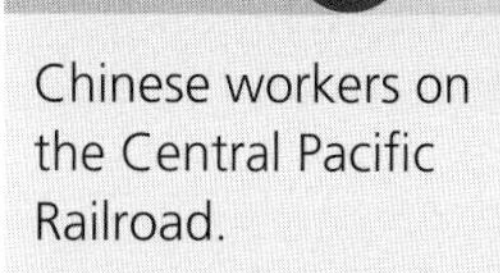

Chinese workers on the Central Pacific Railroad.

BRAIN BOOST

Draw a timeline, showing the main attempts to improve communications and travel between the East and West coasts from 1840 to 1870.

2.8 What impact did the railways have on the West?

LEARNING OBJECTIVES

In this lesson you will:

- find out what different impacts the railways had on the West
- get practice in answering questions that ask you to explain an aspect of a topic.

The construction of the railroads brought both positive and negative results – the positive ones helped the West develop even more extensively after 1870; the negative ones led to growing conflicts between white settlers and the US army on the one hand, and the Plains' Indians on the other.

The spread of the railways

After the opening of the first transcontinental railway in 1869, there was a great rush to build more railways. Four more major ones were built, along with many smaller branch lines to remoter places – mostly in the West.

The four most important ones were the Southern Pacific Railroad, the Northern Pacific Railroad, the Denver and Rio Grande Railroad, and the Atchison, Topeka and Sante Fe Railroad. Between 1850 and 1890, railtracks increased from 20,000 km to 324,000 km – this was greater than the whole of Europe's rail network, including Britain and Russia. By the 1880s, the journey time from East to West had fallen to four days on the faster trains – though slower trains still took ten days – and over one million people travelled on the railways each year (see Source A).

The growth of the West

The coming of the railways helped the West to develop in a number of ways.

- Cities connected or close to the railways – such as Los Angeles, Dallas and Denver – grew quickly. Some of the temporary shanty towns became permanent settled towns and grew in size, for example Cheyenne and Laramie in Wyoming.
- Thousands of farms were created close to the rail routes – this especially helped homesteaders on the Great Plains (see Lessons 2.9–2.11 on pp. 52–59).
- Cattle ranching and the cattle industry benefited and led to the growth of cow towns such as Abilene and Dodge City, as the cattle could now be transported by rail to the East (see Lesson 3.1 on pp. 66–69).
- Trade and heavy industry profited as raw materials and finished products for export could now be transported easily between East and West. By the 1890s, this had helped the West to be part of the great industrial boom or revolution taking place in the USA. By 1890, the USA had become the world's leading industrial power.
- Quicker access between the ports on the two coasts increased foreign trade, and helped the US become even wealthier.
- The railways helped the West become more law-abiding and developed – as federal law officers, judges, government officials and teachers could get there more easily.

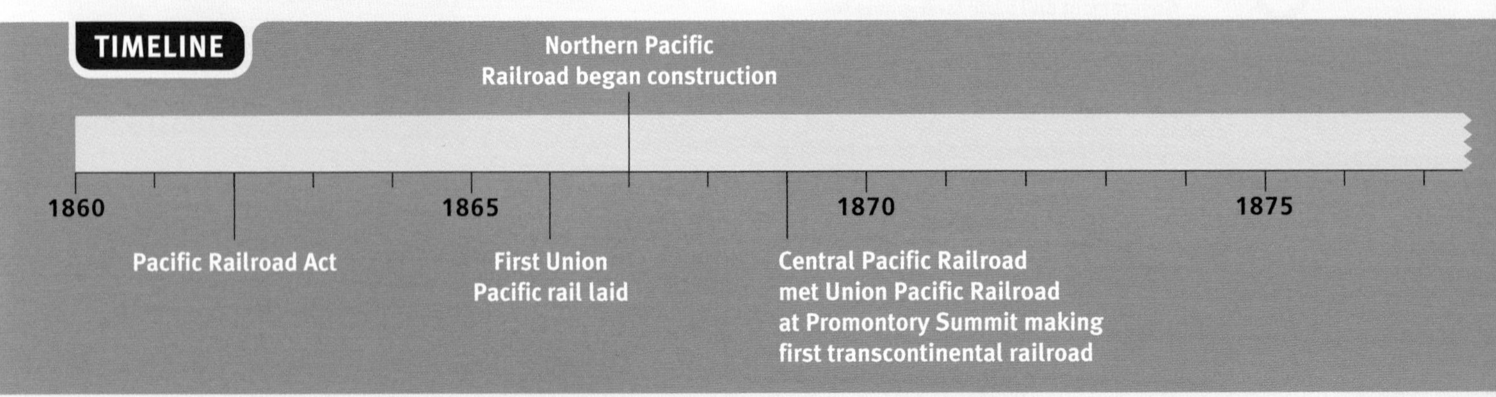

All of these things made it easier for increasing numbers of people to go to the West and settle. This led to a second major migration West, this time on to the Great Plains themselves, rather than just across to the West coast and adjoining areas.

Problems caused by the growth of the railways

The coming of the railroads created several problems, including the following.

- There was growing conflict between white settlers and the US army on the one side, and the Plains' Indians on the other, after 1870. This was because the railroads disrupted the great buffalo herds and thus the Plains' Indians' traditional way of life. Thousands of settlers now wanted to live on the Indians' traditional hunting grounds.
- Competition from the trains greatly affected the stagecoach and freight wagon companies – though they did continue to provide services from the railheads to those remote settlements on the Plains which had no branch lines.
- Some farmers felt the rail companies charged high prices for a poor service.
- Towns not on or near the railway lines often became deserted, and the businesses in them collapsed.

After 1870, many railroad companies spent huge amounts on advertising – not just to get people to travel on their trains, but also to settle in the West (see Source A). The more people and businesses in the West, the more customers they would have for their services!

SOURCE A

1869. May 10th. 1869.
GREAT EVENT
Rail Road from the Atlantic to the Pacific
GRAND OPENING
OF THE
Union Pacific
RAIL ROAD,
PLATTE VALLEY ROUTE.
PASSENGER TRAINS LEAVE
OMAHA
ON THE ARRIVAL OF TRAINS FROM THE EAST.
THROUGH TO SAN FRANCISCO
In less than Four Days, avoiding the Dangers of the Sea!
Travelers for Pleasure, Health or Business
LUXURIOUS CARS & EATING HOUSES
ON THE UNION PACIFIC RAIL ROAD.
PULLMAN'S PALACE SLEEPING CARS
RUN WITH ALL THROUGH PASSENGER TRAINS.
GOLD, SILVER AND OTHER MINERS!
CONNECTIONS MADE AT
CHEYENNE for DENVER, CENTRAL CITY & SANTA FE
THROUGH TICKETS FOR SALE AT ALL PRINCIPAL RAILROAD OFFICES!
Be Sure they Read via Platte Valley or Omaha

A poster advertising the opening of the first transcontinental railway in 1869.

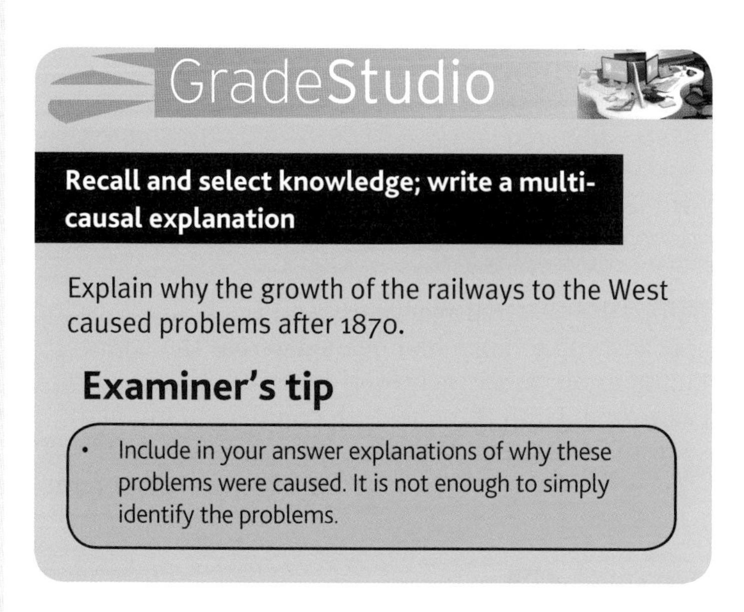

Recall and select knowledge; write a multi-causal explanation

Explain why the growth of the railways to the West caused problems after 1870.

Examiner's tip

- Include in your answer explanations of why these problems were caused. It is not enough to simply identify the problems.

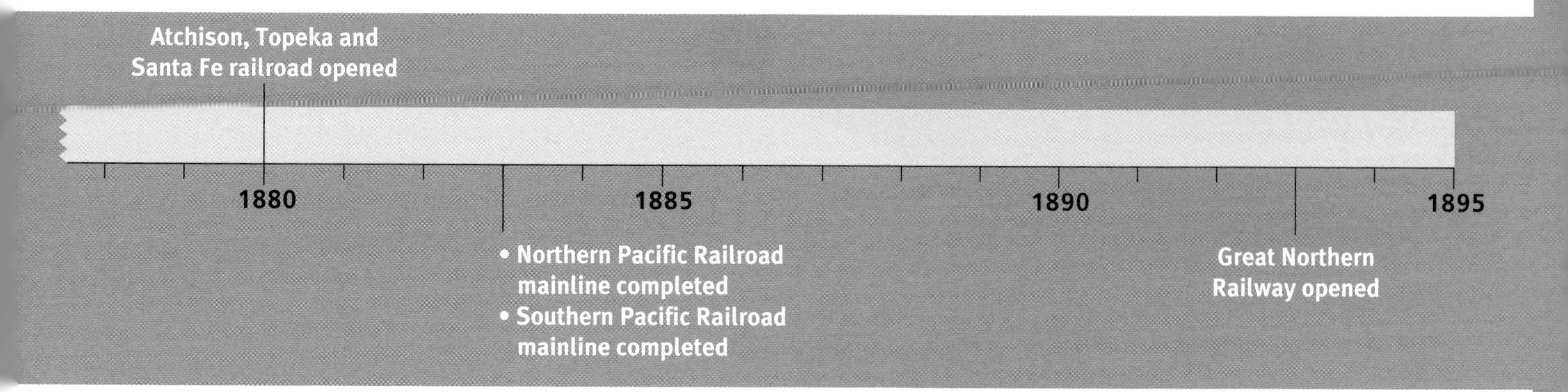

2.9 Why did people want to settle on the Great Plains?

LEARNING OBJECTIVES

In this lesson you will:

- find out why so many people wanted to settle on the Great Plains after 1860
- get practice in answering questions that ask you to explain the usefulness of a source.

KEY WORDS

Demobilised soldiers – *soldiers released from service (and so often made unemployed) once a war is over.*

Indian Territory – *the area/areas of land which successive US governments said the Indians could keep – this land was not to be settled on or mined, and sometimes not even crossed, by whites. The size of this land was continually reduced, until Indians were left with much smaller reservations.*

Before the US Civil War, early settlers going West and wishing to farm had headed across the Great Plains to the newly acquired states of Oregon or California. Until the mid-19th century, many had seen the Great Plains as the 'Great American Desert' – but then perceptions began to change (see Lesson 1.2 on pages 6–9).

SOURCE A

European immigrants on a flatcar provided by a railway company, being shown possible farming sites in Kansas.

During the 1860s, the US government began to encourage people to settle on the Great Plains. From then on, larger numbers headed West to the Great Plains – and on to land that had been promised by the government to the Plains' Indians who lived there.

Reasons for moving West

As with the earlier migration of pioneers West (see Lesson 2.2), there was a combination of 'push' and 'pull' factors which, after 1850, led thousands of people to travel great distances – thousands of miles in some cases – to build a new life for themselves on the Great Plains. Land continued to be scarce and expensive in the East, while many were seeking a more prosperous life. At the same time, there were problems of land shortages, poverty and unemployment in many European countries, which resulted in thousands wanting to emigrate to the USA and start a new life. Others – for instance, Jewish people – wished to escape religious persecution. These, too, saw the USA as their salvation.

The US government itself was keen for American citizens – and immigrants from across the world – to populate the West. It passed a series of acts in the 1860s and 1870s making millions of hectares of land on the Great Plains available to encourage people to settle. By 1895, there were nearly 450,000 new homesteads (small farms) on the Great Plains (see Source A).

The numbers of settlers greatly increased following the end of the American Civil War in 1865. Thousands of **demobilised soldiers** and their families, whose lives had been disrupted by the war – especially in those parts of the South which had been devastated by the war – were looking for a new life There were also thousands of newly freed slaves who wanted to move from the South, where they were often persecuted by white Americans (see Source B). To both these groups, the West seemed the place to go, away from the problems in the East and the South. Some wanted to be farmers, while others soon found employment building railroads, working as cowboys on the new cattle ranches on the Plains, or working in the mines.

The building of the transcontinental railroads, which linked the East and West, and reduced travelling time, made journeys much safer than the earlier method of travel by wagon trains, and so meant it was easier to move West. After 1869, more and more railroads were built. In addition, the railway companies often sold off the land granted to them by the US government in order to raise extra money. This meant land could be bought cheaply. Consequently, the numbers wishing to move to the West increased greatly after 1869. Railway companies also advertised widely to spread news about the benefits of moving West, as did many of the new territories and states.

Finally, as with the previous migrations West, the first to go then wrote letters back to their families and friends still in the East, saying how life was better and encouraging them to come and join them.

US government actions

The first act passed by the US government after 1860 to encourage people to move on to the Great Plains was the Homestead Act of 1862. This gave all heads of households, and all males over 21, about 160 acres (about 80 hectares) in the West if they built a house (homestead) on their plot and worked on it for five years. In addition, they had either to pay a $10 entry fee, or pay $1.25 per acre. This led to the biggest growth in farming in US history – with over 65 per cent of farms resulting from the 1862 Act.

Another important action of the US government – especially after the Civil War had ended – was to break treaties made previously with the Plains' Indians which had confirmed the Great Plains as '**Indian Territory**'. Instead, they began to force the Plains' Indians to accept smaller areas, called reservations, where they were to stay (see Lesson 4.2 on pp. 98–99). These actions were increasingly enforced by the US army, who protected the new settlers and fought the Plains' Indians. Land 'cleared' in this way was then made available to the new settlers.

SOURCE B

All Colored People

THAT WANT TO

GO TO KANSAS,

On September 5th, 1877,

Can do so for $5.00

IMMIGRATION.

WHEREAS, We, the colored people of Lexington, Ky,. knowing that there is an abundance of choice lands now belonging to the Government, have assembled ourselves together for the purpose of locating on said lands. Therefore,

BE IT RESOLVED, That we do now organize ourselves into a Colony, as follows:— Any person wishing to become a member of this Colony can do so by paying the sum of one dollar ($1.00), and this money is to be paid by the first of September, 1877, in instalments of twenty-five cents at a time, or otherwise as may be desired.

RESOLVED. That this Colony has agreed to consolidate itself with the Nicodemus Towns, Solomon Valley, Graham County, Kansas, and can only do so by entering the vacant lands now in their midst, which costs $5.00.

RESOLVED, That this Colony shall consist of seven officers—President, Vice-President, Secretary, Treasurer, and three Trustees. President—M. M. Bell; Vice-President —Isaac Talbott; Secretary—W. J. Niles; Treasurer—Daniel Clarke; Trustees—Jerry Lee, William Jones, and Abner Webster

RESOLVED, That this Colony shall have from one to two hundred militia, more or less, as the case may require, to keep peace and order, and any member failing to pay in his dues, as aforesaid, or failing to comply with the above rules in any particular, will not be recognized or protected by the Colony.

A poster urging black people to leave the South after the Civil War and go to Kansas.

GradeStudio

Analysis of sources

Study Source B.

What does this source tell you about why people moved to the Great Plains after 1860. Use the source and your own knowledge to explain your answer. **[7 marks]**

Examiner's tip

- Remember to use information from the source to explain how and why people moved to the Great Plains – and remember to use your own knowledge to support your comments with precise facts.

VOICE YOUR OPINION!

What do you think about the US government's actions after 1860 in relation to encouraging people to settle on the Plains?

2.10 What problems did the homesteaders face on the Great Plains?

LEARNING OBJECTIVES

In this lesson you will:

- find out about the problems faced by the homesteaders and how the homesteaders and the US government tried to solve these problems
- get practice in answering questions that ask you to describe an aspect of a topic.

KEY WORDS

Homesteaders – *those settlers who gained land on the Plains for their homes and farms (homesteads); particularly applied to those who moved onto the Plains after the 1862 Homestead Act.*

Despite all the encouragement and help given to migrants to settle on the Great Plains, they faced many problems. These were of two main types – the actual living and farming conditions on the Great Plains, and problems with the 1862 Homestead Act.

Farming on the Great Plains

Though the area of the Great Plains was not the 'Great American Desert' as once thought by many Americans, it was not always ideal farming land. The soil was often dry and not very fertile – even ploughing the land was difficult, as the prairie grasses had thick tangled roots, and the early cast-iron ploughs were often damaged.

Even building a house was a problem because there were very few trees, unless you were lucky enough to have a plot in a river valley. Only the well-off could afford to import timber from the East. Consequently, timber shortages meant many lived in sod houses or dug-outs. Sod houses were made from pieces of turf (sods) cut into large bricks, with roofs made from timber which was then covered with more sod and grass (see Source A). These were more permanent and better than the dug-outs, which were a quick, short-term solution to living on the Plains – they were just dwellings hollowed out of the sides of hills, with a wall of turf and the opening (see Source B).

Also, because of the lack of wood, there were no fences, so it was difficult to keep cattle – or buffalo – off the growing crops. The lack of clearly marked boundaries sometimes led to conflicts with neighbours.

Another important problem in many areas was the lack of water: there were very few rivers or lakes that could be used for irrigation, in the way the Mormons had at Salt Lake City. While some **homesteaders** had been able to settle near streams, others were dependent on ponds or buffalo wallows, which often dried up. This could mean the loss of crops, and bankruptcy or even starvation. While some tried to overcome this by digging wells, many found it expensive, extremely hard work and often almost impossible – in some parts of the Great Plains, the water table was 60 metres below ground. This meant not only problems for growing crops, but also for keeping clean and washing clothes.

Lack of fuel was another problem – there were few trees and no coal. So homesteaders did what the Plains' Indians did – used the dried dung of the buffalo (buffalo chips) instead. Additional problems were caused by insects such as grasshoppers which ate the crops and vegetation – and clothing, curtains and farm implements as well. In 1871, 1874 and 1875, there were serious plagues of grasshoppers on parts of the Great Plains, which destroyed thousands of hectares of corn. There were also snakes and scorpions to cope with.

In addition to all this, there were extreme climate variations – including spring floods, and droughts in the summer, which brought the added risk of prairie fires that could destroy crops. In Kansas, for instance, there was no rain at all from January 1859 to November 1860. There were also tornados known as 'twisters', and deep snow and extremely low temperatures in winter (often as low as –40°C). While the Plains' Indians coped with these problems by moving camp with the seasons, the homesteaders had to stay in one place if they were to retain their plot and harvest their crops.

Problems with the 1862 Homestead Act

In addition to practical difficulties faced by the homesteaders, there were problems with the 1862 Homestead Act. The prices set by the act – a $10 entry fee paid up front or $1.25 an acre for 160 acres (about 80 hectares), to be paid for in six months (this came to $200) – were too high for many ordinary people. Since much of the land was of poor quality, the homesteaders needed considerably more than 160 acres to be able to farm successfully. As a result, speculators and railroad companies bought up most of the best land. Some speculators got round the act by having rough shacks on wheels, which they moved from plot to plot, and so were able to obtain a great deal of the available land. Consequently, many genuine homesteaders were left with poor land which was far from the towns and railways.

Fact file

Sod houses and dug-outs attracted insects, mice and snakes, and were impossible to keep clean. They were also damp, and easily became muddy. Consequently, disease was a constant problem – especially for children. However, they were warm in winter and cool in summer.

SOURCE A

A sod house in Nebraska in 1887.

SOURCE B

A dug-out in Nebraska in 1890.

BRAIN BOOST

Use the information on these two pages to make a spider diagram of the main problems facing homesteaders on the Great Plains.

When you've done this, use two different colours to show which were natural problems, and which were caused by human activity. Remember to do a key!

How the homesteaders overcame their problems

Some of the early problems faced by the first homesteaders were solved as the years passed – but many of them were not really solved until the 1880s. Consequently, some homesteaders – especially those on very poor soil – gave up after a year or two. But most stayed on after their first year, and were able to benefit from a number of changes and new farming machinery and techniques.

Early government action

Once the US government became aware of the problems with the 1862 Homestead Act – and how speculators were getting around it – it tried to improve matters by passing further acts. The main ones were:

- the Timber Culture Act, 1873 – this gave an extra 160 acres (about 80 hectares) if trees were planted on 25 per cent of the land. This was also intended to help with the timber shortage on the Great Plains.
- the Desert Land Act, 1877 – this allowed people to buy 640 acres (about 300 hectares) in certain dry areas for $1.25 an acre if they improved it over three years.

Fact file

Despite these new acts, much of the land was eventually bought up by speculators and the big ranchers.

The importance of the railways

The coming of the railroads in the 1870s (see Lesson 2.7) also helped the homesteaders because not only did many rail companies sell to settlers the land granted to them by the government but also, more importantly, the improved railway network meant crops could be transported quickly and often more cheaply to the big cities in the East or for export to countries such as Britain (see Source C).

Later developments in homesteading

The early homesteaders (known as 'sodbusters' by the cowboys) on the Great Plains planted wheat and corn. But their farming methods were more suited to the better climate and fertile soil of the East, while their ploughs and other farming equipment were often not up to the harsher conditions found on the Plains.

However, from 1870, several developments made life easier and farming more profitable for thousands of homesteaders. As the problems were overcome, the Great Plains became covered with wheat and corn fields. The main developments were:

1 Barbed wire

One problem had been the growth of cattle ranching on the 'open range' (see Lesson 3.2, pp. 70–71), with roaming herds often ruining crops. Wood was too scarce and expensive for fencing, leading to conflicts between homesteaders and ranchers. Then, in 1874, barbed wire was invented and was soon mass-produced. This gave a cheap and effective solution to protecting crops but, though this was popular with homesteaders, many ranchers objected (see Lesson 3.7, pp. 82–83).

2 Windmills

Lack of water was overcome by an invention of 1874 – the self-governing windmill, which was used to pump water from under the ground and which could withstand the strong winds of the Great Plains. This soon led to a drop in the price of wind pumps which, at first, had been too expensive for most homesteaders: by the 1890s they had dropped to $25. This meant deep wells could be dug, allowing irrigation, which overcame the drying winds of the Great Plains.

3 'Dry farming' techniques

'Dry farming' techniques, via deep ploughing, were another way in which the water problems of homesteading were overcome. Homesteaders ploughed the land while it was still wet from heavy rain or snow, so that a layer of dust formed on top of the land, helping to keep the moisture in. The land was then left fallow (unplanted) until the next year. In addition, by the early 1880s, the use of hardier wheats – such as Turkey red brought by Russian immigrants – rather than the corn which the earlier homesteaders had used, also made farming easier. This wheat was better suited to the conditions on the Great Plains. Homesteaders who grew it got better yields – allowing them to produce a surplus that could then be sold to buy better equipment.

SOURCE C

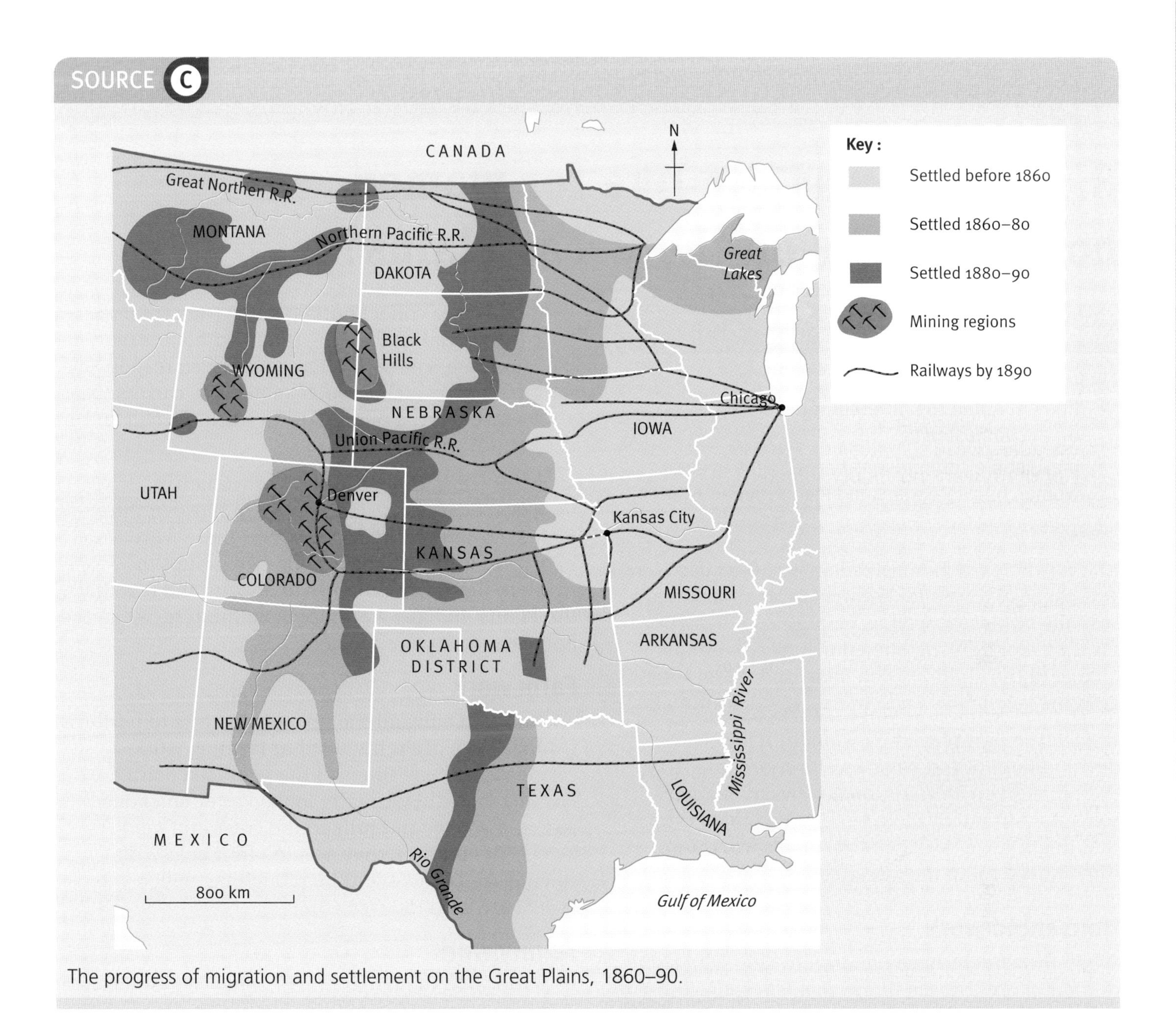

The progress of migration and settlement on the Great Plains, 1860–90.

4 Better and cheaper farming machinery

During the 1870s and 1880s, the Industrial Revolution in the East meant cheaper and better mass-produced farming equipment – especially ploughs. Stronger ploughs were developed, which could cope with the tough prairie grass roots – unlike the earlier ploughs. Especially important was the John Deere 'sod-buster'. In addition, there were cheaper and better harrows, reapers, binders and threshers. Because of the railroad expansion, these could be transported quickly and cheaply to the Plains.

Thus, by the 1890s, this combination of factors – plus the determination and hard work of the homesteaders – meant most of the problems of farming on the Great Plains were overcome. The majority of homesteaders who had stayed became quite prosperous and bought more land. The Great Plains soon became an important wheat-producing area.

Fact file

By the time most of these improvements took place, many homesteaders had already had to mortgage their farms to survive – or even sell and become tenant farmers or labourers. In addition, severe droughts in the 1870s and 1880s in some parts of the Great Plains led to many homesteaders going bankrupt and having their farms repossessed by the banks.

ACTIVITIES

Draw an ideas map to show how each problem faced by the homesteaders was eventually solved.

2.11 What was life like for women homesteaders on the Great Plains?

LEARNING OBJECTIVES

In this lesson you will:

- find out about the different roles played by women on the homesteads
- make some comparisons between the lives of women homesteaders and Plains' Indian women.

Life for the early homesteaders was very hard – this was especially true for women. Women had many responsibilities: as well as helping with heavier farming work during busy times, they were in charge of the children, the house, clothing, cooking, growing vegetables and tending smaller animals.

In fact, the part played by women in the development of the West was far more important than that given by traditional views of women's roles. In particular, most women had to do things that might have been seen as 'men's work' until they moved on to the Great Plains.

Household work

While they might have children to help with some of their chores, it was the woman's responsibility to organise things. In addition to having responsibility for looking after the children and keeping the house clean, women had many hard jobs to do. All tasks were very time-consuming. For example, doing the family laundry took all day. There was no running water for most families, so water had to be taken from a well (if they had one) or from ponds or streams – this was hard physical work. In addition, many women even had to make their own soap.

Women also made the family's clothes, using looms and spinning wheels – this, too, was very time-consuming. Later, sewing machines made this task a little easier.

Preparing and cooking food for the family took much more time than it would today. In addition to the lack of water, very few homesteaders had stoves. So cooking was usually done on an open fire, using spits for meat, and big iron kettles and pans.

Women had to collect buffalo chips (dung) for fuel for cooking and for heating their sod houses or dug-outs (see Source A). They were also responsible for growing vegetables such as turnips, carrots, peas and beans – it was often hard to work the soil and keep it watered.

In many ways, then, the roles of women homesteaders were very similar to those of the Plains' Indians women. However, there were also many differences between the two groups of women: these were mainly to do with the fact that the Plains' Indians were nomadic hunters, while the homesteaders were farmers.

Farm work

As well as having all the household tasks to perform, women were often involved in farming work, especially at busy times of the year (see Source B). For instance, they usually looked after chickens, pigs and sheep, and milked the cows and made butter. In addition, they would often help with sowing seeds and even the ploughing, which was especially hard (Source C).

Family work

In addition to the harsh practicalities of everyday living, many early homesteaders were often very isolated as they had no near neighbours. Doctors were scarce at first, so childbirth was often faced alone or, at best, with the help of a neighbouring wife. Even so, it was a risky business in sod houses which were difficult to keep clean.

Coping with illness – especially of children – was difficult. Infant mortality was high – almost 30 per cent of homesteaders' children died before the age of one. Women often had no proper medicines when nursing the sick, so relied on herbal remedies.

Fact file

Turpentine was used to clean wounds, warm urine to cure earache, a roasted mouse to deal with measles, and chicken meat to suck out snake bites.

SOURCE A

A woman homesteader in the 1880s, collecting buffalo chips for fuel in Kansas.

Community work

Later, as more people came to the Plains, small communities grew up, and dances, social evenings and plays were organised. Women also began to form 'sewing bees' as a way of meeting other women.

They played a big part in bringing the Christian religion to the Plains – often establishing churches, organising Sunday schools and Bible readings, and even persuading the men to attend. They campaigned for schools to be set up for their children, and so played an important role in bringing formal education to the Great Plains. Many of the first teachers were women, as it was not considered to be men's work.

SOURCE B

6 April [temperature: 98°F] – We planted pea, turnips and squash on our claim.

5 May – There was a white frost this morning. The water froze in the water pail. Mamma and I planted 81 hills of melons. At night I drove Mr. Ray's cattle away from our garden with buffalo bones.

10 May – We planted potatoes.

Some extracts from the diary of Luna E. Warner, aged 15, about her family's life in Kansas,1871.

ACTIVITIES

1. Look at the information given above about the various roles played by women on the homesteads. Now try to produce a spider diagram which divides the roles into four main categories: Housework, Family work, Farm work and Community work.
2. Look back to Lesson 1.7 on pp. 22–23 and re-read the information about the roles of Plains' Indian women. Then, using that information, and the information from this lesson, draw a chart that shows the similarities and differences between the work and lives of these two groups of women.

SOURCE C

A woman homesteader driving a binder.

2.12 How important was 'Manifest Destiny' in the 1860s and 1870s?

LEARNING OBJECTIVES

In this lesson you will:

- find out how the idea of Manifest Destiny grew after 1845
- get practice in answering questions that ask you to comment on the usefulness of a source.

Manifest Destiny

During the 1860s and 1870s, the idea of 'Manifest Destiny' seemed to have been fulfilled in many respects. When the phrase was first used by the newspaper editor John L. O'Sullivan in 1845, he was referring to the idea of taking over and occupying as much of the land as possible between the East and West coasts – and even to dominate the whole of the Americas. His ideas caught the public imagination, and many newspapers began to say similar things.

In the year that O'Sullivan printed his statement, the USA had grown considerably when Texas became one of its states.

The idea of Manifest Destiny caught on, and soon many white Americans saw it as their 'god-given' duty – and right – to spread across the whole of the continent of North America. Soon, anyone who opposed this came to be seen as traitors to the USA and to God (see Source A).

The growth of the USA

By 1850, much of this had been achieved:

- In 1846, the USA finally persuaded Britain to sell the area in the north-west known as Oregon.
- In 1848, after a war against Mexico, the USA had obtained the huge area in the south-west known as California.

Once these territories had been acquired, the US government, as part of its belief in Manifest Destiny, began to encourage people to go West and settle there. In addition, the defeat of Mexico had led to an increased nationalism in the USA, with many wanting to have one huge nation, stretching from coast to coast and from north to south, especially after gold was discovered in California.

However, because of the problems of travel between one coast and the other across the Great Plains, the US government then began to put money into improving communications. In particular, it wanted a transcontinental railway to connect the East and West coasts – not just for economic reasons, but also to control these new areas more effectively, by sending out judges and law enforcement officers.

Plans for such railroads were disrupted and slowed by the outbreak of the American Civil War in 1861, which lasted until 1865. Once the war was over, an extra effort was made and the plan was finally successful in 1869 with the joining of the Central and Union Pacific Railroads. Other important railways followed.

The 'Great American Desert'

For most of this time, there had been little white American interest in the Great Plains – hence the willingness in 1832–34 to allow this to be 'Indian territory', as it was seen as useless and therefore unwanted by most white Americans. However, as the population of the USA grew – the number of immigrants coming from Europe in the period 1830–90 rose from 500,000 to 5.25 million – some people began to reconsider the earlier belief that the Plains were just the 'Great American Desert' and therefore worthless. There was also the belief that the great numbers of settlers moving West should be protected.

Many people believed that the Plains' Indians were not only 'savages' who needed to be civilised by being converted to the Christian religion, but also that they had no right to the land as they 'wasted' it by not farming, or by not farming as intensively as they could because they also hunted (see Source B).

Homesteaders

Once it became clear that at least part of the Great Plains could be farmed or used to raise cattle, the idea of settling large numbers on the Plains grew. The US government passed acts to make this easier for as many people as possible. The railway companies also encouraged this. Consequently, from 1860 many people settled on the Plains to set up homestead farms.

SOURCE A

Manifest Destiny, a painting by John Gast, 1872. Note in particular the references to railways and homestead farmers.

The Plains' Indians

However, the Plains' Indians, who had lived on the Great Plains for generations and had been told these were to be recognised as 'Indian territory' by the US government, increasingly came to resent these new settlers who, unlike earlier ones who had simply crossed the Plains to the West coast, now wanted to stay.

As part of its belief in Manifest Destiny, the US government – and many individuals – came during the 1860s and 1870s to think that it would be necessary to make the Plains' Indians agree to live in much smaller areas. If necessary, they believed it was their god-given duty to do this by force. As part of Manifest Destiny, then, it would be necessary to fight for control of the Great Plains, to link up the territories in the east, west and south (see Source C). There was even more reason for this after it was discovered that the Plains were very good for cattle ranching.

SOURCE B

The average Indian of the prairies is a being who does little credit to human nature. As I passed over those magnificent [valley] bottoms of Kansas which form the reservations of the Delaware, Potawatomies [Eastern coast Indian nations who earlier had been forcibly removed to the Plains] – the very best cornlands on earth – and saw their owners sitting around the doors of their lodges at the height of the planting season... I could not help saying, 'These people must die out – there is no help for them. God has given the earth to those who will tame and cultivate it.'

An extract from H. Greeley, *New York to San Francisco*, 1859. Greeley was a journalist who travelled across the Great Plains.

VOICE YOUR OPINION!

Do you think the Plains' Indians were justified in resisting settlement on the Great Plains after 1860?

SOURCE C

North America will... expand and fit itself to the continent; to control the oceans on either hand, and eventually the continents beyond.

The views of William Gilpin, in 1858.

GradeStudio

Analysis of sources

Study Source A.

What did white American people think about 'Manifest Destiny' by 1870? Use the source and your own knowledge to explain your answer.

[7 marks]

Examiner's tip

- Remember to use information from the source to explain reasons AND remember to use your own knowledge to support your comments with precise facts.

You have now completed this unit which has focused on various aspects of the way in which white Americans began to travel through and then settle on the Great Plains after 1840. You have also had practice in answering questions designed to prepare you for your exam. Below is an example of one type of exam question, with some hints to help you write a top-scoring answer.

Fact file

In the exam, you will be asked to answer two questions from Section B, the Depth Study: a source-based question and a structured question. The source-based question is divided into three parts – **a**, **b** and **c**.

b Study Source A.

Source A

A savage cartoon, published in the 1840s, attacking the Mormon practice of polygamy.

How useful is this source in telling you about why the Mormons experienced hostility from non-Mormons? Use the source and your own knowledge to explain your answer. **[6 marks]**

Examiner's tip

Remember, in questions that ask you to explain something, the examiners are expecting you to extract information from a source, AND to show both *knowledge* and *understanding* of a particular topic or aspect of your course. This means more than just 'listing' two or three bits of information from the source OR simply identifying a couple of reasons. You need to *use* your knowledge to show AND explain *why* the source is and is not useful, by pointing out reasons from the source AND by giving information about other reasons not shown/mentioned by the source.

For *explain* questions like the one above, the other important thing to do in order to reach the higher levels is to make sure you try to identify AND explain at least TWO different reasons – from the source AND from your own knowledge. While explaining reasons based on the source, OR just using your own knowledge to explain a few reasons without using the source, will get you half marks or more, it will NOT get you the highest mark available.

Before you write your answer, below are two things to help you start on the right lines.

First look at the simplified mark scheme. This should help you write your answer in a way which will allow you to get the full 6 marks available.

Simplified mark scheme

Level	Skill	Mark
Level 0	No answer or irrelevant answer	0
Level 1	Vague or general answer/unsupported assertion	1
Level 2	Just describes the details shown in the source, but doesn't give any reasons	1
Level 3	Identifies reasons in the source OR gives other reasons from own knowledge, but doesn't explain them	2–3
Level 4	Uses own knowledge to explain the usefulness of the source OR uses own knowledge to explain other reasons, with little reference to what the source shows	4–5
Level 5	Uses BOTH sources AND own knowledge to explain the usefulness of the source	6

Second, look at the sample answer below, noting especially the examiner's comments.

Candidate's answer

This source is useful for telling why the Mormons experienced hostility because this cartoon shows what many non-Mormons thought about polygamy: lots of women fighting, lots of babies and chaos. This was why there was hostility against the Mormons – the fact the cartoon was published shows how angry some people were.

Polygamy was the belief that some men could have more than one wife. This idea was first put forward by the Mormon leader, Joseph Smith, in 1844, when he said he had had a revelation from god telling him that certain Mormons could do this. By then, he already had more than one wife while his bodyguard, John Scott, had five.

This angered some of the Mormons who, by then, were living in the town of Nauvoo (Commerce) in Illinois. A breakaway group then attacked Smith's idea in their newspaper. Smith retaliated by destroying the newspaper's printing press. The issue of polygamy soon became known to non-Mormons in Nauvoo who were angry as they thought it was immoral and against the Bible, and would lead to chaos and confusion in society. Mobs began to roam the streets, so Joseph Smith and his brother, Hyrum, fled to Carthage and sought protection in the jail. But a mob of non-Mormons stormed the jail on 27 June 1844 and shot them dead.

Examiner's comment

The first highlighted part of the answer (green) gets the candidate into Level 3, as one reason is identified from the source. The candidate has also wisely begun by commenting on the *usefulness* of the source – this is what the question is about. This is a good habit to get into, as it should help make sure that you answer the question set.

The second highlighted part of the answer (red) is providing useful and precise supporting own knowledge and so is *explaining* the reason which has been identified from the source. This gets the candidate into Level 4. However, only ONE reason is explained, so this does not get the full marks available in this level.

Look again at the mark scheme above, and you should be able to see what that candidate could have done to push this good answer from a low Level 4 (about half marks) into Level 5 and so score the full 6 marks available.

You will see that in order to get into Level 5, and score 6 marks, all the candidate needed to do was *identify* and *explain* at least one more reason – either from the source OR from their own knowledge, using some precise knowledge to support the point(s) being made.

Once you think you have fully understood what was needed to improve this candidate's answer, write your own answer. However, don't use the source and the issue of polygamy given above in the sample answer. Instead, try to explain – using precise own knowledge – OTHER reasons why the Mormons encountered hostility from non-Mormons: there are several more.

Before you start, look back at Lesson 2.4. Then try to write your answer without looking at the relevant pages.

Chapter 3

What were the consequences of the spread of cattle ranching to the Plains?

This chapter focuses on the growth and spread of cattle ranching, from its origins in Texas in the south, to the Great Plains in the years after 1840. It also looks at the lives and experiences of the cowboys on the cattle trails and on the **open range**, and the problems of law and order in the cattle or cow towns which grew up. In particular, it will look at the conflicts that broke out between the cattle **ranchers** and the homesteaders.

SOURCE A

The Stampede, a painting by Robert Lindneux, showing cowboys trying to control a herd of cattle frightened by a thunder storm.

KEY WORDS

Open range – *cattle ranching took place over huge areas of land: often between 7500 and 250,000 hectares, and sometimes much more. There were no fences, so cattle and people were free to roam.*

Ranchers – *people who owned or managed a cattle ranch.*

GETTING STARTED

For many people – especially those who like to watch Western films – the cowboys seem to symbolise the Wild West. Yet many of these Western films give only a partial view of what life was really like. Often, the life of a cowboy is shown as being free and exciting – yet the reality was often very different. In particular, very few films show that as many as 25 per cent of the cowboys were black – former slaves who had received their freedom after the end of the American Civil War.

Many people, when asked about the West, immediately think of gunfighters and rustlers – the cow town of Dodge, with its connections with Wyatt Earp, has often been an important part of such films. This unit will explore the reality of the Wild West and its famous characters. These include Billy the Kid, John Wesley Hardin, Jesse James and his brothers, and Buffalo Bill – as well as women such as Belle Starr, Etta Place, Annie Oakley and Calamity Jane.

In groups of four, take a blank piece of paper and write down what you know about five of the people mentioned in the paragraph above.

At the end of the five minutes, share these with the rest of the class to see what points have come up most frequently.

Sources A, B, C and D are common examples of the ways in which many people view the lives and activities of cowboys and others in the Wild West.

SOURCE B

Gunfight, a painting by Charles M. Russell, 1902. Russell lived and worked for a time as a cowboy on the Great Plains.

SOURCE C

A Wanted poster for two of the James brothers, Frank and Jesse.

$5,000.00

REWARD

Wanted by the State of Missouri

JESSE & FRANK JAMES

For Train Robbery

Notify AUTHORITIES
LIBERTY, MISSOURI

HISTORY DETECTIVE

Try to find out more about the life of a cowboy by visiting www.heinemann.co.uk/hotlinks and entering the code 1433P, or watch at least one Western film, such as *Butch Cassidy and the Sundance Kid*, *Young Guns* or *The Left Handed Gun!*

SOURCE D

Painting the Town Red, a painting by Rufus Zogman, 1886.

3.1 How did the early cattle trade begin?

LEARNING OBJECTIVES

In this lesson you will:

- find out about how and why the cattle trade began in the USA
- get practice in answering questions that ask you to explain the usefulness of a source.

KEY WORDS

Railhead towns – *towns where the railways had reached. The most important ones were Sedalia, Missouri, Abilene and Dodge City in Kansas. They grew quickly, and were often notorious for their lawlessness.*

Texas Longhorns – *cattle that resulted from interbreeding between Criollos (the Spanish cattle of Texas) and other breeds, like the English Longhorns. The early cattle trade began in south Texas. At first, cowboys drove millions of cattle across the Great Plains on the Long Drive. Later, cattle ranches were set up, but the cattle boom ended in the late 1880s.*

Texas and the early cattle industry

Cattle, like horses, had been introduced into America by the Spanish at the end of the 15th century. By the early 19th century, cattle ranching – on the open range – was well-established in Mexico which, before 1845, included the area now known as Texas. In 1836, the Texans rebelled against Mexican rule and, in 1845, Texas became part of the USA. The Mexican ranchers left or were chased out, leaving many of their cattle behind – these were taken by Texan farmers. In addition, some cattle had escaped over the centuries, and there were large herds of unclaimed cattle roaming free. These were the **Texas Longhorns**: thin and stringy, but strong, and hardier than other breeds (see Source A). They were well-suited to being driven long distances over rough country and, unlike many other breeds, were immune to Texas fever (a disease carried by ticks).

At first, because beef was not a very popular meat, Texan ranches were quite small – with the cattle being used mainly for their hides and tallow fat. Also, it was very difficult to transport cattle to the big cities in the East, and the population in the West was so low, there was little incentive to round up these cattle. But, during the 1850s, beef became more popular and the price began to rise.

Before 1861 and the start of the Civil War, there were some limited attempts to drive cattle along the Shawnee Trail to the Mississippi ports. However, these were small-scale – and remained so until the problems of transport between East and West were overcome. There was also opposition from homesteaders in these areas, as their cattle would die if they caught Texas fever from the ticks of the Texas Longhorns.

However, by the time the Civil War ended in 1865, there were about five million Texas Longhorns – many had roamed free during the Civil War, and had continued to breed. Most of

SOURCE A

A Texas Longhorn.

them were still unbranded and so could be taken by almost anyone. As the South – including Texas, which had fought on the losing side – had been devastated by the Civil War, some people began to think that they could make their fortunes from these cattle as, during the previous 20 years, things had begun to change in the USA.

In particular, by then, the USA was undergoing an industrial revolution in the towns of the north-east – the growing populations of factory workers and their families wanted beef. This, plus the growing numbers of soldiers, miners and settlers in the West – and the growing numbers of Native Americans forced on to reservations – who also needed feeding, led to a greatly increased demand for meat (see Source B). By 1870, the US government was buying 50,000–60,000 cattle a year as rations for the various Native American reservations.

BRAIN BOOST

Make a list of the main factors that explain why Texas was able to become important in the early cattle industry. Call it 'Reasons why Texas became the centre of the early cattle industry'. Number the factors – and then try to learn them.

SOURCE B

Cowboys driving a cattle herd from Texas to Kansas on the Chisholm trail, 1870s.

The early cattle trails

Cattle that could be bought for about $3 in Texas could be sold in the north for about $30 – this offered the chance to make huge profits if the cattle could be driven to these railhead towns. So the Longhorns were rounded up and driven on the Long Drive (see Lesson 3.5 on pp. 76–77) north to **railhead towns**. From there, they could be transported by train to the East or elsewhere.

The main early cattle trails were:

- the Chisholm
- the Sedalia (formerly the Shawnee)
- the Goodnight–Loving.

Fact file

When the Plains' Indians agreed to move to reservations, they were expected to give up hunting to become farmers. In return, the US government gave them grants so they could buy beef rations. (To find out more about the life of the American Indians on reservations, see Lesson 4.4 on pp. 102–103.)

At the same time, more and more railroads were pushing West. By 1865, the Missouri Pacific Railroad had reached Sedalia in Missouri; the line was soon extended by other companies into Kansas. This now meant it was much easier to transport cattle to the growing populations of the East, and – as these towns were further to the west – without coming into contact with the animals of the homesteaders.

Fact file

Much of Abilenes rapid growth was due to Joseph G. McCoy, an Illinois meat dealer, who decided to make Abilene, Kansas, into his base for buying cattle. Although Abilene was undeveloped at first, it was on the railroad, and water and good grazing were plentiful. Stockyards were built and the growth of Abilene soon saw the Chisholm Trail eclipse the Sedalia Trail. Although McCoy eventually went bankrupt, he had played a big part in the development of the cattle industry.

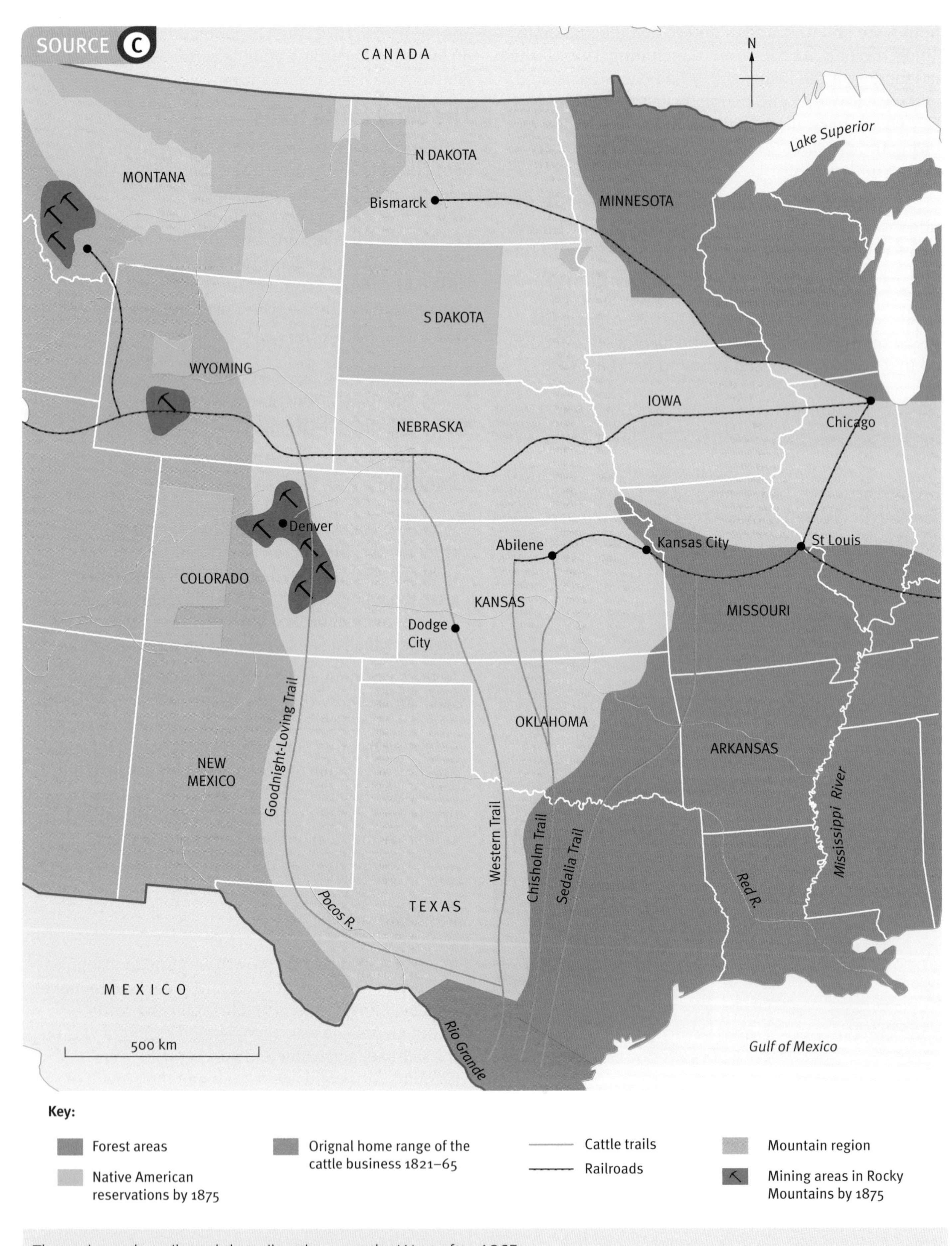

The main cattle trails and the railroads across the West after 1865.

The Sedalia and Chisholm Trails

The Sedalia Trail was one of the first cattle trails: in 1866, 250,000 cattle were driven north from Texas, through Indian Territory, to Sedalia, Missouri.

More important was the Chisholm Trail (named after Jesse Chisholm, the son of a Scottish man and a Cherokee woman), which ended in Abilene: in 1867, 35,000 cattle were driven north to this town; by 1871, this had risen to over 600,000 a year.

SOURCE D

Suddenly, the right conditions fell into place... the Civil War brought an increased demand for beef... settlers learned that cattle could thrive on the native grass and survive the drastic changes in climate; the transcontinental railroads pushed to the Pacific...

An extract from W.E. Hollon, *The Great American Desert*, 1966.

The Goodnight–Loving Trail

The Goodnight–Loving Trail was developed by two Texan ranchers, Charles Goodnight and Oliver Loving. By the end of the Civil War in 1865, Goodnight had a herd of 8000 cattle. In 1866, he and Loving drove the cattle from Texas to the mining camps around Denver, Colorado, via New Mexico – where some were sold to the US army to give to Navajo Indians who were near starvation on their reservation. This was repeated in 1867; and, although Loving was killed by Comanches, Goodnight continued to supply the mining camps and army forts and Indian reservations in Colorado (see Source C).

From 1875, the Western Trail had overtaken the Chisholm Trail – this saw Dodge City, Kansas, become a major cow town as the Western Trail ended there. Other cow towns emerged later.

GradeStudio

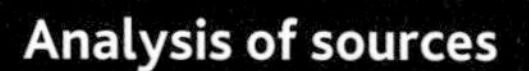

Analysis of sources

Study Source C.

How useful is this source in telling you about why the cattle industry began to grow after 1865. Use the source and your own knowledge to explain your answer.

Examiner's tip

Remember – in order to get into the top level, you need to do TWO things:

- Use the source AND your own knowledge to explain your reasons.
- Comment on the reason(s) provided by the source AND use your own knowledge to explain other reasons NOT provided by the source.

3.2 Why did ranching begin on the Great Plains?

LEARNING OBJECTIVES

In this lesson you will:

- find out why cattle ranching spread from Texas on to the Great Plains and what cattle ranching on the open range meant
- get practice in answering questions that ask you to explain the role of a key individual.

When the railroads first came, the Texan pioneers in the cattle trade made great fortunes by driving herds of cattle across the Great Plains to market. Then, during the 1860s and 1870s, as the number of railways increased, many began to raise cattle on large farms called ranches on the open range of the Great Plains, in order to avoid the Long Drive (to find out about the Long Drive, see Lesson 3.5 on pp. 76–77). Cattle ranching soon spread.

Reasons for growth

There were several different factors involved in the spread of cattle ranching on to the Great Plains, including the following.

- The railroads continued to extend their networks across the Plains to the west and north, making it possible to transport cattle more easily to huge slaughter houses in cities such as Chicago.
- The development of cold storage and refrigerator cars on trains meant it was even easier to transport meat from Chicago to big markets further away in the East.
- New healthier and meatier breeds of cattle were developed, which were better able to withstand the cold winters and other conditions of life on the Plains. This was done by cross-breeding the thin Texas Longhorns with other breeds such as Hereford or Angus cattle. This resulted in cattle that produced greater quantities of more tender meat.
- At the same time as the cattle industry was beginning to take off, homesteaders were establishing themselves on the Plains. Very often, their farms cut across and even blocked the routes used on the cattle drives. In addition, many cattle owners were becoming fed up with the dangers and difficulties often encountered on the long drives from Texas.
- During the 1860s, 1870s and 1880s, the Plains' Indians were being defeated by the US army and forced on to smaller reservations – this meant there was more land available.
- Finally, as part of the campaign to defeat the Plains' Indians, the large herds of buffalo were being wiped out by commercial hunters encouraged by the US government (see Lesson 4.5 on pp. 104–107). This meant there was plenty of grazing for cattle.

The open range

The start of large-scale ranching on the Great Plains is often associated with John Wesley Iliff (see Source A) who developed this in Wyoming. He had tried gold mining in Colorado but had been unsuccessful. He then discovered that Texas Longhorns could successfully overwinter on the Plains – and that this killed off disease-carrying ticks. So he began to build up a herd of his own – often buying cattle from those settlers travelling West on the Oregon Trail. In 1867, he won a contract to supply beef to the workers on the Union Pacific Railroad. He bought $45,000 worth of cattle from Charles Goodnight. This increased his herd to 35,000 – and he then sold them at a good profit. In 1868, he won a government contract to supply beef to the Sioux reservations being established.

The fortunes made by people like Iliff encouraged many more to try ranching on the Great Plains. Texas Longhorns were bought for $7 a head, then crossbred with Herefords. The healthier animals which were born as a result could be sold for over $50 a head. In 1870, Charles Goodnight began ranching with Texas Longhorns in Colorado – where, at the beginning, he and Loving had driven their cattle. Although this was unsuccessful, he moved back to Texas where, by 1877, he had a ranch covering about 500,000 hectares, with over 100,000 head of cattle.

SOURCE A

A painting of John Wesley Iliff, 1888.

Fact file

If a rancher controlled a river or stream, he usually controlled all the land next to it, as land without water was almost worthless. These rivers and streams often acted as boundaries between the ranches. The fact that the ranches were unfenced did cause some problems – in particular, as the cattle wandered all over the open range, the only way for ranchers to identify their cattle when it was round-up time was to have a distinctive sign branded on the cattle. There was also the problem of the rustling (stealing) of herds by outlaws – or Plains' Indians who refused to go on to reservations or who had left them in order to return to their traditional way of life.

ACTIVITIES

Make an ideas map to show the reasons for the spread of cattle ranching on to the Great Plains after 1860.

In addition, land was cheap – in many cases, would-be ranchers just took what they wanted. As shown in Lesson 2.9 on pp. 52–53, the US government made grants of land only to farmers who would grow crops and settle permanently on the land. The rest of the Plains was seen by white Americans as land available for anyone to use.

GradeStudio

Recall and select knowledge

Early cattle ranchers on the Great Plains made important contributions to the development of the cattle industry.

Briefly describe the actions taken by John Wesley Iliff in the development of cattle ranching on the Great Plains.

3.3 What impact did cattle ranching have on the Great Plains?

LEARNING OBJECTIVES

In this lesson you will:

- find out what impact the rapid growth of cattle ranching in the 1880s had on the Great Plains, and why the open range came to an end
- learn how to produce high-scoring answers to questions that ask you to extract/infer information from sources about an aspect of a topic. You will find below some useful tips about how to do this, and a question that gives you practice at answering such questions.

KEY WORDS

Cattle barons – *those cattle ranchers who managed to gain control of huge tracts of land, with great herds of cattle. They sometimes used their wealth and power against smaller ranches.*

As a result of the developments and factors mentioned in Lesson 3.2, the number of cattle on the Great Plains increased – from about 100,000 in 1860 to over four million by 1880. Many huge ranches soon appeared on the open range, and the massive profits attracted even more people into cattle ranching, especially as land on the Great Plains was either cheap or often just free for the taking.

Overcrowding on the open range

From 1880 to 1885, there was a boom in the cattle industry which saw ranching on the Plains reach a peak (see Sources A and B). At first, there were many small ranches on the Plains, as well as bigger ones. These were mainly set up during the late 1870s and early 1880s, especially in Wyoming.

Those with money to invest often put it into the cattle industry. Thousands of people wanting to be ranchers and make big profits headed West – even if

SOURCE 

The Haylie Ranch, Wyoming.

they knew very little about cattle. The result of this creation of many small cattle ranches was overcrowding. The hugely increased numbers of cattle on the Great Plains eventually led to overstocking, which began to significantly reduce the amount of grass available for cattle. Also, as more people became involved in cattle ranching, the cost of cattle increased – this eventually led to decreased profits. While the industry continued to boom, this was not a great problem, but, later, when the price of beef began to fall as a result of overproduction, serious problems began to emerge.

As the 1880s continued, it became increasingly necessary for ranchers to spend money on fencing because of the growing numbers of ranchers and to try to prevent the spread of disease. However, this was particularly difficult for the smaller ranchers.

Ranching corporations

As with mining, these problems and costs resulted in smaller ranchers finding themselves squeezed out by the bigger ranchers – the **cattle barons**. Soon, large ranching corporations were established, and the wealthier ranchers formed powerful cattle associations to protect their interests. When the cattle industry began to experience difficulties after 1885, conflicts between these powerful cattle associations and the smaller ranchers began to increase in number and in scope.

The end of the open range

Although the cattle industry was still booming in the early 1880s, many new ranchers had little experience. In the late 1880s, the industry began to collapse. Lack of experience led to many smaller ranches being taken over by large ranching corporations.

There were also droughts in 1883 and two terrible winters in 1886 and 1887, in which thousands of cattle died in the cold and blizzards. Though the cattle industry continued, the boom was over. However, as profits began to decline, competition between large and smaller ranchers led to tensions and even violent conflicts on the Great Plains (see Lessons 3.7 and 3.8).

Fact file

The ranching corporation Swan Land and Cattle Company was set up by Alexander Swan in 1883. He bought three ranches in Wyoming and formed them into one huge operation, with over 100,000 cattle. This made Swan a powerful force in Wyoming.

SOURCE B

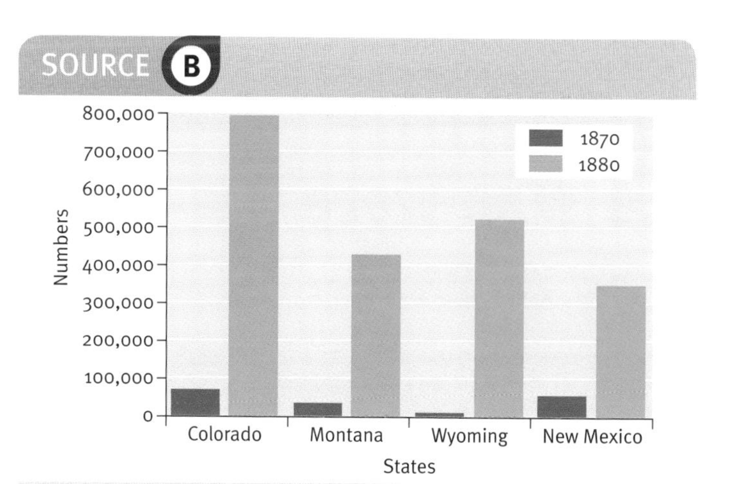

Increase in the numbers of cattle on the Great Plains, 1870–1880.

BRAIN BOOST

Draw up a numbered list of the main effects of the rapid growth of cattle ranching on the Great Plains during the early 1880s.

ACTIVITIES

1. What information in Sources A and B suggests that cattle ranching may have caused problems on the open range of the Great Plains?
2. Look carefully at the sources. What pieces of information can you get from them straight away?
3. Is there anything you can *infer* or *intelligently guess* from them? (What might be the *implications* or *consequences* of the information given by the sources?)

GradeStudio

Recall and select knowledge

Briefly describe the main effects of the rapid growth of cattle ranching on the Great Plains during the early 1880s.

Examiner's tip

- Remember, you need to do more than simply identify or name these effects. Use specific own knowledge to describe these effects.
- Also, remember to give several different effects. Don't think you've finished once you have dealt with just one!

3.4 Who were the cowboys and what did they do?

LEARNING OBJECTIVES

In this lesson you will:

- find out what kind of people became cowboys, the skills they needed and what kind of work they did
- get practice in answering questions that ask you to describe an aspect of a topic.

KEY WORDS

Lasso (or lariat) – *the rope used by cowboys to catch cattle for branding etc.*

Vacqueros – *cowboys (from the Spanish word for cow).*

Who were the cowboys?

The first cowboys were the Spanish **vacqueros** who, in the early 19th century, looked after the Longhorn cattle on the open range in Mexico, which in 1845 became the US state of Texas. It was in these areas that cattle rearing first began in the Americas. Because the Mexican ranchers did not keep their cattle in fenced-off areas, cowboys were employed to look after them.

After 1845, when Texas became part of the USA, the cattle herds of the Mexican farmers were taken over by white American ranchers: they, too, needed cowboys to help them control their animals. Later, it was the cowboys who took the cattle from Texas on the Long Drive north across the Plains; and afterwards worked on the ranches that were established there from the mid-1870s.

The word cowboy, in fact, didn't become widely used until the 1870s – it described the men who worked with the cattle on the cattle drives and on the ranches. Most of these first cowboys were from Texas and other states in the south of the USA. Consequently, despite what has been depicted in many films and comics, many of the first ones were Spanish-Mexicans, or Mexicans. After the Civil War ended in 1865, many white southerners were keen to leave the war-devastated south; while black veterans of the Unionist army, and newly freed slaves in the South, also looked for a new life. Later, others came from Europe, the East coast or other parts of America, looking for work, and signed on as cowboys.

A cowboy's work

Cowboys had to be both physically tough and skilled horseriders – the Texas Longhorns were often bad-tempered and, with horns up to 2.1 m long, needed to be handled carefully. These cowboys soon came to symbolise much about life on the Great Plains and in the Wild West – which was seen as exciting and dangerous. However, the reality of their lives and work did not always match up to the various myths that grew up about them.

Their main work was based around the cattle – as the lives of the Plains Indians were with the buffalo. Because the cattle grazed on the open range, the cowboys spent most of their time on horseback, looking after them. In winter, they were sent out to line camps along the boundaries of the ranch, often living in tents or shacks – sometimes alone, but usually in pairs. The role of these line riders was to help any cattle in trouble in the deep snows and to protect them against wolves. Later, as barbed wire came into use, they also became fence riders, responsible for repairing fences. When the snows melted, they then had to look for cattle trapped in mud or caught in the newly swollen rivers and streams.

The hardest work for a cowboy on a ranch was the round-up: this was done twice a year. In spring, the young calves were separated from the herd and lassooed, so they could be branded – as the open range of a ranch was often huge, this could take two to three months. Then, in late summer, there was another round-up, when cattle were sorted out for the Long Drive north. This was especially dangerous because the cattle had roamed freely on the Plains and were almost like wild animals. During this time, the cowboys lived in camps on the range.

The Long Drive and cattle ranching on the Plains

The work on the Long Drive and, later, on the ranches, was also done by cowboys. They received low wages and poor food – it was not the glamorous life often shown in modern Western films.

As cattle ranching on the Great Plains began to spread from the mid-1870s, some cowboys began to live more settled lives, working on one ranch. However, the work was still hard, mostly dull and low paid. In 1883, cowboys in Texas went on strike – but the strike was broken up by the big cattle corporations.

SOURCE B

Poor cowboys, eating a very basic meal.

Equipment and clothing

The equipment needed to do the hard and skilled work of a cowboy was expensive, but had to be provided by the men themselves (see Source A). The most important item was the saddle, which could cost over $30. Also important was the **lasso** (or **lariat**), used for catching and roping steers; and the tools needed for branding cattle and dealing with horse's hooves. Cowboys had to provide their own plates, cutlery and bedding (see Source B). This all came to a lot of money for people whose wages were often low.

In addition, some of their clothing was expensive. Particularly important were: leather boots; leather chaps (pronounced 'shaps'), worn over their trousers, to protect their legs; leather gloves and wrist cuffs, to protect them from rope burns when roping cattle; and bandanas (neckerchiefs) to protect against sun or dust.

A typical cowboy's equipment and clothing.

Fact file

Many words associated with cowboy's come from the connection to the early Spanish-Mexican period: for example, *lariat* (a cowboy's rope), and a slang word for cowboy – buckaroo – is a corrupted version of the word *vacquero*.

3.5 The Long Drive

LEARNING OBJECTIVES

In this lesson you will:

- find out about what happened on the Long Drive
- get practice in answering questions that ask you to explain why one factor/aspect might be more important than another.

KEY WORDS

Jayhawks – *another name for cattle rustlers.*

Stampede – *when cattle, terrified by a noise or event, rush off in all directions. Many were lost, killed or so badly injured that they had to be shot.*

The Long Drive is the name given to the movement of cattle north across the Plains along the various cattle trails (see Lesson 3.1 on pp. 66–69). The early cowboys from Texas had mostly gained experience looking after cattle, before the Civil War, on the Texas ranches – most of which were relatively small. Some had also been involved on the small number of attempts to drive cattle to the Mississippi before 1861. However, after 1865, many more were required as greater numbers of cattle were driven north, to the new railhead towns (see Source A).

Life and work on the Long Drive north was hard and difficult. On the Sedalia Trail, for instance, heavy rains often made things difficult for both cowboys and cattle; much of the route was heavily wooded – the Texan Longhorns did not like to be surrounded by trees; and the Native Americans wanted to be paid for allowing the cattle to pass through their lands. The first drive along this trail in 1866 was not a success – only 35,000 out of 250,000 cattle survived.

The hazards of the Long Drive

Cowboys on the cattle drives faced many hazards – some hazards, such as Native American attacks, blizzards and drought, and difficult river crossings, were faced by all those who tried to cross the Great Plains.

Natural hazards

There were also hazards that particularly affected those trying to herd cattle long distances, such as **stampedes**. A very common cause of a stampede was thunder and lightning, but even the striking of a match could start one. Cowboys trying to catch and calm down the cattle might be trampled and badly injured or crushed to death. The cattle often panicked during river crossings, if the water was deep or fast-flowing – again, not only were cattle lost or injured, but the cowboys were at risk too.

Conflicts on the Long Drive

As well as natural hazards faced by cowboys on the Long Drive, there were conflicts – sometimes violent – with other groups of people living on the Great Plains. White American rustlers or cattle robbers (**jayhawks**) tried to steal cattle or the money carried by trail bosses which was used to pay the cowboys. There were also conflicts with homesteaders, who bitterly resented the damage sometimes done to their crops and land by the large herds of cattle; and the homesteaders' attempts to fence their land, which sometimes cut off access to water for the herds, angered the cowboys.

Life on the Long Drive

Between 10 and 20 cowboys were employed on the Long Drive, depending on the number of cattle in the herd – the average was about one cowboy for 300–350 steers. Cowboys on the Long Drive usually rose at dawn. The herd would be driven until the hottest part of the day, when they stopped for water and grass. After the temperature had cooled a bit, the herd was driven on. At sunset, they stopped and made camp, and the cowboys had their main meal of the day. During the night, a rota was worked out, with cowboys taking it in turn to keep watch over the herd and camp – usually in two-hour shifts (see Source B). In some cases, cowboys worked almost a 24-hour day.

Fact file

Herds were usually about 3000, though some could be as large as 15,000 or as small as 600.

Relations with the Plains' Indians varied. While some tribes would trade with or even assist the cowboys, others demanded a toll (tax) of several head of cattle to pass through their lands, or started stampedes, attacked riders or tried to steal cattle.

The Long Drive could take from two to four months from Texas to Abilene – the average distance covered was about 20–25 km a day. To be successful, good organisation and routine were essential. From the mid-1870s, when ranches began to be established on the Great Plains, the average time dropped to one month.

SOURCE A

An example of a cattle drive.

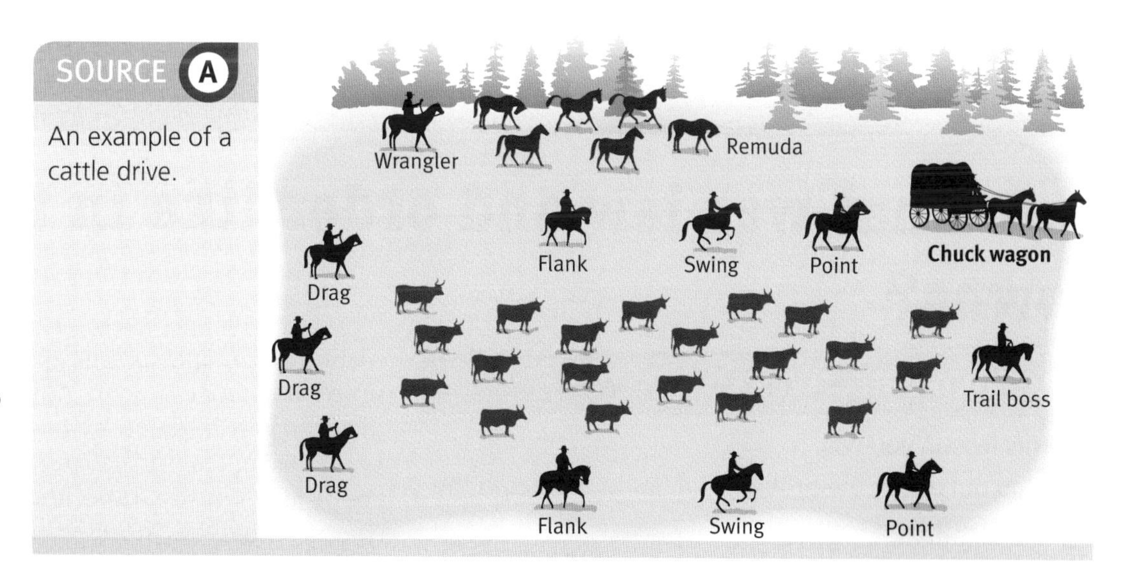

SOURCE B

Cowboys on a cattle drive in the 1880s – the relief watch is being woken up to watch the cattle.

BRAIN BOOST

Make two lists of (a) the natural hazards and (b) people with whom cowboys came into conflict. Number each of your points – and learn them.

SOURCE C

The ethnic origins of cowboys, 1866–85.

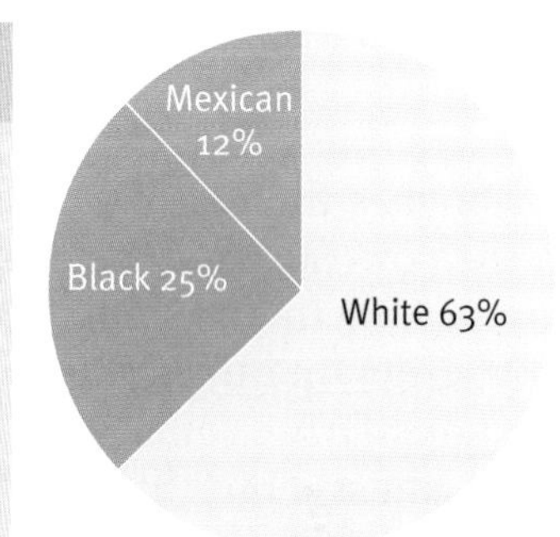

GradeStudio

Explanation and analysis

Which type of hazard presented the greatest dangers for cowboys on the Long Drive: natural hazards or the risk of conflict?

Examiner's tip

You have to do several things with questions like this if you want to score full marks:

- Give specific reasons – using details from your own knowledge – to *explain* why BOTH factors/aspects can be seen as dangerous/important. In other words, you need to do more than just describe/give facts about the factors.
- Once you have explained why both factors/aspects can be seen as dangerous/important, you need to make a balanced/informed *judgement* about why one was more dangerous/important than the other.

3.6 What was law and order like in the cow towns?

LEARNING OBJECTIVES

In this lesson you will:

- find out about the problems of law and order in the cow towns
- get practice in answering questions that ask you to explain the usefulness of a source.

KEY WORDS

Posse – *a group of people 'sworn in' by a law officer (e.g. sheriff, marshal) in the West to track down/ arrest suspected/actual criminals.*

Perhaps one of the biggest myths surrounding cowboys is their rowdy and often lawless behaviour in the cow towns, once they had finished the Long Drive. Cow towns such as Abilene, and later Dodge City, grew up quickly, and cowboys relaxing after the Long Drive sometimes caused disorder and lawlessness – but this has been greatly exaggerated.

The end of the trail

As the cattle neared the cow town, they were allowed to fatten up, and then the dealer met the trail boss to agree a price. Once this was done, the cowboys drove the cattle through the town, firing their guns in celebration that the Long Drive was over.

Once they got their pay, the cowboys looked for ways to spend it. This mostly took the form of drinking alcohol in saloons, gambling and visiting prostitutes (see Sources A and B). Consequently, drunkenness and brawls were common – and gunfights were not unusual.

Abilene

The first cow town to get a bad reputation was Abilene, which was at the end of the Chisholm Trail in Kansas. In 1867, Abilene was just a collection of huts but, because of its position on the Kansas Pacific Railroad and at the north end of the Chisholm Trail – and the foresight of Joseph McCoy – it grew rapidly (see Lesson 3.1 on pp. 66–69). From then until 1872, it became a booming cow town.

Although prosperity increased, so did law and order problems. Once a year, Abilene – like other cow towns – was invaded by cowboys at the end of the Long Drive. Its normal population in winter was about 500 – but in June it could jump to 7000 as the cowboys arrived, along with those who wanted to make money out of them.

As well as the traditional view of drunken cowboys and the occasional gunfight, there was an added cause of violence: most of the cowboys were from Texas and elsewhere in the south, so there was often Confederate–Union rivalry between the cowboys and the citizens of this northern town.

Yet the picture of Abilene – and other cow towns – as lawless has been greatly exaggerated, according to modern historians. At its height as a cow town, Abilene had only ten saloons or taverns, three brothels and one dance hall. But as with the mining towns, it was difficult to do much about law and order problems until the population had grown large enough to support a system of local government. For instance, Abilene did not even have a mayor until 1870 – he then appointed a town marshal, Tom Smith, to clean up the town. Smith managed to stop cowboys bringing guns into town, but violence continued, and he was eventually killed in 1871 by a settler. Tom Smith was replaced as marshal by a more famous law officer, Wild Bill Hickok. By the 1870s, families were beginning to move to Abilene and, in 1872, the people of Abilene banned cowboys altogether.

Fact file

Wild Bill Hickok had made his reputation as a gunfighter in 1865, when he killed at least three men, and for a time had been marshal of Hays – until he was forced to flee, after having killed a soldier of the 7th Cavalry. Although paid $150 a month as town marshal of Abilene, he also gambled, drank heavily and lived with a number of prostitutes. But he did try to enforce the 'no guns' law. However, in a gunfight, he killed a man and, accidentally, his own deputy: because of his unpopular behaviour, his contract was not renewed.

SOURCE 

The bar-room, the theater, the gambling room, the bawdy house, the dance house, each and all come in for their full share of attention... Such is the manner in which the cowboy spends his hard-earned dollars.

An extract from a description by Joseph McCoy on what took place in Abilene.

Once they had been banned from Abilene, the cowboys on the Chisholm Trail went to other cow towns, such as Ellsworth and Wichita. However, for a time, it was Dodge City in Kansas that came to represent the lawlessness of a typical cow town. Dodge City was originally on the Western Trail but, after Abilene banned cowboys in 1872, cattle were often diverted there from the Chisholm Trail. Yet Dodge City, though it did have a law and order problem for a time in the early 1870s, was not packed with prostitutes and gunfighters. Even during its wildest time, it had only eight saloons or taverns and two dance halls.

Although Dodge City was a place where cowboys finishing the Long Drive came to relax, and there was fighting and disorder, it was no more violent than many other places. There was only one case of vigilante justice – in 1881. Between 1870 and 1885, 45 men were recorded as having been killed in all the Kansas cattle towns – and 16 of these were killed by law officers. This is quite a different picture from that of the frequent shoot-outs shown in most Western films.

SOURCE B

Just a Little Pleasure, a painting by Charles M. Russell, c.1898.

HISTORY DETECTIVE

Try to find out more about Abilene and its law and order problems.

SOURCE 

During his whole stay here he occupied a place of high social standing and was regarded as a high-minded, honorable citizen. As Marshal of our city he was ever vigilant in carrying out his duties: he was brave, unflinching, and on all occasions proved himself the right man in the right place.

Extract from a petition about Wyatt Earp to the judge, signed by the people of Dodge City, 1881.

At first, Dodge City had been the haunt of buffalo hunters, and it was from this that it began to acquire its lawless reputation. This increased after 1872, when it became an important cow town. Local business people did try to control things – for instance, a campaign in 1881 to ban alcohol led to the election of an anti-alcohol campaigner as mayor. For a time, after 1878, Wyatt Earp was assistant marshal in Dodge City (see Source C). Another famous law officer in Dodge City was Bill Masterson. Like Wyatt Earp, he moved there in 1876 and became county sheriff. His brother, Ed, became town marshal but was killed by a drunken cowboy in 1878. Bill Masterson later followed Wyatt Earp to Tombstone.

Law and order in the 1880s

The cases of Hickok in Abilene and of Earp and Masterson in Dodge City illustrate the early problems of law and order in the Wild West – in that often outlaws and gunfighters became law officers, while law officers very often became gunfighters. However, as transport and communications improved, populations increased, and towns and counties began to have proper forms of local government, it was easier for state and federal authorities to impose law and order.

After 1865, most of the lands west of the Mississippi were still federal territories, as opposed to full states – this was because their small populations could not raise enough taxes to pay for a proper system of local government and law enforcement, so the federal government in Washington recognised these areas as federal territories, and it then became the federal government's job to ensure law and order (see Source D). The distances involved, and the initial lack of reliable law enforcement officers, made this a difficult task at first. (To find out about law and order in the mining towns, see Lesson 2.6 on pp. 46–47.)

SOURCE D

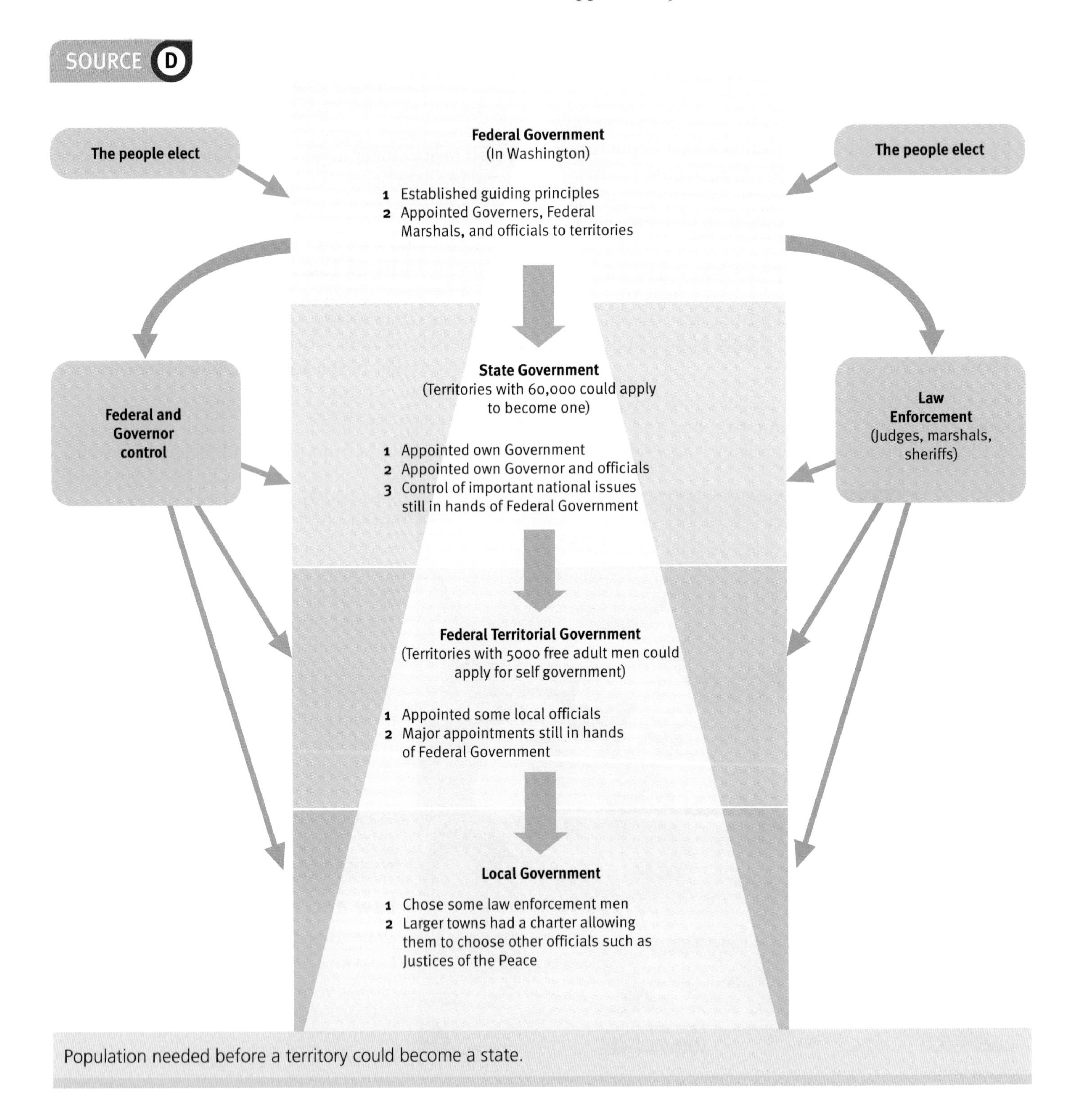

Population needed before a territory could become a state.

Law officers

The main forces of law and order in the federal territories of the West were:

- US marshals, who were appointed by the US president to take charge of a state or territory. Marshals had responsibility for a huge area – to help them, they appointed deputy marshals, who worked more closely with counties and towns.
- sheriffs, who were appointed by the people of a county, for a period of two years at a time. They, too, had a wide area to cover, so needed under-sheriffs and deputies. They could also swear in local people as a **posse** to chase criminals.
- town marshals, who were appointed by the people of a town, often for one year at a time. They too could appoint deputies.
- judges, who were appointed by the US president to try cases – each state or territory had three. For such large areas, this was not many, so cases often took a long time to come to court. Sometimes, vigilantes had already taken the law into their own hands and lynched the suspects.

In addition to the law officers, there were various law enforcement organisations.

- In Texas and in Arizona, small armies of law enforcers were employed to enforce the law – the Texas Rangers were set up by the Mexicans as early as 1820, 25 years before Texas became a US state.
- There were private companies that could be employed to protect banks and stage coaches or to catch particular criminals or gangs. The most famous was the Pinkerton Detective Agency.
- Some communities set up vigilance committees, where there were no regular law enforcement officers – but these vigilantes often broke the law themselves, and frequently lynched innocent people. They were, however, more common in the mining districts than in the cow towns.

HISTORY DETECTIVE

Do you think the problems of law and order and violence in cow towns has been exaggerated? Give reasons for your judgement.

GradeStudio

Analysis of sources

Study Source C.

What does this source tell you about the law and order problems of cattle towns in the 1870s and 1880s? Use the source and your own knowledge to explain your answer. **[7 marks]**

Examiner's tip

Remember – in order to get into the top level, you need to:

- Use the source AND your own knowledge to explain your reasons.

3.7 Why was there conflict between ranchers and homesteaders?

LEARNING OBJECTIVES

In this lesson you will:

- find out why conflicts between ranchers and homesteaders broke out
- get practice in answering questions that ask you to briefly describe some aspect of a topic.

There were often serious conflicts on the open range of the Great Plains between cattle ranchers and homesteaders, largely because they were competing for the same land at more or less the same time.

Reasons for conflict

Such violent disputes came about for a number of reasons: destruction of crops by cattle, disagreements over water access, water rights and ownership of land once permanent ranches were being established.

Cattle drives

From the 1850s, when the first small-scale cattle drives had begun, both groups wanted to use the Great Plains – but for different purposes. In the early days, homesteaders had wanted to stop the cattle drives to the Mississippi area because they were afraid that the cattle would damage their crops or infect their animals with Texas fever. This opposition deepened after 1861, when the number of cattle being driven north from Texas on the Long Drives greatly increased because of the railroads pushing West.

Problems caused by ranching on the Great Plains

Then, from about 1870, other problems and tensions began to emerge as a result of the growth of cattle ranching on the open range. In particular, as wood was often scarce and hence expensive for fencing, herds of cattle often ruined the crops of homesteaders. This led to bitter conflicts between homesteaders and ranchers (see Source A).

In 1874, when barbed wire was invented and then rapidly mass-produced, homesteaders could at last afford a cheaper way to fence in and protect their crops from straying or stampeding cattle. Though this was popular with homesteaders, many ranchers objected as, from the 1870s, they wanted the land on the Plains to be open range, and in particular wanted access to water for their cattle. The homesteaders also wanted access to water for themselves and their crops, but fencing sometimes led to access to water being cut off from the cattle. It was this that often led to conflicts.

Later, as some big cattle ranchers began to see the advantages of using barbed wire to fence off their huge ranches, this led to conflict between the large and small cattle ranchers. Fence cutting was often the start of more serious conflicts.

Sheep farming

An additional cause of conflict on the Great Plains arose in the late 1870s and the 1880s. This was the spread of sheep farming on the Plains, particularly in the states in the south-west. In New Mexico it was estimated there were five million sheep, while in Arizona sheep outnumbered cattle 10 to 1. There were also large numbers of sheep in California and Utah.

SOURCE A

There was no love lost between settlers and cowboys on the trail. Those jayhawkers would take up a claim right where the herds watered and charge us for water. They would plant a crop alongside a trail and plough a furrow around it for a fence, and when the cattle got into their wheat... they would come cussing and waving a shotgun and yelling for damages.

The view of a cowboy about why conflicts broke out with homesteaders.

Sheep farming spread quickly as it offered many advantages – sheep were cheaper to buy than cattle, and so people needed less money to get started, while the returns were also quicker. This encouraged many poorer people to try sheep farming (see Source B).

The problem was that the large numbers of sheep ate grass, and so competed with cattle for grazing. Also, they cropped the grass much closer to the ground than cattle, and so left little behind; and the grass therefore took longer to recover. Conflicts also took place here, with cattle ranchers killing shepherds, destroying sheep and burning the hay of farmers who sold fodder to sheep farmers.

Racial and religious intolerance

Another cause of conflict between sheep farmers and cattle ranchers involved racial or religious intolerance. Sheep farmers were often immigrants – some from Europe (such as Scottish people or Basques from Spain), but many were Mexican-Americans, or Navaho Indians. In addition to this racial intolerance, religion too played a role, as many sheep farmers and shepherds – especially in Utah – were Mormons.

SOURCE B

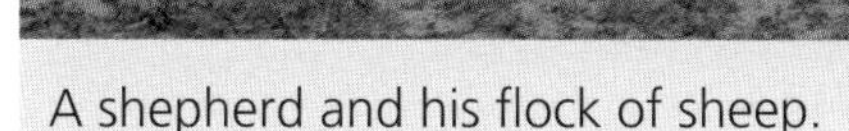

A shepherd and his flock of sheep.

VOICE YOUR OPINION!

Do you think the cattle ranchers were more to blame for the conflicts that broke out than the homesteaders and sheep farmers?

GradeStudio

Recall and select knowledge

Briefly describe the problems which existed between ranchers and homesteaders on the Great Plains.

Examiner's tip

- Remember – you need to do more than simply identify or name these problems. You will need to use your own specific knowledge to *describe* these problems.
- Also – remember to give SEVERAL different problems. Don't think you've finished once you have dealt with just one!

3.8 Why did range wars break out on the Great Plains?

LEARNING OBJECTIVES

In this lesson you will:

- find out about other tensions on the Great Plains, how these sometimes led to range wars, and how outlaws and gunfighters sometimes got involved in these disputes
- get practice in answering questions that ask you to explain something.

KEY WORDS

Range wars – *the serious fighting/armed conflicts which broke out in the West at times, between big and small cattle ranchers, or between cattle ranchers and homesteaders or sheep farmers.*

Range wars and outlaws

Although much of the violence of the Wild West was exaggerated, there were some serious problems. Some of the most famous involved gunfighters and outlaw gangs.

The problems in the West of distance and travel, and the lack of suitable law officers, made it relatively easy for those wishing to break the law. Sometimes, wealthy cattle ranchers hired gunslingers in their disputes with homesteaders, or with other ranchers. Some of these disputes developed into full-scale **range wars**.

The Lincoln County War, 1877–81

In 1877–81, the Lincoln County War in New Mexico was fought not only in courtrooms but also through gunfights, murders and cattle rustlings. In particular, the war attracted outlaws from all parts of New Mexico, Texas, Colorado and south of the Rio Grande – including Billy the Kid (see Source A).

At that time Lincoln County covered nearly one-fifth of the entire territory of New Mexico, and was the largest county in the USA. However, unlike most range wars, this particular one was not a conflict between ranchers and homesteaders, or between cattle barons and small ranchers. Instead, it arose from conflicts between rival New Mexico cattle barons and business people.

The House and the Regulators

During the 1870s a group of merchants had gained control over the economy of Lincoln County, including profitable contracts from the military at Fort Stanton. Major Lawrence G. Murphy and J.J. Dolan, who owned huge cattle ranches in Lincoln County, had a near-monopoly on the cattle and merchant trade. Murphy also had a store in Lincoln. This group and their allies were called the House. The infamous Seven-Rivers gang – of which Jesse Evans, a boyhood friend of Billy the Kid, was a member – fought for the House.

On the other side was John Chisum, the biggest cattle baron in the area, and John Tunstall, a rich English rancher. A rich lawyer, Alexander McSween, was also involved on Chisum's side. This group of cattle barons and business people became known as the Regulators.

Origins of the conflict

The struggle between these rival groups of cattle ranchers had begun in 1877; they fought for economic and political control of the area. Chisum and Tunstall wanted a bigger share of local trade and government beef contracts. In 1877, Murphy's and Dolan's control was challenged by Alexander McSween and John Tunstall, backed by John Chisum. Tension and violent disputes between employees and supporters of the House and the Regulators soon mounted.

At first, Chisum accused Murphy of rustling his cattle, and Tunstall then opened a rival store in Lincoln, and helped Chisum to open up a bank in the town. Their aim was clearly to put Murphy out of business, and so eliminate a business rival. On 18 February 1878, John Tunstall was murdered, apparently by Sheriff Brady who supported Murphy. These disputes then developed into a war in which many were killed.

The war

The significant part of the war lasted until July 1878, ending in a three-day battle in the main street of Lincoln. The connection between cattle ranchers and outlaws is shown by the fact that Billy the Kid was employed by John Tunstall and so fought on the side of Chisum and Tunstall and the Regulators. Initially, he was employed as a cattle guard, and seems to have seen Tunstall as a father figure. But, after Tunstall was killed, he became heavily involved in the violence of the war, after first killing Sheriff Brady. By the end of the conflict, Billy the Kid had built up a formidable reputation as a top gunfighter. He was convicted of killing Sheriff Brady, one of Murphy's supporters. Though he was captured by Sheriff Pat Garrett, imprisoned and sentenced to be hanged, he managed to escape – killing two deputies in order to do so. He was finally tracked down and shot dead by Pat Garrett at Fort Sumner, New Mexico, on 14 July 1881. This marked the official end of the Lincoln County War.

SOURCE A

A tintype photograph of Billy the Kid, 1880.

Fact file

Billy the Kid was born in New York in 1859 (or possibly 1860), and his real name was Henry McCarty, though he often called himself William H. Bonney. Nothing is known about his father, and his mother died when he was about 14 or 15; his first imprisonment – for theft – came soon after, in 1875. He escaped from prison and was said to have killed his first man – who had been bullying him – at the age of 17. For a time, before the Lincoln County War, he appears to have been a cattle rustler. He was only 21 when he was shot dead by Pat Garrett. Though reputed to have killed 21 men by then, modern historians think the true figure was fewer than ten – and possibly as low as four.

SOURCE B

Engraving of Billy the Kid shooting an enemy in a saloon bar.

GradeStudio

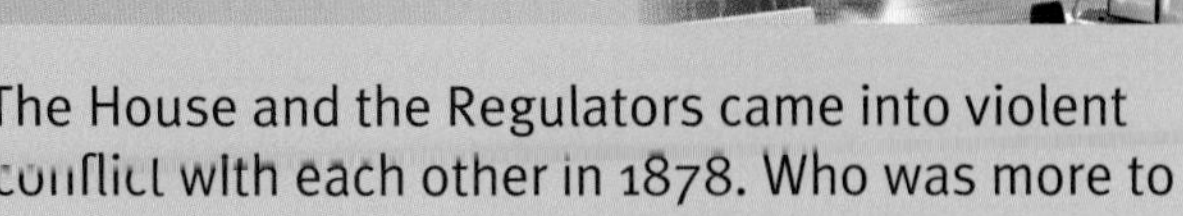

Analysis of sources

Conflict often broke out between cattle ranchers and homesteaders. Sometimes, conflicts also arose between cattle barons and smaller cattle ranchers.

a) Identify the causes of the Lincoln County War.

b) Use your knowledge to describe one of these causes, and explain how it helped cause the Lincoln County War.

c) The House and the Regulators came into violent conflict with each other in 1878. Who was more to blame: the House or the Regulators? Explain your answer.

3.9 Case Study: The Johnson County War, April 1892

LEARNING OBJECTIVES

In this case study you will:

- find out about the origins of this range war, and its main events
- get practice in answering questions that ask you to explain why something happened.

The Johnson County War, in Wyoming, took place in April 1892. By then, the cattle boom was over because of overproduction and the winters of 1886 and 1887 (see Lesson 3.3 on pp. 72–73), but the cattle barons blamed the small ranchers and the homesteaders whose barbed-wire fences had ended the open range. The war was a struggle between small farmers and the large, wealthy ranchers in the Powder River country. Like the earlier Lincoln County War, it came to symbolise several of the law and order problems of the Wild West. It ended in a shoot-out between local farmers and ranchers, a band of hired killers known as the Invaders, a sheriff's posse and, eventually, the US cavalry. Its story has been retold in many books, novels, TV programmes and films.

Background

Conflict – sometimes violent – over land use was common in the development of the American West. But, as has been seen, it was particularly common during the second half of the 19th century when the West was being settled by different groups of white Americans.

In Wyoming, most of the land was seen as being public land – the rights of the Plains' Indians were not considered – and so open both to homesteading and to cattle raising on the open range.

Fact file

The Johnson County War is also known as the Johnson County Cattle War, the War on Powder River or the Wyoming Civil War.

Property and use rights were usually based on who was first to settle the land, and on the size of the herd. However, large ranching outfits would sometimes band together and use their power to control large areas of land, and so prevent newcomers from settling the area. The large ranchers also acted aggressively against cattle rustling – often by lynching (or threatening to lynch) suspected rustlers.

The cattle associations

Many of the large ranchers set up cattle associations to protect their interests. The cattle barons in Wyoming formed the Wyoming Stock Growers' Association (the WSGA). This was made up of some of the state's wealthiest ranchers, and had considerable political influence in the state and region. The WSGA also employed an agency of detectives to investigate cattle rustling against its members. In 1888, the WSGA was able to get a local law passed known as the Maverick Bill, giving them the sole right to round-up unbranded cattle.

The late 1880s

The tense relations between the larger and smaller ranches became worse after the poor winter of 1887–88, when a series of blizzards and extremely low temperatures had followed an extremely hot and dry summer. Thousands of cattle were lost and the wealthier ranchers began to try to take extra land and water supplies.

Some settlers were forced off their land, and the smaller ranchers were excluded from the annual round-up. The rich ranchers justified their actions by saying it was to deal with rustling. There is some evidence to suggest that some small farmers and ranchers saw nothing wrong with taking unbranded cattle. The Maverick Bill of 1888 made it a criminal offence for anyone not belonging to the WSGA to brand cattle.

Rustling in the area does seem to have increased during the late 1880s, and there were well armed bands of horse and cattle rustlers operating in Wyoming and Montana. In 1889, Montana cattle ranchers declared a war on the rustlers, with Wyoming ranchers doing the same in 1890.

In Johnson County, agents of the larger ranchers killed several alleged rustlers from smaller farms. However, many were killed without any real evidence. Between 1889 and 1891, several small ranchers and homesteaders were killed. Frank M. Canton, who had been the sheriff of Johnson County in the early 1880s – and who then became a gunfighter and detective for the WSGA – was rumoured to be behind many of these deaths (see Source A).

A particularly notorious case was that of Ella Watson and storekeeper Jim Averell, who were lynched in 1889 (see Source B). It was believed that the person responsible was Albert Bothwell, a wealthy rancher who claimed he owned the land they farmed – after their murder, he took the land. This event angered the smaller ranchers, but several other alleged rustlers were lynched in 1891.

Resistance

A group of smaller Johnson County ranchers led by Nate Champion decided to form their own Northern Wyoming Farmers' and Stock Growers' Association (NWFSGA) to resist the power and activities of the WSGA. The WSGA warned them to disband, but the NWFSGA refused. Instead, it announced publicly that it would organise its own round-up in the spring of 1892. There was also a political element, in that most of the WSGA supported the Republican Party, while the smaller ranchers were mostly Democrats or Populists (a smaller party of the time). The determination of these small ranchers and settlers to fight back forced the WSGA to take action.

SOURCE A

Frank M. Canton, the former sheriff of Johnson County, hired by the WSGA to lead the Invaders.

SOURCE B

An artist's impression of the lynching of Ella Watson and James (Jim) Averell, on very dubious evidence that they were rustlers. Averell was an entrepreneur, and had no cattle!

HISTORY DETECTIVE

See if you can find out more about the WSGA, including its leading members and, in particular, its political connections.

HISTORY DETECTIVE

Find out more about the winter of 1887–88, and its impact on cattle ranching.

The Invaders

The WSGA, led by Frank Wolcott, a wealthy North Platte rancher, hired a group of skilled gunfighters – officially to deal with alleged rustlers, and unofficially to break up the NWFSGA. Twenty-three gunfighters from Texas, along with some cattle detectives from the WSGA, were hired. They had the support of several political figures, including a state senator. Other people got involved, and about 50 people were organised for an expedition.

The WSGA then hired Frank M. Canton to lead the expedition. Canton was later found to have a list of dozens of rustlers to be shot or hanged, including Sheriff Red Angus, who supported the small farmers and ranchers. Canton also had a contract that promised to pay the Texan gunfighters $5 a day, and a bonus of $50 for every rustler killed. The group became known as the Invaders (see Source C).

The war

The group travelled by train, and then rode into Johnson County on horses (see Source D). They cut the telegraph lines in order to prevent any alarm being given. Canton and the skilled gunfighters travelled ahead, with Wolcott and the party of WSGA officials following behind.

Nate Champion

Their first target was Nate Champion (see Source E). The Invaders travelled to his KC ranch late at night, on Friday, 8 April 1892. They quietly surrounded the buildings and waited for morning.

Three men besides Champion were at the KC – two men who had spent the night on their way through were captured as they emerged from the cabin to collect water at the nearby Powder River, while the third, Nick Ray (Champion's friend), was shot while standing inside the doorway of the cabin and died a few hours later. Champion was besieged inside the log cabin.

During the siege, while taking cover inside the cabin, Champion kept a journal that contained a number of notes he wrote to friends (see Source F). Eventually, the Invaders stopped firing into the cabin and decided to set it on fire. Nate Champion signed his journal entry and put the journal in his pocket before running from

SOURCE D

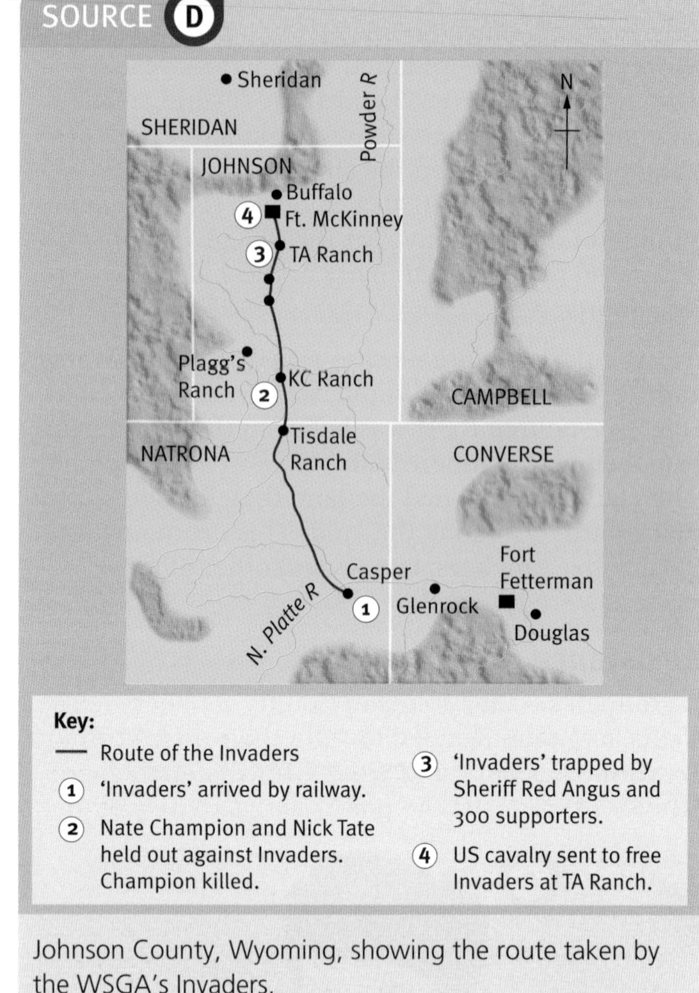

Johnson County, Wyoming, showing the route taken by the WSGA's Invaders.

SOURCE C

The Invaders of the Johnson County (Cattle) War, photograph taken at Fort D.A. Russell, near Cheyenne, Wyoming, 4 May 1892.

HISTORY DETECTIVE

Find out more information about Nate Champion. Is there any evidence that he was involved in rustling?

SOURCE E

Nate Champion – he is the person riding the middle horse.

the back door with a six-shooter in one hand and a knife in the other. As he emerged he was gunned down, and the Invaders pinned a note on his body that read: Cattle Thieves Beware.

The shooting was heard by two passers-by, and local rancher Jack Flagg rode to Buffalo, the county town of Johnson County. He got Sheriff Red Angus to raise a posse of almost 300 men over the next 24 hours and the party set out for the KC ranch on the night of Sunday, 10 April.

On the morning of Monday, 11 April, the WSGA Invaders were at TA Ranch on Crazy Woman Creek, when the posse led by the sheriff caught up with them. A siege then took place, with the gunfighters taking refuge in a barn. Ten of the gunfighters then tried to escape from the barn, but this failed, and the Texan gunfighters were killed in the attempt.

SOURCE F

Boys, I feel pretty lonesome just now. I wish there was someone here with me so we could watch all sides at once...

Well, they have just got through shelling the house like hail. I heard them splitting wood. I guess they are going to fire the house tonight. I think I will make a break when night comes, if alive.

Shooting again. It's not night yet. The house is all fired. Goodbye, boys, if I never see you again.

Some extracts from Champion's journal, including the last entry.

BRAIN BOOST

Make an ideas map/timeline to show the main factors and dates in the period 1880–92 which led to increased tensions between the wealthy and less wealthy ranchers.

The end of the siege

However, one of the WSGA group managed to escape by pretending he was coming out to negotiate, and then riding off. He went to see the acting governor of Wyoming, and pleaded with him to help save the WSGA group. On the second day of the siege, 12 April 1892, Governor Barber telegraphed the US president for help (see Source G). The president (a Republican) immediately ordered action, and the 6th Cavalry from Fort McKinney went to the TA Ranch at once to take custody of the WSGA expedition. The 6th Cavalry rode through the early hours of the morning, and reached the TA Ranch at 6.45 am on 13 April. The expedition surrendered to the 6th – just as the posse had finished preparations to set fire to the barn, using gunpowder (see Source H).

SOURCE G

About sixty-one owners of live stock are reported to have made an armed expedition into Johnson County for the purpose of protecting their live stock and preventing unlawful roundups by rustlers. They are at T.A. Ranch, thirteen miles from Fort McKinney, and are besieged by Sheriff and posse and by rustlers from that section of the country, said to be two or three hundred in number. The wagons of stockmen were captured and taken away from them and it is reported a battle took place yesterday, during which a number of men were killed. Great excitement prevails. Both parties are very determined and it is feared that if successful will show no mercy to the persons captured. The civil authorities are unable to prevent violence. The situation is serious and immediate assistance will probably prevent great loss of life.

The telegram sent by acting Governor Barber to the US president, asking for help for the Invaders.

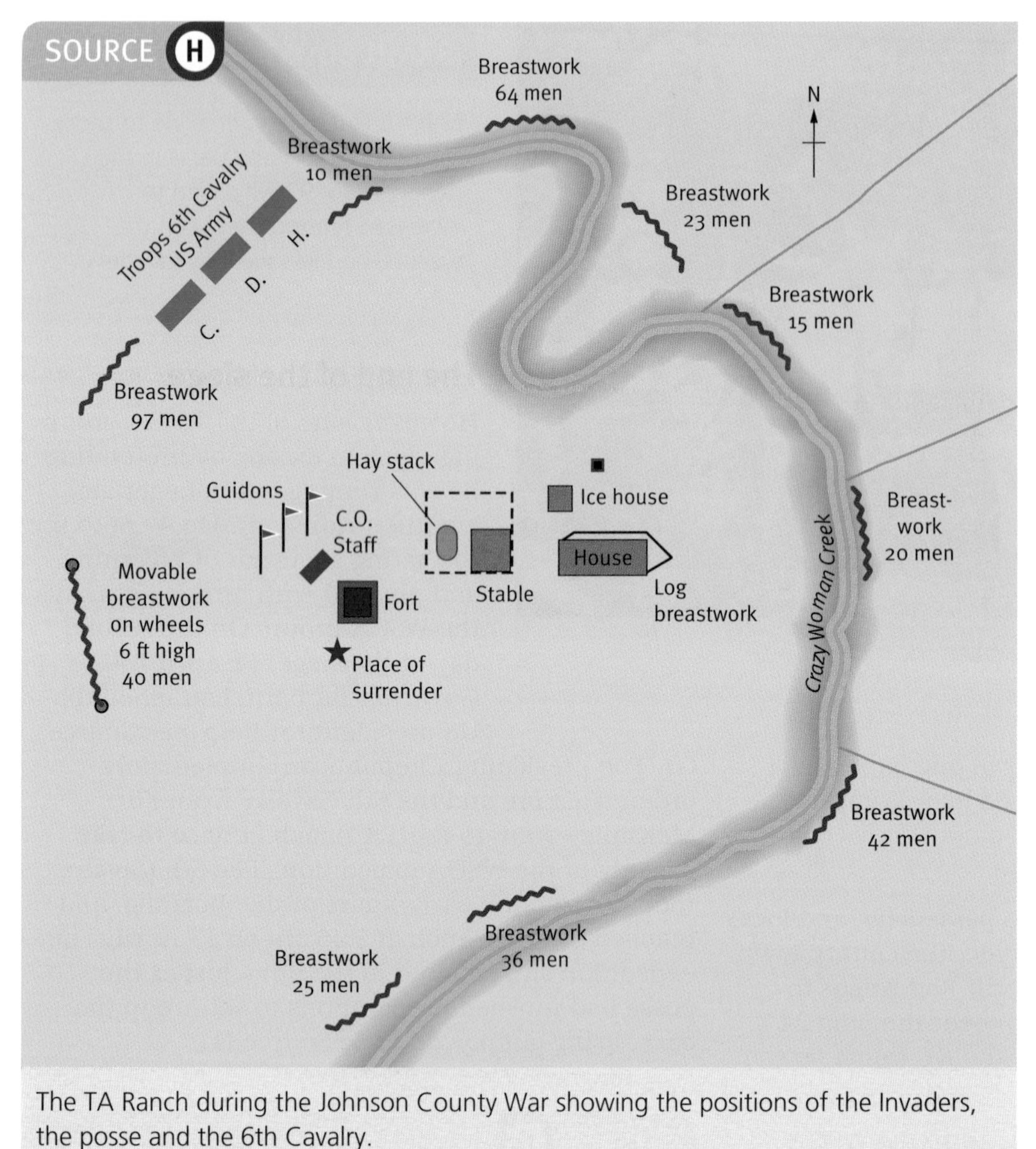

The TA Ranch during the Johnson County War showing the positions of the Invaders, the posse and the 6th Cavalry.

The impact

The WSGA group was held at the barracks of Fort D.A. Russell, because the general in charge of the 6th Cavalry felt that tensions were too high for the prisoners to be kept at the more local Fort McKinney, as the Johnson County officials would have preferred. Indeed, several hundred armed people – supporters of both sides – were reported to have gone to Fort McKinney because they believed the Invaders were being held there.

The prisoners received special treatment, and were allowed to wander about the base by day as long as they agreed to return to the jail to sleep at night.

When details of the WSGA's plan emerged – especially Canton's list of 70 people to be killed – newspapers spoke of important people being charged with aiding and abetting the invasion. These were said to include men high in authority in the State of Wyoming. But, in fact, charges against the politicians in Wyoming who had supported the WSGA were never brought. Eventually the Invaders were released on bail, if they promised to return to Wyoming for the trial. Many of the gunfighters simply fled back to Texas, while, in the end, the WSGA people went free after the charges were dropped because Johnson County refused to pay the costs of prosecution. Partly because of this scandal and the political connections of the Republican Party to the big ranchers, the Democrats won the election for governor of Wyoming in 1895.

Meanwhile, tensions in Johnson County remained high, and the 9th Cavalry of Buffalo Soldiers was drafted in to replace the 6th Cavalry. They had to remain there until November in order to keep the peace. However, emotions continued to run high for many more years. Some saw the large and wealthy ranchers as heroes who took justice into their own hands in order to defend their rights, while others saw the WSGA as no better than vigilantes who had successfully run roughshod over the law of the land, and got away with murder.

Some myths

Supporters of the WSGA claimed Nate Champion was a rustler and a member of the Red Sash Gang of outlaws which, it was claimed, included Jesse James and the Hole in the Wall Gang (see Source I). Modern historians have shown that most of these rumours were false. Though the Hole in the Wall Gang did hide out in Johnson County during this period, there is no evidence that Champion had any connection with them.

On the other hand, those who supported the smaller ranchers claimed that the WSGA had employed some of the West's most notorious gunslingers, including the legendary Tom Horn. Though Horn did briefly work as a detective for the WSGA in the 1890s, there is no evidence he was involved in the Johnson County War.

Although none of the cattle barons or Invaders were ever convicted, their power was broken. This, and the problems of cattle ranching in the late 1880s and 1890s, brought an end to such conflicts.

Fact file

The members of the Wild Bunch/Hole in the Wall Gang were led by Harry Longbaugh and Robert Parker – better known as the Sundance Kid and Butch Cassidy. They operated in Wyoming and Arizona, mainly as train robbers, but also as rustlers. They were known as the Hole in the Wall Gang because of the territory where they hid out. An escarpment of red sandstone known as the Red Wall, in south-west Johnson County, is broken only by one deep V-shaped canyon, called the Hole in the Wall. The valley was used by rustlers to graze stolen cattle, while there were also six cabins used by outlaws wanting refuge from the law. Jesse James is said to have used the Hole in the Wall for a time. Butch Cassidy and the Sundance Kid seem to have died in a shoot-out in Bolivia in 1909.

SOURCE I

The Hole in the Wall gang, also known as the Wild Bunch. The Sundance Kid is on the far left, with Butch Cassidy on the far right.

GradeStudio

Explanation and analysis

Explain why the Johnson County war broke out in 1892.

Examiner's tip

- Remember that with questions like this, you must do more than just identify different reasons – you need to *explain* them, using your own *precise* knowledge.
- Also – remember to explain several reasons – just explaining one will NOT get you the top marks.

VOICE YOUR OPINION!

What do you think about the ways in which the WSGA Invaders were treated after the fighting? How significant were their political connections?

HISTORY DETECTIVE

Find out more about the Hole in the Wall Gang. Is there any evidence that the less wealthy ranchers helped them rustle cattle?

GradeStudio

You have now completed this unit, which has focused on how the cattle trade developed and spread on to the Great Plains, the impact this had, and why there was conflict between the cattle ranchers and the homesteaders. You have also had practice in answering questions designed to prepare you for your exam. Below is an example of one type of exam question, with some hints to help you write a top-scoring answer.

Fact file

In the exam, you will be asked to answer two questions from Section B, the Depth Study: a source-based question and a structured question. The structured question is divided into three parts – **a**, **b** and **c**.

c The cattlemen and the homesteaders were often in conflict with one another. Who was more to blame, the cattlemen or the homesteaders? Explain your answer. **[8 marks]**

Before you write your answer, below are two things to help you start on the right lines.

First, look at the simplified mark scheme for this question. This should help you to write your answer in a way that will allow you to get the full 8 marks available for such questions.

Simplified mark scheme

Level	Skill	Mark
Level 0	No answer or irrelevant answer	0
Level 1	Vague or general answer/general assertions OR identifies reasons, but no precise own knowledge	1–2
Level 2	Just describes relevant aspects about ONE side, but doesn't give any explanation OR just explains some general reasons	2–3
Level 3	Identifies, with specific own knowledge, ways relating to BOTH sides, but doesn't explain them	4
Level 4	Uses specific own knowledge to explain aspects, relating to ONE side	5–6
Level 5	Explains reasons relating to BOTH sides, supported by specific own knowledge	7
Level 6	Explains reasons relating to BOTH sides, supported by specific own knowledge, AND makes a supported/argued overall judgement/decision	8

Examiner's tip

Remember, in order to reach the higher levels in this type of *explain* question, the examiners are expecting you to do TWO things:

- Explain how BOTH sides could be seen as being to blame.
- To come to a judgement to show how, overall, you think one side was more to blame than the other. In such questions, there isn't a right or wrong decision – the important thing is to make a judgement. If you don't, you will not be able to achieve full marks.

They are also expecting you to use *specific* own knowledge AND understanding of the particular topic or aspects of your course to *explain* your points/examples. It is not enough just to *describe* relevant aspects – you must *explain*.

Second, look at the sample answer below, noting especially the examiner's comment

Candidate's answer

I think the homesteaders were to blame as the cattlemen had been on the Great Plains first.
An example of why the homesteaders were to blame is the way they used barbed wire, after it was invented in 1874. Before then, because of the lack of trees and wood, the Plains had been an open range when cattle had either been driven along the cattle trails or, later, raised on the Plains. The homesteaders used the barbed wire to make fences to fence off their land – very often, this meant that the cattle were unable to get to watering holes which they had used in the past.

When the ranchers cut the barbed wire, there were often disputes and, sometimes, violent conflicts between the two groups. This was the homesteaders' fault because the cattle needed to use the watering holes, and the cattlemen had been using these water holes long before the homesteaders arrived on the Great Plains.

Examiner's comment

The first highlighted part of the answer (red) – by itself – gets the candidate into Level 1, as one reason is given but without any supporting *specific* own knowledge identified from the source.

The second highlighted part of the answer (**green**) is providing useful and precise supporting own knowledge, relating to one relevant group, and is *explaining* why that group is to blame. This gets the candidate into Level 4. However, it relates to only ONE group – it does not explain why the other group might also have been to blame, and this also means the candidate is not able to make an overall judgement. Therefore, the candidate does not get into either of the top two levels.

Look again at the mark scheme provided, and you should be able to see what that candidate could have done to push this good answer from Level 4 (5–6 marks) into Level 6 and so score the full 8 marks available.

You will see that in order to get into Level 6, and score 8 marks, all the candidate needed to do was:

- *identify* and *explain* reasons why BOTH sides could be seen as being to blame, using *precise* knowledge to support the points being made, AND
- make an *overall/supported* judgement about one side being *more* to blame than the other.

Once you think you have fully understood what is needed to improve this candidate's answer, write your own answer. However, don't use the issue of barbed wire and water holes given by the sample answer. Instead, try to explain – using *precise* own knowledge – OTHER reasons why BOTH the cattlemen AND the homesteaders could be blamed. Remember, too, to come to an overall judgement which is supported by argument.

Before you start, look back at Lesson 3.8. Then try to write your answer without looking at the relevant pages.

Chapter 4

Why did white Americans and Plains' Indians find it so difficult to reach a peaceful settlement?

This chapter focuses on the growing conflict between white Americans and the Plains' Indians in the period 1840–90. It examines the different attitudes towards Native Americans held by various white Americans, and why US governments frequently changed their policies in relation to the Plains' Indians. It also looks at the government's reservations policy and its impact on the lives of the Plains' Indians, and the deliberate destruction of the herds of buffalo. It deals with various military conflicts, and the different chiefs and commanders. Finally, it examines the situation that the Plains' Indians found themselves in by the end of the 19th century.

Sources A, B, C and D are common examples of the images many people have about the conflict between white Americans and the Plains' Indians.

GETTING STARTED

For many people, one of the most notorious events during the Vietnam War of 1960–75 was the My Lai Massacre, in which a group of US soldiers killed hundreds of Vietnamese women and children. Yet such events were not uncommon during the wars fought in the second half of the 19th century to take the Great Plains from the Plains' Indians. Not only were massacres of Native American villages committed by US troops, there was frequently an element of racism – also present in the Vietnam War. Native Americans were often referred to as 'redskins' or 'red varmints' (vermin) by many white Americans – just as Vietnamese were seen as 'gooks' or 'ginks' by some US soldiers. For some of those involved in the growing conflict on the Great Plains, the belief that the Plains' Indians were somehow inferior or 'subhuman' meant that certain violent and even repellent actions were acceptable in these 'Indian Wars'.

Yet, as with the Vietnam War, there were plenty of contemporaries amongst white Americans who took a different view, and opposed such attitudes and actions. However, they were not usually in a position of power to shape things.

At the same time, as the conflicts became increasingly violent, the Plains' Indians themselves became split. Many of the older leaders felt that the white Americans were too numerous and too strong to fight, so they were prepared to compromise and make peace. However, some younger leaders were opposed to this because it increasingly involved giving up their traditional way of life. Then, when treaties were broken by the US government, such war leaders often ignored their chiefs and whatever agreements they had made, and decided instead to fight to protect what lands remained to their tribe or nation.

In groups of four, take a blank piece of paper and take five minutes to discuss and write down what YOUR views would be in such a situation, when faced with an overwhelmingly strong and powerful enemy: to surrender and make the best deal you can, OR to resist for as long as it takes to force them to give up.

At the end of the five minutes, share your ideas with the rest of the class to see whether the peacemakers or the resisters are in the majority.

SOURCE A

A still from the 1970 film *Soldier Blue*, showing US cavalry attacking a Cheyenne woman during the Massacre at Sand Creek, 28 November 1864.

SOURCE B

A print from an engraving by Frederick Remington, showing US cavalry discovering the bodies of fellow soldiers killed by Native Americans. The bodies have been scalped and shot full of arrows.

SOURCE C

A painting by Charles Schreyvogel, 1868, showing the Massacre of Washita. During the massacre, the Cheyenne chief Black Kettle was killed and scalped by US cavalry.

SOURCE D

A photograph, taken on 1 January 1891, of dead Sioux Indians being buried – against their religious traditions – in a mass grave, following the Massacre of Wounded Knee, 29 December 1890.

HISTORY DETECTIVE

Try to find out more about the Native American wars for control of the Great Plains in the second half of the 19th century by visiting www.heinemann.co.uk/hotlinks and enter the code 1433P.

4.1 Attitudes of white Americans to Native Americans – a clash of cultures

LEARNING OBJECTIVES

In this lesson you will:

- find out how ideas about what land the Plains' Indians could have began to alter after 1840 and the different attitudes about the Plains' Indians held by different groups of white Americans
- practise answering questions that ask you to describe an aspect of a topic.

Background to the struggle for the Great Plains

The conflict between Native Americans and white Americans, which had developed since US independence in 1783, deepened after 1840, and broke out into serious fighting from the 1860s. Yet, when the first white Americans had crossed the Great Plains, relations with the Native Americans who lived there were generally good. This was because, at first, the number of white migrants was small, and groups such as the mountain men lived in a way similar to that of the Plains' Indians – some even married Native American women.

When white Europeans had first settled in the East, they soon forced out the Native Americans who had lived there for centuries. The Plains' Indians, who lived on the Great Plains to the west, had completely different attitudes towards nature and the land from those held by most white Americans. In 1825, the US government had set aside an area for Native Americans called the 'Indian Territory' – in what is now present-day Oklahoma. Then, in 1832, because the US government thought the Great Plains were of little value, the Native Americans were also 'awarded' this huge area.

The first change to this came in 1834, when the border between the USA and the Indian Territory was moved further west, and fixed on the 95th meridian – all land west of this 'Permanent Indian Frontier' (PIF) was known as 'Indian Territory' and was now to be one huge 'Indian Reservation' where Native Americans could live as they wanted.

Fact file

Part of the 1834 'agreement' was the earlier Indian Removal Act of 1830, which had required all Native Americans to leave the fertile wooded lands between the east banks of the Mississippi River and the Appalachian Mountains. This mainly affected the Cherokee, Creek, Chickasaw, Choctaw and Seminole nations – known as the 'Five Cultured Tribes'. They were then forced by the US army to move west to a semi-desert region. Only the Cherokees resisted – they were eventually rounded up, and over 2000 died on their 'Trail of Tears' in 1838–39.

Developments after 1840

During the 1840s, most Indians of the Great Plains did not object to white settlers crossing Indian Territory. Even when the USA gained California and Oregon in the 1840s, most Plains' Indians tolerated the increased numbers crossing their lands on their way to the new US territories along the Pacific. To begin with, most white migrants still saw the Great Plains as the 'Great American Desert'.

However, tensions began to increase when large numbers of white miners and farmers wanted to settle permanently on the Plains – and were increasingly encouraged by the US government to do so. After decades of misunderstanding and racism, the Plains' Indians decided to resist the growing threat to their way of life and very existence.

Different attitudes of white Americans

It would be wrong to think that all white Americans thought about the Plains' Indians in the same way. At first, mountain men were very often sympathetic to their way of life. Also, many individual white visitors to the West – such as the painter George Catlin – felt that the Plains' Indians should be respected and treated well.

However, by the 1840s, many white Americans – settlers, miners, railroad companies, ranchers, the US army and government – had begun to see the Plains' Indians as a 'problem' which needed to be 'solved'. But there were different ideas about how to do this.

KEY WORDS

Genocide – *the destruction, or attempted destruction, of an entire group or race of people, such as the attempt by the Nazis to wipe out all Jewish people in Europe.*

Indian agents – *white people appointed by the US government to run the reservations in which the Plains' Indians were to live. They were mostly unsympathetic to the culture, beliefs and problems faced by the Indians, and were often corrupt.*

'Humanitarians' versus 'exterminators'

One group favoured a humanitarian approach and negotiation as the way to solve what they saw as the 'Indian problem'. Most – but not all – of these 'humanitarians' tended to live in the East: some settlers and **Indian agents** had come to understand and respect the culture of the Plains' Indians (see Source A). These humanitarians believed – especially after the end of the American Civil War in 1865 – it was best to avoid fighting if possible. Hence they believed that the Bureau of Indian Affairs should control policy – not the Department for War and the US Army, which often took a more aggressive line. They wanted to negotiate agreements with the Plains' Indians and then, by a humanitarian policy of education and religious missionary work, try to change the culture and way of life of the Plains' Indians – from hunters into farmers.

However, while some white settlers on the Plains had respect for the way of life of the Plains' Indians, most did not. They saw them as 'primitive savages' and 'heathens', and so favoured a more aggressive policy. Many of the settlers, miners, ranchers and those who won contracts to supply the Plains' Indian reservations believed there was much land to be gained if the Plains' Indians could be pushed into smaller and smaller areas – and even exterminated (see Sources B and E). This was also the belief of many of the US troops brought in in increasing numbers to protect the settlers as attacks by Plains' Indians on settlers increased in the 1850s.

These 'exterminators' came increasingly to favour a policy of total destruction of the Plains' Indians – what in more modern times would be called **genocide** (see Source B). Such settlers in the West – and many in the US Army – felt responsibility for policy towards the Indians should be taken from the Bureau of Indian Affairs, and handed over to the US army, who would take stronger action.

SOURCE A

The attempt to cajole and bamboozle [trick] the Indians as if they were deficient in intelligence ought to be abandoned. Faithlessness on our part in the matter of treaties, and gross swindling of the Indians, are at the bottom of all this Indian trouble.

An extract from the *New York Times*, 8 June 1870.

SOURCE B

We must act with vindictive earnestness against the Sioux, even to their extermination – men, women and children.

An extract from comments made by General Sherman of the US army.

SOURCE C

US General William Tecumseh Sherman.

SOURCE D

The Indian is a savage in every sense of the word; not worse, perhaps, than his white brother would be similarly born and bred, but one whose cruel and ferocious nature far exceeds that of any wild beast of the desert.

An extract from *My Life on the Plains* by US General George Custer; the book was published in 1874.

SOURCE E

We have come to the point in the history of our country that there is no place beyond the white population to which you can remove the Indian, and the precise question is will you exterminate him, or will you fix a lasting place for him.

An extract from a speech to the US Congress, made by Senator Morrill in 1867.

ACTIVITIES

Link the sources in this lesson to one of the two groups of white Americans: 'humanitarians' or 'exterminators'.

4.2 Why did US government policy towards the Great Plains and the Plains' Indians change in the period 1840–50?

LEARNING OBJECTIVES

In this lesson you will:

- find out how US government policy towards the Plains' Indians began to change after 1840
- learn how to produce high-scoring answers to questions that ask you to compare/contrast the information provided by two sources, and to consider/explain different attitudes. You will find below some helpful tips about how to do this, and a question that gives you practice at answering such questions.

KEY WORDS

Atrocities – *events in which large numbers of people are killed, and/or acts such as torture, mutilation and rape are committed – usually on non-combatants – by military/armed forces.*

By 1850, the population of the USA was more than 20 million. At the same time, there were only about 350,000 Plains' Indians – who came increasingly to be seen by white Americans and the US government as standing in the way of 'Manifest Destiny' and hence a barrier to further westward expansion (see Lesson 2.12 on pp. 60–61).

From the 1840s, because of the expansion of mining, farming and the railroads in the West, this developed into a war for control of the Great Plains. For the Plains' Indians, though, it was more than a war for control – it was a war for the survival of their culture and way of life, and even for their very existence.

Fact file

Many Native American chiefs thought they had been cheated and betrayed by US officials – and often found it hard to control younger warriors who wanted to fight to maintain their traditional way of life.

Early US government policy

At first, US governments were prepared to let the Plains' Indians keep the Great Plains, and promised that no white migrants would be allowed to settle on the Plains. Initially, some groups – such as the Lakota Sioux – were content to demand tolls from those non-Indians crossing the Plains.

However, from the mid-19th century, the numbers of miners and settlers crossing the lands of the Plains' Indians increased significantly.

SOURCE A

Attack on the Emigrant Train, a painting by Charles Wimar, showing Indians attacking a wagon train crossing their lands on the Great Plains.

Consequently, US governments frequently broke the 1832–34 agreements with the Indians, in order to give miners, settlers and railroad companies access to land west of the so-called 'Permanent Indian Frontier'.

As attacks by Native Americans on wagon trains and miners' camps increased (see Source A), the US government dropped the policy of 'one big reservation' – that the Indians could have all of the apparently worthless Great Plains.

Manifest Destiny and the expansion of the USA after 1845

US governments instead decided that the Indians of the Great Plains should not be allowed to stand in the way of Manifest Destiny and the development of the West. This attitude hardened after 1845, when the USA expanded greatly by obtaining Texas, California and Oregon in the south and west. Then, in 1848, gold was discovered in California and later Colorado. So the numbers of miners and settlers crossing Indian Territory on trails such as the Oregon Trail, and disturbing and hunting the buffalo herds, hugely increased. In addition, these migrants often carried diseases, and some white traders sold whisky to the Indians, causing extra problems (see Source B). The US government then began to encourage white migrants to settle on the Great Plains themselves.

Native American attacks on the wagon trains and mining camps increased. Not surprisingly, the migrants demanded protection from the US government against what they saw as unprovoked attacks. However, although the government sent in cavalry units and established forts, tensions and clashes continued to grow. Often the slightest incident could spark off a major confrontation – with both sides sometimes committing **atrocities**. This was not helped by the fact that many army officers and soldiers were ignorant of the culture and way of life of the Plains' Indians, and showed little sensitivity when dealing with incidents. Many were also racist, and saw the Plains' Indians as being almost sub-human.

SOURCE B

When the trail to Oregon was opened to wagon trains in the early 1840s, the resulting annual flow of travellers brought critical new problems to the Indian tribes... friction between the travellers and the tribes soon built up to danger point, and minor conflicts erupted all along the way. Most problems between red men and white resulted directly from the white man's firm belief that an Indian had no rights of any kind, even in his own land.

An extract from F. Haines, *The Plains' Indians*, Collins, 1976, p. 39.

Fact file

At first, US army forts and outposts were built along the PIF. Later, as the number of migrants and settlers increased, and following further agreements, these forts were built on Indian lands.

ACTIVITIES

1. How do Sources A and B reflect the reasons why US government policy towards the Plains' Indians changed in the period 1840–50?
2. What do Sources A and B have in common concerning the reasons for increased tensions and possible US government concerns? And how do they differ?
3. What information does Source B provide which is not mentioned in Source A?
4. Why might the producers of these two sources have different attitudes?

Recall and select knowledge

Briefly describe the main changes in US government policy towards the Plains' Indians in the period 1840–50.

Examiner's tip

- Remember, with questions that ask you to describe something, always try to identify several points/aspects.
- Don't just 'list' these points, try instead to use a few precise bits of information to describe your points.

4.3 How successful was the Treaty of Fort Laramie, 1851?

LEARNING OBJECTIVES

In this lesson you will:

- find out how the Treaty of Fort Laramie, 1851, tried to solve the growing problems outlined in the last lesson
- get practice in answering questions that ask you to explain the usefulness of a source.

The growing tensions and occasional outbreaks of violence between some Plains' Indians and the migrants crossing the Great Plains led the US government in Washington to take action. At this stage, it believed the best policy would be to negotiate with the Plains' Indians. However, this was not easy, as tribes within a nation, and bands within a tribe, had a lot of independence. Consequently, war parties – often involving only small numbers of warriors – might decide not to accept agreements made by senior chiefs.

The Treaty of Fort Laramie, 1851

Eventually, at Fort Laramie, Wyoming, in 1851, a major peace council was held: more than 10,000 Plains' Indians attended. The US government agent and fur trader Thomas Fitzpatrick, who was trusted by many Native Americans, met with the chiefs of the main Great Plains' tribes. Most important were the Sioux, and their Northern Cheyenne and Northern Arapaho allies.

By the Treaty of Fort Laramie, 1851, the US government promised the chiefs gifts and an annual payment of $50,000 to the tribes for the next ten years (though this was later reduced to five), as compensation for each tribe agreeing to live, in peace, in smaller tribal areas or reservations. These were to be clearly defined – in part, also as an attempt to limit conflict between the different Plains' nations and tribes. It was also stated that the Plains' Indians would be free to leave their reservations at certain times to hunt buffalo on certain areas of the Great Plains.

The most pressing concern of the Plains' Indians – that of restricting the numbers of white settlers – was also addressed by the Treaty, as the US government said that white migrants could not enter or settle on these reservations, and promised to protect Indians against any crimes committed by US citizens. In return, the Plains' Indian chiefs agreed to give up the previously agreed right of unlimited access to the Great Plains, and to leave open the main routes through Kansas and Nebraska for settlers – such as the Oregon Trail (see Source A). They also agreed to allow the US army to build roads and forts on Indian Territory to protect the travellers across the Plains. Afterwards, a delegation of 11 chiefs was taken to Washington to meet the US president.

After the treaty

The acceptance of individual reservations divided and separated the different nations and tribes, and made it more difficult for them to band together. For the same reason, this policy of concentration made it much easier for the US army to control the movements of the Plains' Indians. By 1854, the US army had 52 forts in the West, though only a few at first had more than 100 men or real fortifications. However, as the numbers of white settlers crossing the Plains increased, the numbers of soldiers in the forts increased also.

SOURCE A

They are in terrible want of food half the year. The travel upon the road [trail] drives the buffalo off or else confines them to a narrow path during the period of migration... Their women are pinched with want and their children are constantly crying with hunger.

An extract from a report to the US government made in 1853 by Thomas Fitzpatrick, the Indian agent who had helped bring about the Treaty of Fort Laramie, 1851. He is commenting on the impact of the wagon trains on the Oregon Trail, crossing Indian lands.

Very soon, the US government began to demand more land concessions from the Plains' Indians – to a large extent, it had never seriously intended to abide by the terms of the 1851 treaty. As early as 1854, both Kansas and Nebraska were 'opened up' by the US government for white settlers – thus further reducing the Indians' lands.

Increasingly, Plains' Indian leaders felt that they had been cheated and betrayed yet again. In addition, chiefs did not have control over all their warriors, many of whom objected to the Treaty which restricted their traditional hunting and their right to roam freely across the Great Plains.

The Grattan Incident, 1854

These bad feelings were increased by the Grattan Incident. When a skinny cow that had wandered away from a Mormon wagon train bound for Utah was killed by High Forehead, an Indian from a Brule Sioux village, the cow's owner went to Fort Laramie to complain. A young and inexperienced lieutenant, John L. Grattan, led a troop of 30 cavalry to the village to arrest High Forehead, and to deal with other issues. When discussions with the village chief, Conquering Bear, seemed to be going nowhere – partly owing to Grattan's drunken and anti-Indian interpreter – the soldiers opened fire, killing the chief and others, including other Sioux waiting for the annual money payments promised by the Treaty of Fort Laramie. But the village warriors fought back and killed the entire troop in revenge – their bodies were then mutilated.

Early in 1855, while the Plains' Indians were still in their winter camps, a US army unit of 600, led by General William Harney, massacred 86 Sioux Indians in a camp at Blue Water in Nebraska in retaliation for this. Many others were injured, and dozens were taken prisoner – one Sioux warrior who was angered by this was Crazy Horse.

The speed with which such a small initial incident so quickly led to armed conflict showed how tense the situation was. By the 1860s, the situation became worse for various reasons.

VOICE YOUR OPINION!

Do you think the US government genuinely thought that the Treaty of Fort Laramie, 1851, was a final agreement with the Plains' Indians?

SOURCE B

Indians Watching the Wagon Train, a painting by Oscar Berninghaus.

Analysis of sources

Study Source B.

Did the Treaty of Fort Laramie, 1851, solve the problems between the white settlers and the Plains' Indians? Use the source and your own knowledge to explain your answer.

Examiner's tip

- Remember to use the source AND your own knowledge when trying to explain if the Treaty of Fort Laramie solved the problems.
- Also, remember that in the exam you can refer to other sources given on the exam paper, IF they are relevant to the question, AND provided you do use the one mentioned in the question! Do you think Source A could help you write your answer?

4.4 Why were there problems with life on the Indian reservations?

LEARNING OBJECTIVES

In this lesson you will:

- find out about some of the problems on the reservations
- get practice in answering questions that ask you to explain an aspect of a topic.

From 1825, as has been seen, US governments had developed a policy of Indian reservations on the Great Plains. These reservations were supervised by government-appointed Indian Agents, selected by the Indian Bureau. Their roles were to distribute food and money, and to encourage Native Americans to give up hunting, and to live as farmers instead – although, at first, some Indians were allowed off the reservations at certain times to hunt buffalo. Later, this 'right' was removed.

Many Indians soon came to resent being confined, for most of the time, to reservations – which were much smaller than the land they'd previously lived on. The idea of this confinement – or imprisonment – was, of course, to keep them away from the growing numbers of settlers on the Plains.

Life on the reservations

Once on the reservations, they were strongly encouraged to grow crops – but often this was on poor land, or in unhealthy areas which, for the time being at least, the settlers did not want. This made it difficult for the Indians to feed themselves. They were also pressured to abandon their language, customs and beliefs – in particular, children were to be taught English and American values, and wear European clothes (see Source A).

They also hated the idea of becoming dependent on the distribution of beef rations and other supplies, which had to be bought with the annual payments sent by the US government after the 1851 Treaty of Fort Laramie. Many yearned to be free to follow and hunt the buffalo wherever they went. For many, they felt their culture, way of life and even their self-respect and dignity were being destroyed. This was especially true for the younger men because they had previously been able to gain and maintain status and honour in their group by the skill and bravery shown in hunting or warfare.

Corrupt government agents

To make matters worse, many of the government-appointed white Indian Bureau agents who ran the reservations were incompetent or even corrupt (see Source B). Such agents often stole money intended for the Indians or sold part of their food rations to white traders or settlers. As a result, food on the reservations was poor and often in short supply. At first, the US government allowed the chiefs to distribute the food rations. This later changed, with the government getting the heads of families to collect the rations instead. Later, in 1887, the Dawes Act allocated land to individual families. This was a deliberate way of destroying – or at least undermining – Native American culture and power structures. It was known as 'deculturisation'. It was intended to turn them into christian 'Americans'.

Medical treatment was often inadequate and many Indians suffered greatly from diseases such as measles, whooping cough and influenza. The fact that they were often poorly fed just made matters worse.

Finally, of the two government bodies dealing with Native Americans, the War Department was much more hostile than the Indian Bureau. Most senior army officers – Sherman, Sheridan, Custer and Chivington – were extremely prejudiced against

SOURCE A

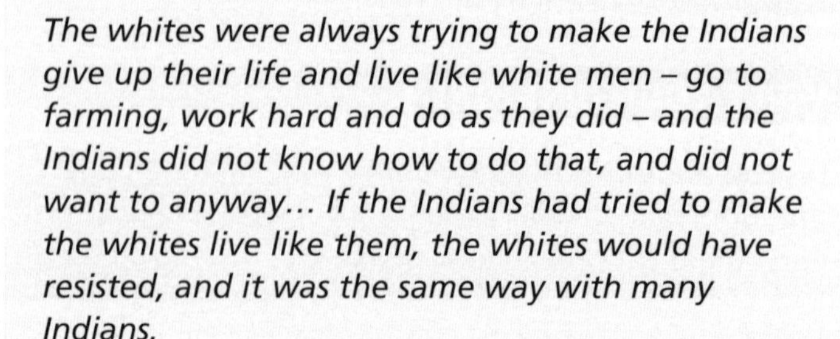
The whites were always trying to make the Indians give up their life and live like white men – go to farming, work hard and do as they did – and the Indians did not know how to do that, and did not want to anyway... If the Indians had tried to make the whites live like them, the whites would have resisted, and it was the same way with many Indians.

A comment by Big Eagle of the Dakota Sioux.

Indians. Sherman later advocated a dual or 'double' policy of 'peace within their reservation and war without'.

Continual encroachments

Even after the 1851 Treaty, the Plains' Indians came under increasing pressure to give up parts of the lands they had been granted, to make room for settlers who continued to pour on to the Plains in great numbers (see Source C). For instance, the Dakota Sioux on the northern Plains were forced to give up part of their reservation in 1858, when Minnesota became a state of the USA. Their 'choice' was either to agree to this or to risk losing all their lands to the settlers.

The increasing pressure from white settlers on the Great Plains led to more and more violent incidents. Initially, because of the distractions of the American Civil War, these tensions did not develop into serious warfare. However, even before the Civil War was over in 1865, the 'War for the Great Plains' had begun.

SOURCE B

A cartoon attacking corrupt Indian agents. Although this cartoon dates from 1890, it illustrates problems on reservations that were there from the beginning.

The results

The earlier removals, and the later policy of smaller and smaller reservations, were very demoralising. Added to the poor conditions and the problems on reservations, alcoholism, depression and even suicide among the Indians – especially amongst young males – became increasingly common.

BRAIN BOOST

Make a spider diagram of the main problems faced by Native Americans on the reservations.

GradeStudio

Explanation and analysis

Explain why many Indians disliked living on reservations.

Examiner's tip

- Remember – you need to do more than simply identify or 'list' reasons – you must use your own specific knowledge to *explain* your reasons.
- Also – don't just explain one reason – you must try to consider at least TWO reasons.

SOURCE C

The rapid progress upon the continent [of North America] will not permit the lands which are required for civilisation to be surrendered to savage tribes for hunting grounds. The government has always demanded the removal of the Indians when their lands were required for agricultural purposes by advancing settlements.

An extract from comments made by the US secretary of the interior, 1862.

4.5 The Wars in the central and southern Plains, 1860–75

LEARNING OBJECTIVES

In this lesson you will:

- find out about what happened on the central and southern Plains in the period 1860–75 and the importance of the Great Plains' Massacre of the buffalo
- get practice in answering questions that ask you to describe an aspect of a topic.

Disputes between the Plains' Indians and white Americans began to arise when, in breach of the 1851 Fort Laramie Treaty, large numbers of miners and settlers began to move into the areas that had been promised to the Plains' Indians in 1851. Eventually, in the 1860s, this led to the start of the Plains Wars. These wars continued, on and off, for the next 30 years. By 1890, the wars had ended, and the Plains' Indians had lost their Great Plains.

War for the central Plains

During the 1860s, a series of conflicts broke out between the US army and the Cheyenne and Arapaho in the central Plains, and the Comanche and Kiowa in the southern Plains.

In 1861, by the Treaty of Fort Lyon (also known as the Treaty of Fort Wise), Cheyenne and Arapaho chiefs agreed to give up their 1851 reservations in return for a smaller reservation at Sand Creek, Colorado. However, much of the land was of very poor quality, and was dry and infertile, making it almost impossible for the Plains' Indians to survive there, and the growing hardships of life on the reservation made it increasingly difficult for the Cheyenne chief, Black Kettle – who felt the whites were too well-armed and who realised the buffalo were declining – to control the younger warriors.

These Cheyenne warriors became angrier when Colorado was opened up for white settlement later that year. During 1861–62, some of them left the reservation to roam the area in search of buffalo and other animals to hunt. But there was little to be found and, in 1863, Black Kettle led the Cheyenne out of their Sand Creek reservation. This was the beginning of the Cheyenne uprising of 1863. Faced with starvation, they began to carry out attacks on wagon trains in order to steal food – at first, the travellers were left unharmed. But soon the attacks escalated, and mining camps, railway surveyors and mail coaches were also attacked – inevitably, several white Americans were killed in these attacks.

Many people – including the US army – had little sympathy for the plight of the Cheyenne, and in 1864 it was decided to send out a military unit under Major Jacob Downing to punish them by attacking one of their villages in Cedar Canyon. Black Kettle sent out peace parties to negotiate, but these were shot and the village was wiped out.

The Sand Creek Massacre

As most regular soldiers were still fighting in the Civil War, the governor of Colorado recruited a militia of volunteers, under the control of Colonel J.M. Chivington (see Source A). The army then said all Cheyenne wishing for peace should report to army forts. On 28 September 1864, their leader, Black Kettle, agreed to return to Sand Creek. But, in October, Chivington – who openly stated that he wanted to kill as many Indians as possible – decided that Black Kettle had not surrendered properly as he had failed to report to an army fort. Instead, at dawn on 29 November, Chivington's unit of Colorado Volunteers attacked Black Kettle's camp at Sand Creek, while the 600 or so Cheyenne were still asleep (see Sources B, C and D).

Although numbers are disputed, it would appear that at least 160 Plains' Indians were massacred in the attack – two-thirds of them women and children – even though Black Kettle raised the US flag and a white flag above his tipi to show he wanted peace.

Fact file

Those taken prisoner following the Sand Creek Massacre were later displayed to American theatre audiences during the intervals, along with the scalps of dead Cheyenne taken by Chivington's troops.

SOURCE A

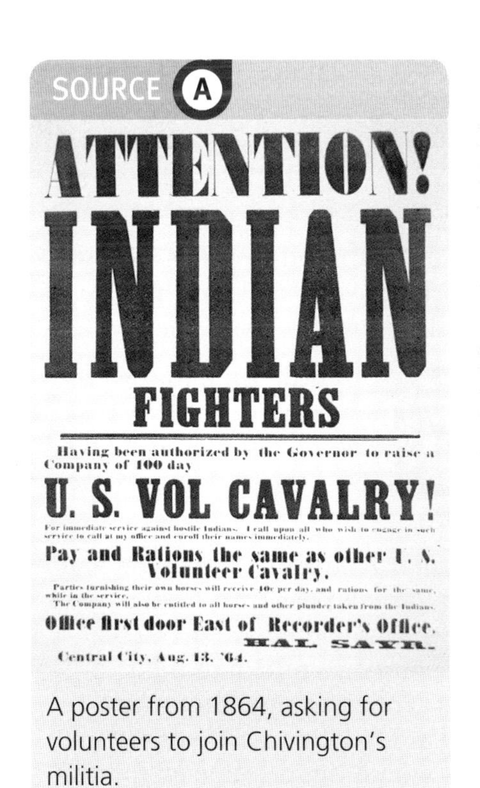

A poster from 1864, asking for volunteers to join Chivington's militia.

Fact file

It is estimated that the US government spent $30 million on fighting the Plains' Indians in the period 1864–67 as the fighting spread. The Plains' Indians had nothing like these resources.

SOURCE B

They were scalped, their brains knocked out; the men used their knives, ripped open women, clubbed little children, knocked them in the head with their guns, beat their brains out, mutilated their bodies in every sense of the word.

Part of an account of the Sand Creek Massacre given by John Smith, a trader who witnessed it.

Later, when news of the massacre reached the East, and it became clear to Chivington that he might face a court martial, he resigned before he could be charged.

The wars on the central and southern Plains after 1864

The Sand Creek Massacre outraged the Cheyenne 'dog soldiers', and they began to attack white settlements and wagon trains. Black Kettle, who managed to escape from his camp, and the Cheyenne teamed up with the Sioux to the north, while the Comanche and Kiowa allied in the south also joined forces and took part in the war.

The war saw increasing attacks on white settlements and, as far as the nations on the central and southern Plains were concerned, it lasted until 1867. At first, with most of the USA's professional soldiers involved in fighting the Civil War, the Plains' Indians had some successes against volunteer units. But, after 1865, the US army was able to concentrate its forces and resources on destroying the resistance of the Plains' Indians.

The Treaty of Medicine Lodge Creek, 1867

Eventually, the Cheyenne and most of their allies realised their resistance could not continue, and the conflict was ended in 1867, by the Medicine Lodge Creek Treaty. The treaty gave the Cheyenne and Arapaho one shared reservation, and the Comanche and Kiowa another – this separated and concentrated the different nations even more, and so made alliances more difficult. They also agreed to settle permanently in them, in return for regular food and being taught how to farm, and the right occasionally to hunt buffalo outside the reservations.

SOURCE C

Cheyenne and Arapaho chiefs in 1864. Black Kettle is in the middle of the front row. The man kneeling to the right is Silas Soule, who refused to take part in the Sand Creek Massacre.

SOURCE D

It looked too hard for me to see little children on their knees begging for their lives, having their brains beaten out like dogs.

Part of comments made by Captain Silas Soule, who was present but refused to take part in the massacre at Sand Creek.

BRAIN BOOST

Make an ideas map showing the main causes of the serious fighting which broke out in 1864.

KEY WORDS

Great Plains' Massacre – *the deliberate attempt, encouraged by the US government, to hunt the buffalo on the Plains to extinction, so the Indians would be forced to give up hunting, and to live on reservations instead.*

Total war – *this did not mean the deliberate killing of women and children but did mean waging war against the whole population. This was to be done by destroying all the animals, food, shelter and clothing of the Indians. They would then be faced with two choices – starvation, or surrender and a return to their reservations.*

The winter campaign, 1868

Many younger warriors refused to accept the limitations imposed by the new treaty of 1867. Also, the numbers of white settlers continued to increase. In 1868, fighting broke out again, when some Cheyenne in Kansas and Nebraska began to attack settlers. The US army officers in charge of dealing with this new outbreak of fighting were General William Sherman and General Philip Sheridan. As the violence continued, the Department of War began to exert more influence than the Indian Bureau.

Using their experiences of the American Civil War, they decided to adopt a strategy of **total war** against the Cheyenne. Realising that Plains' Indians never fought in winter, when food supplies were lower and hunting much more difficult, Sherman decided on a winter campaign against the Cheyenne. Both he and Sheridan favoured 'extermination' as the way to solve the 'Indian Problem'.

The Battle of Washita

In November 1868, Generals Sherman and Sheridan recalled General George Armstrong Custer, who had been court-martialled in 1867, to duty – he was another 'exterminator'. Together with Sheridan, he planned a surprise winter attack on Black Kettle's camp on the Washita River. The majority of Cheyenne had not been involved in the recent attacks on settlers – and Black Kettle's village was flying the white flag to show they were peaceful.

Fact file

The strategy of total war against the Plains' Indians actually predated the Civil War – General Harney had used it against the Sioux after the Grattan Incident (see Lesson 4.3 on pp. 100–101).

HISTORY DETECTIVE

See what you can find out about General Custer and his career.

But, as at Sand Creek, Custer and his 7th Cavalry unit launched a surprise dawn attack on the Cheyenne camp, while everyone was asleep.

In the Battle of Washita, with little time to organise any defence, the Cheyenne were overwhelmed – Black Kettle and his wife were among those killed. Over 100 Indians were killed – the majority of them women and children.

The Cheyenne, and their Arapaho, Comanche and Kiowa allies, decided to seek peace. In January 1869, a new agreement was signed at Fort Cobb, whereby the Indians agreed to return to their separate reservations. The new agreement was similar to that signed at Medicine Lodge Creek – except that now they would not be allowed to hunt off their reservations.

The Great Plains' Massacre of the buffalo

As part of the total war strategy, and the desire to end the ability of the Plains' Indians to continue their traditional way of life, the US government decided on a new policy. From the early 1870s, it supported the wholesale slaughter of the buffalo – this became known as the **Great Plains' Massacre**. It is estimated there were about 60 million buffalo on the Plains in 1860; by 1870, the numbers had dropped to 15 million; and by 1883, the buffalo had almost vanished from the Plains. By 1890, numbers had dropped to 250, and to fewer than 100 by 1900.

The policy was designed to force the Indians to accept new terms and smaller reservations, so that more settlers and ranchers could have land. This eventually led to the near-extinction of the buffalo, and the final stages of the defeat of all the Plains' Indians (see Source E).

SOURCE E

These [buffalo hunters] have done more in the past two years, and will do more in the next year to settle the vexed Indian question, than the entire regular army has done in the last 30 years. They are destroying the Indians' food supply... for the sake of a lasting peace, let them kill, skin and sell until the buffalos are exterminated.

An extract from a speech made by General Sheridan in 1873, to the Texas legislature.

Fact file

The hunters included William Cody, who was employed by the Kansas Pacific Railroad Company to clear buffalo from the tracks, and to provide the workers with meat. He became known as Buffalo Bill – and claimed to have shot over 4000 in less than 18 months.

Fact file

The Oklahoma Land Rush

Problems for the Indians living on the southern Plains did not end in 1875. By the 1880s, many settlers wanted the lands of the Indian Territory reservation. Some took the law into their own hands and just grabbed the land they wanted – they were known as 'Boomers'. In 1889, the US president gave into white pressure and announced that, on 22 April, the Oklahoma District would be opened up to white settlers. More than 100,000 people turned up to grab their share of this 'vacant' land. After only a few hours, the Oklahoma District was settled.

SOURCE F

A pile of buffalo hides, Dodge City.

The numbers of buffalo on the Plains had begun to decline before 1870, for a number of reasons. The Indians killed more each year once they had horses, and their horses competed with the buffalo for grass. But more important reasons for their decline were to do with the numbers of settlers moving West. The railroads scared the buffalo; settlers and ranchers drove them away and destroyed their habitat; and the ranchers' cattle spread diseases among them.

Also, in 1871, it was discovered that buffalo hide could be turned into good-quality leather. Later, professionally trained groups of hunters were sent out by companies to kill buffalo by the thousands – often leaving the bodies to rot on the Plains (see Source F). Later still, homesteaders and crews of bone-pickers gathered the bones to send East (see Source G), where they were made into fertilisers, glue and other products such as buttons. It also became fashionable to hunt buffalo for sport – with many whites from the East shooting them from the trains as they travelled West.

The Red River War, 1874–75

The mass slaughter of the buffalo resulted in the Red River War in 1874–75, the last outbreak of fighting on the southern Plains, involving the Kiowa, led by Santana, and the Comanche, led by Quanah Parker.

This war broke out after clashes between some warriors and US army units who were protecting the buffalo hunters. It was seen by the Plains' Indians as their 'war to save the buffalo'. In the summer of 1874, about 700 warriors attacked the buffalo hunters near Adobe Walls in an attempt to drive them off the Plains, but the powerful rifles possessed by the hunters – some could kill at a range of 1.5 km – meant the attack was beaten off.

During the war, the Kiowa chief, Santana, was arrested and sentenced to hang. His case became famous throughout the USA, and public pressure forced the governor of Texas to pardon him. But the fighting continued, and over 3000 extra US troops were sent in. The Plains' Indians' war to save the buffalo ended in defeat: by the end of 1875, the survivors agreed to return to their reservations. Indian resistance on the central and southern Plains was over – and the southern herds of buffalo had virtually disappeared.

ACTIVITIES

Draw a timeline to show the main events, treaties and developments on the central and southern Plains, 1860–75.

SOURCE G

Buffalo skulls, showing the scale of the buffalo slaughter in the 1870s.

4.6 How did the wars for the northern Plains begin?

LEARNING OBJECTIVES

In this lesson you will:

- find out about the first part of the wars for the northern Plains
- get practice in answering questions that ask you to explain an aspect of a topic.

Just as the 1860s saw the start of violent conflict on the central and southern Plains, there was increasing military action on the northern Plains. These wars mainly involved the Sioux, and – once the Cheyenne, Arapaho, Comanche and Kiowa nations had, by 1875, been defeated to the south – the northern Plains saw the last major Native American resistance to white expansion in the West.

Little Crow's War, 1862

Fighting in the northern Plains broke out in 1862 in what became known as Little Crow's War (see Source A). The causes of this provide a good illustration of the problems Native Americans experienced on reservations. In many ways, this was a war against reservations, and the corrupt government agents, delayed annual payments and late food distribution.

Trouble began to build in 1858, when Minnesota became a state, and the Dakota were persuaded to give up some of their reservation for the thousands of new settlers pouring into the state in return for extra payments.

Then, in the early 1860s, conditions on the reservation became worse. In part, this was because the outbreak of the American Civil War in 1861 led to reductions and delays in the annual payments. In addition, there were problems with corrupt traders – such as Andrew Myrick – who often cheated the Indians out of part of their payments (see Source B). Also, the corn harvest of 1861 failed, and there was little game on the reservation to hunt. By 1862, Little Crow's people were facing starvation – but still the annual cash payment and food promised by Washington failed to arrive. They were forced to live on credit but, in June 1862, the Agency stopped giving them credit. Yet they knew the Agency warehouses had food (see Source C).

Many also came increasingly to resent the Christian missionaries and US government officials who tried to get them to assimilate to white American ways. As well as this, the younger Dakota were resentful of the fact that life on a reservation gave them no real opportunities to gain status or honour.

Anger mounted in 1862 when the payments did arrive. The government agents decided to pay traders who claimed the Dakota owed them money; the money left over was not enough to buy the food needed. Little Crow tried to control the mounting anger but, in August 1862, violence finally broke out when four young Sioux men killed five settlers – three men and two women.

Little Crow, the most respected Dakota war chief, was appalled by their actions as he knew the white authorities would come seeking revenge. But he was also angry about the way his people were being treated. Believing that attack is the best form of defence, on 17 August 1862 he reluctantly began his war.

The war, which lasted six weeks, resulted in the death of about 600 settlers – and, eventually, many more Dakota. At first, the Dakota took over the reservation agencies, killing about 20 men and capturing ten women and children. The warehouses were raided for food, and then they set fire to the Agency buildings. A party of 45 soldiers sent to deal with the uprising was ambushed, and 21 were killed.

The Dakota then began to chase many settlers from their homesteads. They also attacked Fort Ridgely and the town of New Ulm, which was near their reservation. Eventually, soldiers from Forts Snelling and Ridgely moved against the much smaller Dakota forces and won an important victory near Wood Lake.

On 26 September 1862, the majority of the Dakota were forced to surrender at Camp Release. About 1700 Dakota – both 'friendly' and 'hostiles' – were held prisoner during the cold winter of 1862.

In all, 307 of them were put on trial, with most 'cases' lasting no more than five minutes, and were sentenced to hang. However, eventually, most were pardoned by President Lincoln, who realised the Dakota had been badly treated. But 38 were executed on 26 December 1862 (see Source D). Many of those watching the execution laughed and jeered at the Indians.

About 3000 Dakota, most of whom had not joined in the fighting, fled west to join the Yankton and Lakota Sioux, in fear of white revenge. Also going west were Little Crow and some of his followers. The feared revenge was not long in coming, with the US army sending punishment expeditions under Generals Sibley and Sully, with about 1600 troops.

Little Crow himself eventually fled to Canada, but returned to Minnesota in June 1863. He was shot and killed by a settler, who took his scalp in order to receive the $500 bounty reward.

The Forfeiture Act, 1863

Because of this conflict, the US government passed an act on 16 February 1863, which cancelled all Dakota rights under the 1851 Treaty of Fort Laramie, confiscated most of their lands in the south, and forced all Dakota to move into the smaller part of what remained of their northern reservation in 1864. Conditions there were even worse, and about 400 Dakota died during the first winter. One Sioux leader who paid a visit to this reservation was Sitting Bull: it made a big impression on him. The bitterness caused by this relatively small war set the scene for the much bigger conflicts that were to engulf the northern Plains in the later 1860s and 1870s.

SOURCE A

Little Crow in 1862, photograph taken by Joel E. Whitney.

SOURCE B

We made a treaty with the government, and beg for what we can get, and can't get that till our children are dying with hunger. It is the traders who commenced it. Mr. A.J. Myrick told the Indians that they could eat grass or dung.

Comments by Little Crow in 1862.

SOURCE C

We have waited a long time... We have no food, but here are these stores, filled with food. We ask that you, the agent, make some arrangement by which we can get food from the stores, or else we may take our own step to keep ourselves from starving. When men are hungry, they help themselves.

Little Crow's comments in August 1862 to Thomas Galbraith, the government agent on the reservation.

SOURCE D

A contemporary engraving of the mass execution of Dakota warriors.

GradeStudio

Recall and select knowledge

Briefly describe the main problems facing the Dakota on their reservation in 1862.

Fact file

Andrew Myrick was killed in the attack on the Agency: his body was mutilated and his mouth stuffed with grass.

4.7 What was Red Cloud's War about?

LEARNING OBJECTIVES

In this lesson you will:

- find out about why fighting broke out on the lands of the Lakota Sioux in 1866
- get practice in answering questions that ask you to explain an aspect or the development of a topic.

The Sand Creek Massacre of 1864 had seen some of the Lakota Sioux join forces with the Cheyenne in their uprising on the central Plains (see Lesson 4.4 on pp. 102–103). However, when the Cheyenne and most of their other allies signed the Treaty of Medicine Lodge Creek in 1867, the Lakota (Teton) Sioux did not. The chief of the Oglala tribe of the Lakota Sioux was Red Cloud.

Growing problems, 1862–66

One of the reasons that Red Cloud had allied with the northern Cheyenne was because his people were already experiencing difficulties on the land that had been granted to them by the 1851 Treaty of Fort Laramie.

Although the 1862 Homestead Act did not result immediately in a huge migration onto the Plains, that same year saw the discovery of gold in the remote north-west, in the Rocky Mountains in Montana. Serious problems resulted from this discovery of gold, as the US government wanted to develop the area economically, while many miners were anxious to rush there – and the government made no attempt to stop them.

The Bozeman Trail

There was no direct route to the area at first, until a gold miner called John Bozeman blazed a new trail which broke off north-west from the Oregon Trail to go directly to Montana (see Source A). This created problems as the new trail passed right through the hunting grounds promised to the Oglala Sioux in 1851. Red Cloud was angered by the 1851 agreement being broken (see Source B). This, and the events of Little Crow's War – especially the execution of 38 Dakota Sioux – and the Sand Creek Massacre, made the Sioux determined to resist. Soon, travellers on the Bozeman Trail were being attacked.

Red Cloud's War, 1866–68

This war began in 1866 – though some historians refer to it as the Powder River War, 1865–68.

In 1866, the US government decided to take action to stop the attacks. It began negotiations with Red Cloud but – at the same time – ordered an army force under Colonel Carrington to begin building a line of three forts along the Bozeman Trail to protect travellers using it. This was clearly in breach of the 1851 treaty. Red Cloud withdrew from the talks, and the attacks on travellers resumed. More importantly, the Sioux also began to attack the workers building the new forts and the soldiers protecting them. Red Cloud said he would not make peace until the soldiers left the land given to the Sioux. Two other important Sioux war leaders supported him – the younger Sitting Bull and Crazy Horse.

The Fetterman Massacre

The Sioux had several successes during 1866. Then, on 21 December 1866, a detachment of soldiers was sent, under Captain William Fetterman, to protect woodcutters building Fort Philip Kearney. A Sioux war party lured them into an ambush, coordinated by Crazy Horse. Fetterman and about 80 of the soldiers were killed and their bodies mutilated. However, more than 200 Sioux were killed in the fighting – a result of the superior weaponry of the US troops.

The Sioux – with some northern Cheyenne and Arapaho bands as allies – under Red Cloud's leadership, now waged the most successful of all Indian wars against the forces of the US government. Red Cloud even managed to get the various bands to continue fighting during the winter months. The US government then decided to negotiate with Red Cloud. So, in the spring of 1867, the US government agreed to withdraw the army from the area, and to abandon the three forts. Although it seemed as if Red Cloud had won, the army was both humiliated and angry, and was determined to deal with the Sioux once and for all.

The Fort Laramie Treaty, 1868

The fighting continued while more formal negotiations began. Then, in November 1868, Red

SOURCE A

The Bozeman Trail and the line of army forts ordered by the US government in 1866.

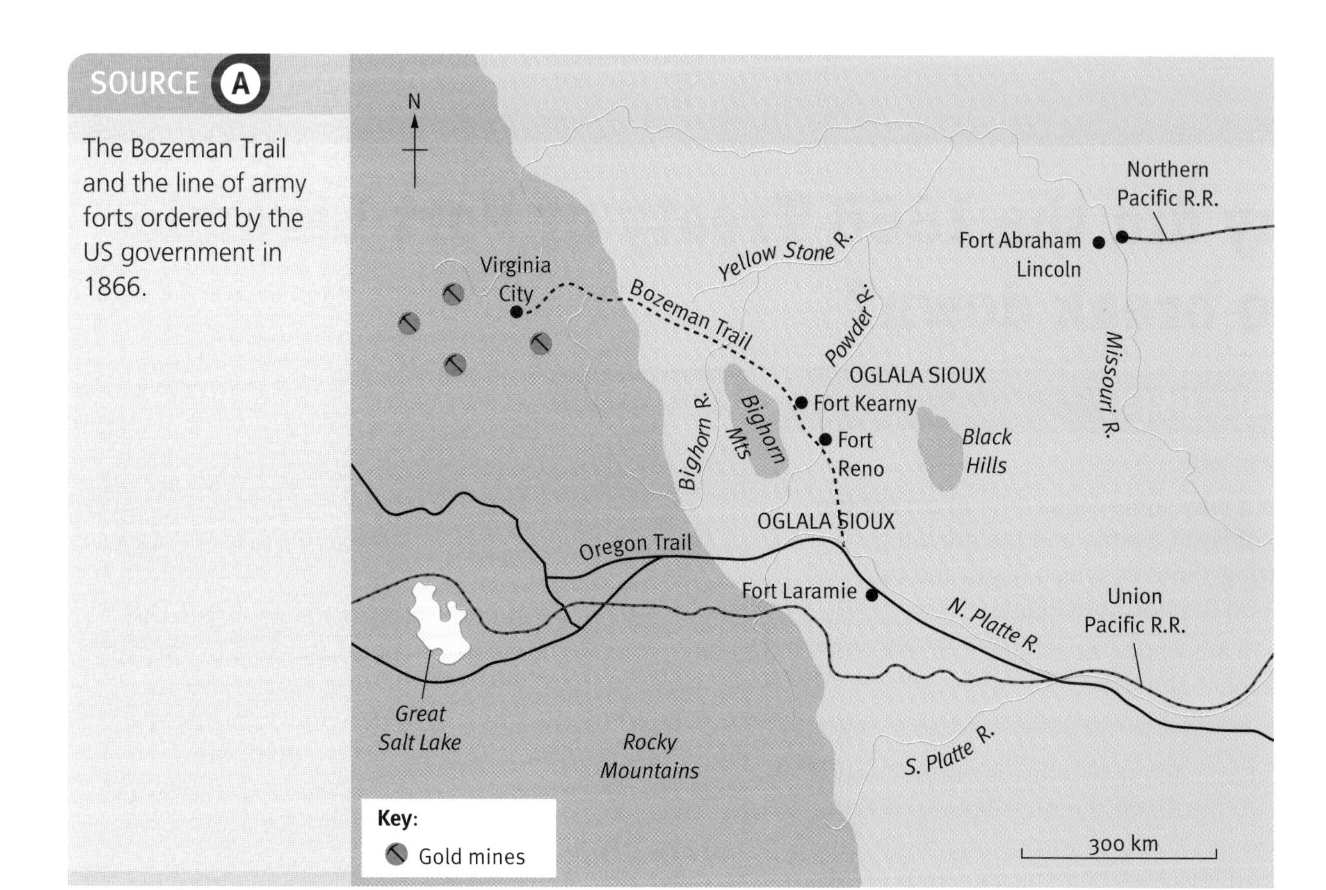

Cloud agreed to a revision of the earlier 1851 agreement in a second Treaty of Fort Laramie.

In return for an end to the fighting, the Sioux were granted the whole of South Dakota west of the Missouri River. This Great Sioux Reservation was to include the Bighorn Mountains and the Black Hills of Dakota – lands which were sacred to the Sioux. The US government said that no white settlers would be allowed to enter these lands and also agreed to stop further work on the Bozeman Trail: by then, an alternative route to the Montana gold-mining areas had been opened. It seemed that after two years of warfare, Red Cloud had won a great victory.

SOURCE B

The white men have crowded the Indians back year by year until we are forced to live in a small country north of the Platte, and now our last hunting ground, the home of the People, is to be taken from us. Our women and children will starve, but for my part I prefer to die fighting than by starvation.

Red Cloud's comments on the encroachments on Sioux hunting grounds.

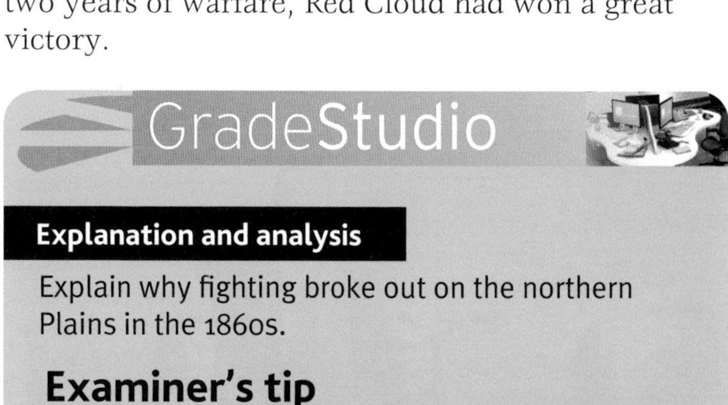

GradeStudio

Explanation and analysis

Explain why fighting broke out on the northern Plains in the 1860s.

Examiner's tip

- Remember – you need to do more than simply identify or list reasons – you must use your own specific knowledge to *explain* your reasons.
- Don't just explain one reason – you must try to consider at least TWO reasons.

4.8 Why did the 1868 Treaty of Fort Laramie start to break down?

LEARNING OBJECTIVES

In this lesson you will:

- find out about why some Sioux did not accept the 1868 Treaty of Fort Laramie and the growing tensions during 1868–75 which finally led to another war on the northern Plains
- get practice in answering questions that ask you to explain an aspect of a topic.

KEY WORDS

Renegades – *those Plains' Indians who refused to accept agreements made by their chiefs, or who left the reservations to go hunting.*

While Red Cloud and about two-thirds of the Lakota Sioux accepted the terms of the new Treaty of Fort Laramie (see Source A), there were some Sioux bands who did not. Younger chiefs such as Sitting Bull, of the Hunkpapa Sioux, and Crazy Horse of the Oglala Sioux, could not accept the idea of being restricted to the confined space of this Sioux reservation.

In 1870, Red Cloud went to Washington to meet US President Grant. There, he discovered that he had been misled as to the full terms of the treaty.

Red Cloud (centre) in Washington to meet President Grant in 1870.

However, he decided to honour his promise and accept it, and returned to spend the rest of his time on a reservation. In 1880, he was successful in showing how the government agent running the Sioux reservation was corrupt. He died, on a reservation, in 1909.

Treaty breaches

As early as 1871, white Americans began to break the terms of the new treaty. In the summer of that year, surveyors of the Northern Pacific Railroad began to move west through the hunting grounds of the Lakota – they were given military escorts to protect them. Then, in 1874, the US government ordered Custer to take a detachment of the 7th Cavalry to survey the Black Hills, in South Dakota, for gold.

The discovery of gold led to thousands of miners pouring into the Black Hills, in breach of the recent treaty. By 1875, there were more than 1000 miners there. However, the US government made no real efforts to prevent this, or to remove those who settled on Lakota lands. Soon, some Sioux began to attack the miners.

At the same time, the US government tried to persuade the Sioux to sell the Black Hills (see Source B). On 20 September 1875, a commission of politicians, missionaries, traders and soldiers met with the Sioux to discuss terms. At first, Red Cloud was prepared to listen, but many other Sioux chiefs and their followers were not. In the end, they refused to sell their sacred land – despite being offered $6 million; they also refused to sell the mineral rights for $400,000 a year, as this would have allowed miners to dig in the Sioux's sacred burial grounds. The commissioners gave up on 23 September and returned to Washington, recommending to Congress that the views of the Sioux be ignored, and a price be fixed and presented to them as a final offer.

Meanwhile, despite the refusal of the Sioux to sell or grant permission for mining, mines and towns continued to spring up, and relations between the Sioux and the US government became increasingly tense. In December 1875, President Grant began to take a harder line. He ordered meat rations to be withheld if any reservation Indians became involved in fighting to resist these new developments, and demanded all Sioux return to their reservation by 31 January 1876, giving them precisely 60 days.

However, as it was winter, the snow prevented many from returning, while not every band received the order. In fact, many Indians did not want to go back to the reservation. In the meantime, leadership had passed to Sitting Bull and Crazy Horse, who had never accepted the 1868 treaty. About 7000 Indians were still living in the Powder River country – not only Sioux, but also some northern Cheyenne and Arapaho. Sitting Bull, in particular – ever since his visit in 1863 to the reservation that the Dakota Sioux had been forced to accept following Little Crow's War – had become deeply suspicious of and hostile to US authorities (see Lesson 4.6 on pp. 108–109).

The US government then authorised the army, under General Sheridan, to take military action against all 'hostiles' or **renegades** roaming outside their reservation. This led to the War for the Black Hills, 1876–77, or the Great Sioux War (see Sources C and D).

SOURCE A

No white person or persons shall be permitted to settle upon or occupy any portion of the territory, or without the consent of the Indians to pass through the same...

No treaty for the cession of any part of the reservation herein described... shall be of any validity or force... unless executed by at least three-fours of all the adult male Indians, occupying or interested in the same.

Extracts from the Treaty of Fort Laramie, made with Red Cloud in 1868, relating to the Great Sioux Reservation.

SOURCE B

One does not sell the earth upon which the People walk.

Crazy Horse's comment on hearing of the US government's offer to buy the sacred lands of the Black Hills.

SOURCE C

Troops should be sent against these uncivilised Indians in the winter, the sooner the better, and whip them into subjection.

An extract from a report by E.T. Watkins, special inspector for the Indian Bureau, 9 November 1875.

SOURCE D

Said Indians are hereby turned over to the War Department for such action as you may deem proper under the circumstances.

A telegram sent by President Grant to the secretary of war.

GradeStudio

Recall and select knowledge

Despite the Treaty of Fort Laramie in 1868, problems between the Lakota Sioux and white settlers continued in the period 1868–75.

Briefly describe the main problems arising on the northern Plains, 1868–75.

Fact file

The price offered for the Black Hills was in fact very low – just one mine yielded over $500 million in gold!

BRAIN BOOST

Draw a timeline to show the various problems that arose between 1868 and 1875 to undermine the 1868 Treaty of Fort Laramie.

4.9 Case study: How did the War for the Black Hills, 1876–77, begin?

LEARNING OBJECTIVES

In this case study you will:

- find out about the immediate causes and main events of the war for the Black Hills
- get practice in answering questions that ask you to explain the usefulness of a source.

HISTORY DETECTIVE

Try to find out more about Sitting Bull.

Once the 31 January deadline for all Sioux to return to their reservation had expired, a chain of events followed that would end in the final defeat of the Lakota Sioux. However, it would also result in the greatest defeat ever experienced by the US army in its wars against the Native Americans.

Early actions

On 7 February 1876, the War Department authorised General Sheridan to begin military action against all renegade Sioux who had not returned to their reservation. The following day, he ordered Generals Crook and Terry to move against Crazy Horse and his allies.

Both Crazy Horse and Sitting Bull had said they might return to the reservation once the snows had gone – in fact, even if they had returned as ordered, their bands would have faced near-starvation as supplies of food were short. By the spring of 1876, the Sioux alliance under Sitting Bull and Crazy Horse had camps in the Powder River area: there were about 7000 people in total – of these, about 2000 were warriors.

On 17 March 1876, one of General Crook's advance columns under Colonel Reynolds attacked a peaceful camp of Northern Cheyenne and Oglala Sioux at dawn, while the camp was sleeping. Reynolds believed it was Crazy Horse's camp but he was far away. The survivors of this attack managed to make their way to Crazy Horse's camp, after three days of hard travel through deep snow and extremely low temperatures. Crazy Horse then led his group to the mouth of the Tongue River, where Sitting Bull was camped. As the weather improved, this huge camp began moving north, in search of game to hunt. They camped by the Rosebud River, where they were joined by others who had left their reservations.

In June, the Sioux received reports of large numbers of cavalry approaching from three directions – according to a plan devised by General Sheridan. There were to be three columns: Crook was coming from the south with a force of over 1000 cavalry and infantry; Colonel Gibbon with a force of 450 from the west; and Generals Terry and Custer with a force of 1000 – including Gatling guns, an early type of

Fact file

George Custer (1839–76) was from Ohio and had a mixed military career. He fought for the Union in the American Civil War and was promoted to Lieutenant-Colonel of the 7th Cavalry. He was twice court-martialled – for poor treatment of his troops, and for desertion to visit his wife. He also made an enemy of President Grant by testifying against his brother in a court case. Known as 'Long Hair' by the Indians, Custer was particularly hated by both the Sioux and the Cheyenne: he had been in charge of the cavalry forces at the Battle of Washita in 1868 in which Black Kettle had been killed; and he had led surveyors and gold miners on to the sacred Sioux lands of the Black Hills in 1874.

machine-gun on wheels – from the east. Sheridan's plan was to trap the renegades between these three columns (see Source A).

The Battle of the Rosebud

Despite his plans, Sheridan had made significant mistakes: no real communication was possible between his three units and, more importantly, his estimate of the total number of Sioux warriors being only about 800 was too low.

On 17 June, Crook's column was resting by the Rosebud Creek when Crazy Horse led a charge of about 1500 warriors. His tactics surprised the cavalry troops and divided them: normally, the Plains' Indians did not fight pitched battles; instead, they usually fought delaying actions to allow their women and children to escape, and then withdrew. After six hours of heavy fighting – during which Crook's troops fired 25,000 rounds of ammunition – the Sioux and Cheyenne warriors had inflicted a defeat on the cavalry forces in the Battle of the Rosebud. Crook was forced to retreat to Fort Fetterman, having casualties of 28 dead and 63 wounded. The losses suffered by the Sioux and Cheyenne were 36 dead and 63 wounded.

Crazy Horse and the other chiefs then decided to move west, to the valley of the Little Bighorn River, where there was plenty of grass for their horses, and antelope to hunt. By then, some historians have estimated there were about 10,000 Indians, of whom about 3500 were warriors – but most agree on 7000 and 2000, respectively.

Meanwhile, on 21 June, Gibbon and Terry met on the Yellowstone River and had a conference, not knowing that Crook had been forced to retreat. At the conference, Terry decided to divide his forces, knowing that the Sioux were camped in the Little Bighorn valley. His plan was for the infantry to follow the Yellowstone River, and to approach the Little Bighorn from the north, while Custer was to follow the Rosebud River and approach the Little Bighorn from the south. The Sioux would then be trapped between two strong forces.

SOURCE A

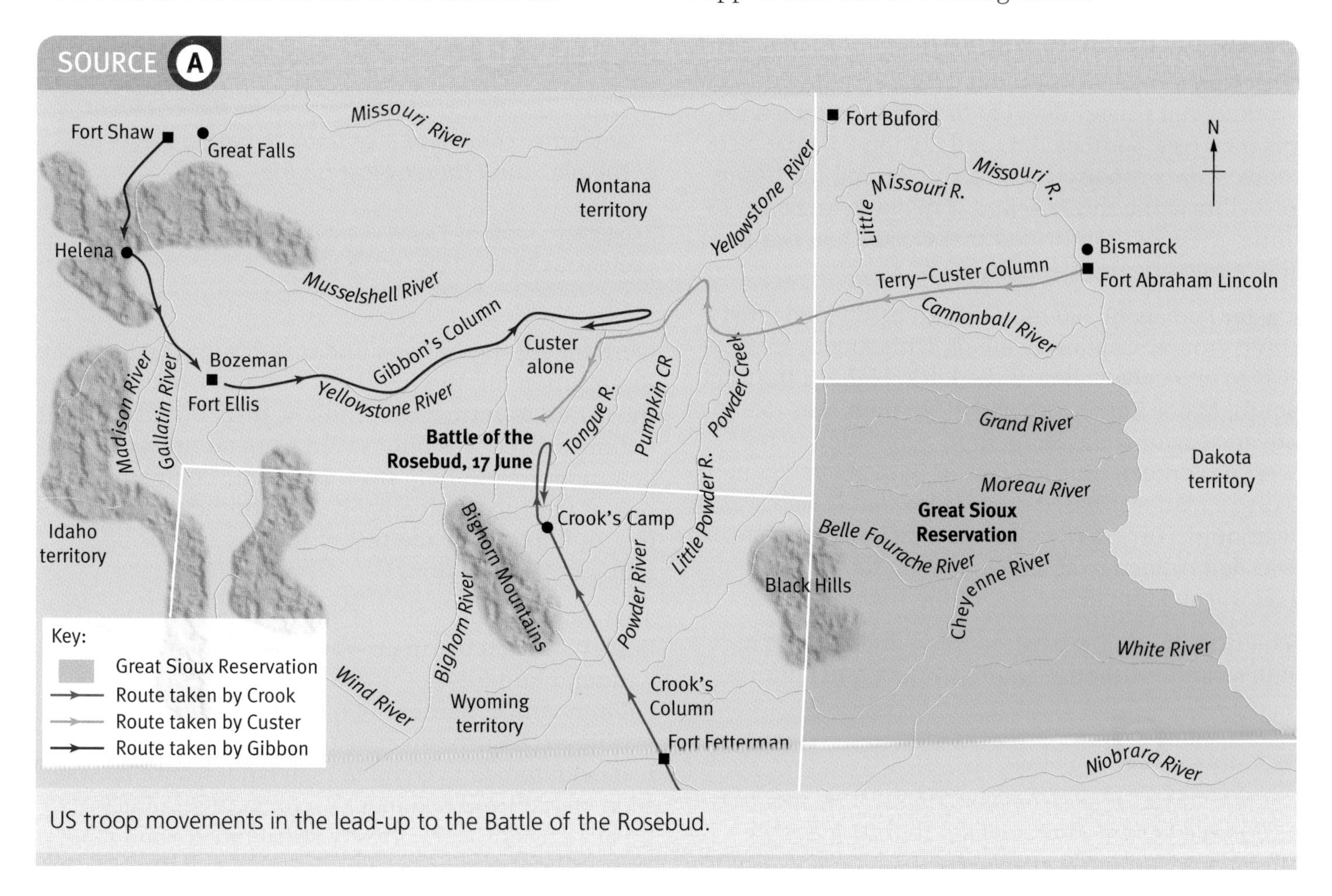

US troop movements in the lead-up to the Battle of the Rosebud.

SOURCE B

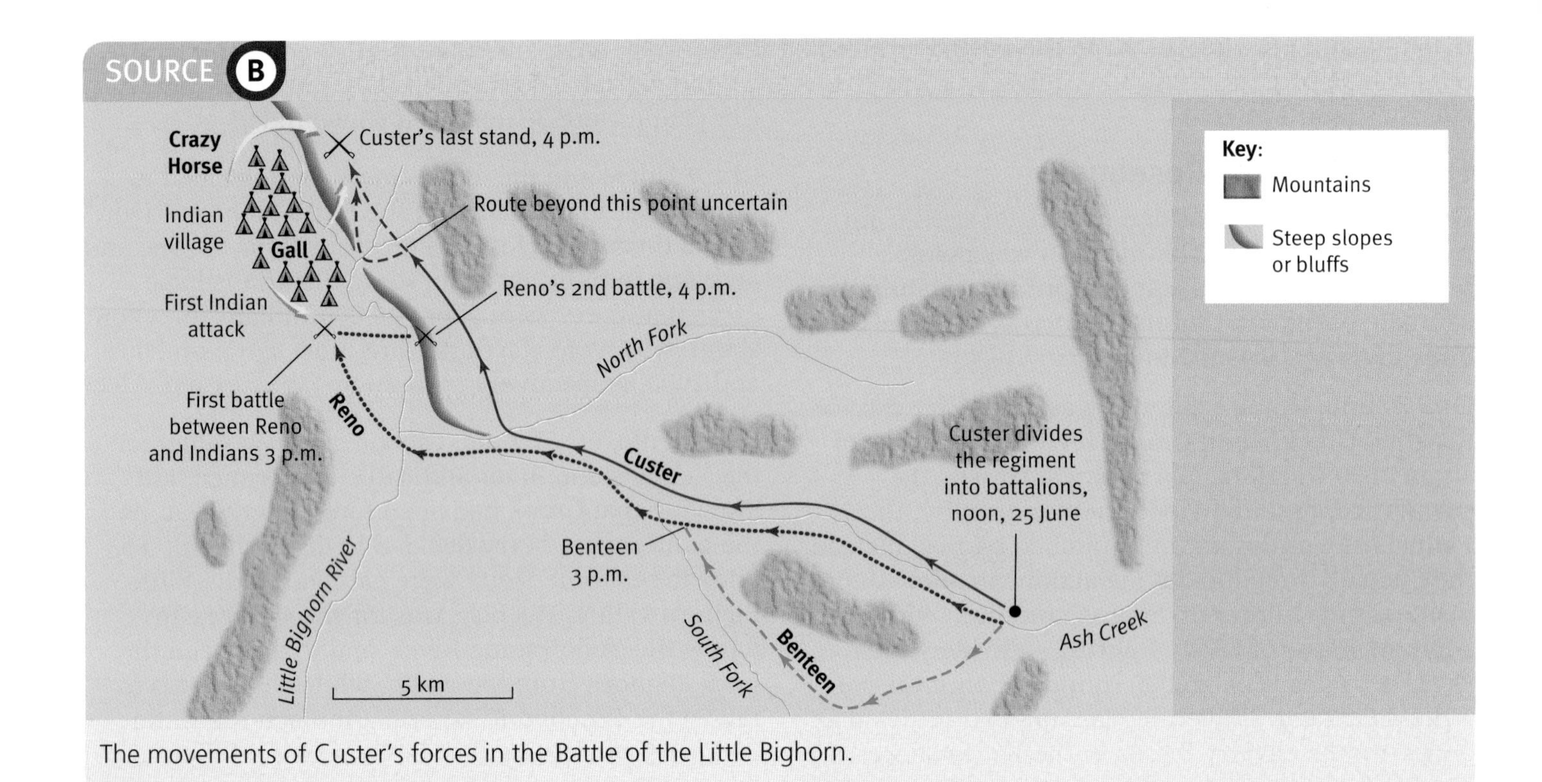

The movements of Custer's forces in the Battle of the Little Bighorn.

Battle of the Little Bighorn

The plan of attack worked out by Terry might have worked, but Custer decided to begin the attack on his own (see Sources B, C and D). On 24 June 1876, Sioux scouts reported seeing Custer and his troops prowling along the Rosebud. The following day, 25 June, they were informed that Custer had begun to move towards the Little Bighorn.

Custer had about 600 men, whom he divided into three groups: Captain Benteen, with about 125 men, was to enter the valley of the Little Bighorn from the south; Major Reno, with about 125 men, was to advance against the Sioux from a direction to the west of Benteen; this left Custer with about 265 men. Terry's plan was based on the idea that Custer was to wait until Terry arrived before attacking. But Custer was determined to attack first, even though his scouts had warned him of the size of the Indian camp.

The first fighting was when Reno attacked Sitting Bull's camp. Although many women and children were killed, the Indians under Gall's leadership beat Reno's men off, forcing them into the woods. When they tried to retreat, the Indians turned it into a rout – Reno's force was only saved from complete destruction with help from Benteen. Their surviving troops then found themselves surrounded, and fought fiercely for the rest of the day, suffering many more casualties.

SOURCE C

Custer acted under a misapprehension. He thought that the Indians were running. For fear that they might get away, he attacked without getting all his men up, and divided his men so they were beaten.

Comments made by General Terry, supporting Custer's actions at the Battle of the Little Bighorn.

SOURCE D

Custer disobeyed orders because he did not want any other command... or body to have a finger in the pie... and thereby lost his life.

Comments made by Captain Benteen about Custer's actions before the Battle of the Little Bighorn.

This allowed Gall – Sitting Bull's adopted brother and lieutenant, and the main war chief of the Hunkpapas – to send hundreds of warriors to attack Custer's column which, because of quicksands, had been unable to cross the river as planned. Instead, Custer had been forced to go on to high land, where he was soon spotted and had quickly come under attack. Custer's troops were already surrounded and facing a determined attack from Crazy Horse and Two Moon, chief of the Cheyenne, when Gall's warriors arrived from the south (see Sources E and F).

Custer sent an order for Reno and Benteen to come to his aid, but they did not – afterwards, they said

SOURCE 

This painting, by William Herbert Dunton in 1915, is one of almost 1000 that have been produced about the Battle of the Little Bighorn. Unusually, it shows the battle from the Indian position – Custer's troops are on the hill in the top right corner.

they'd been unable to help because they were surrounded themselves. Not one of Custer's men survived the battle, which is often referred to as 'Custer's Last Stand'. Not only were they outnumbered – there were about 2000 American Indian warriors – but several of the American Indians had Winchester repeating rifles which were superior to those issued to the US troops.

There is some debate amongst historians as to how Custer died. Several Native Americans claimed later to have killed him, including White Bull of the Minneconjou, while an Arapaho warrior claimed he was killed by several Indians acting together. But there is also evidence that he may have committed suicide just before the warriors closed in, as his body was untouched.

GradeStudio

Analysis of sources

Study Source E.

How useful is this source in telling you about what happened at the Battle of the Little Bighorn? Use the source and your own knowledge to explain your answer.

Examiner's tip

- Remember you MUST use the source by *explaining* what it shows/doesn't show about the events.
- You also need to use your own knowledge to explain how the source is AND is not useful, for example, are there things it does not show/refer to?

SOURCE F

The Battle of the Little Bighorn, painted in about 1890 by Kicking Bear, a Lakota warrior who fought in the battle.

ACTIVITIES

Draw a chart giving evidence and arguments to show how Custer was (and was not) mainly to blame for the defeat at the Battle of the Little Bighorn.

4.10 Case study: How did the War for the Black Hills end?

LEARNING OBJECTIVES

In this case study you will:

- find out about how the war finally ended
- get practice in answering questions that ask you to describe/explain an aspect of a topic.

The aftermath of the Little Bighorn

Despite the defeat of Custer's units at the Battle of the Little Bighorn, the forces under Reno and Benteen were still holding out. They were surrounded by the Sioux who kept watch through the night and, in the morning of 26 June, they renewed their attacks. Meanwhile, the Sioux sent out scouts to see what other US troops were in the area. During the day, these scouts brought reports of a large force under General Crook approaching the Little Bighorn. A council was held and, as most warriors had used up virtually all their ammunition, it was decided to break camp because arrows and lances would be no match for the large number of US troops approaching. The women were told to begin packing and, by the end of the day, the tribes split up and went in different directions. The Battle of the Little Bighorn was to prove the last of their victories in this war.

Response of the US government

Despite their victories at the battles of the Rosebud and Little Bighorn, the Sioux and their allies had not won the War for the Black Hills. The year they had these victories – 1876 – was also the centenary of the American Declaration, signed in 1776. When news of Custer's Last Stand reached the East, in the middle of these celebrations, there was both shock and outrage (see Source A). Newspapers carried story after story of this 'massacre' and demanded revenge. This suited the army and those politicians who favoured a policy of extermination as the way to finally 'solve' the 'Indian Problem'.

On 22 July, General Sherman persuaded the US Congress to place the northern reservations under the absolute control of the military, and government agents on the reservations were replaced by army officers. Even peaceful Plains' Indians were to be treated as hostiles or prisoners of war – their guns, other weapons and horses were to be confiscated; and many were to be imprisoned.

On 15 August, the US government decreed that all Plains' Indians had to agree to give up the Powder River country and the Black Hills, on the grounds that they had broken the 1868 Treaty of Laramie by going to war against the USA. In September 1876, a government commission was sent out to get the chiefs to sign their agreement to this, and to move them to smaller reservations on the Missouri River.

When the chiefs pointed out that the 1868 Treaty required three-quarters of the male adults to agree to any changes, the commissioners said that all those warriors still off-reservation with Sitting Bull and Crazy Horse were hostiles and therefore not covered by the treaty. They also threatened to stop all food supplies to the reservations. Reluctantly, Lakota leaders such as Red Cloud and Spotted Tail signed. A month later, the army, under Colonel Mackenzie, moved into the reservations and began the confiscations and arrests. However, Sitting Bull and Crazy Horse still had bands that supported them, and these refused to give in.

The war continues

While these legal and political actions were taking place, the US army began to pursue the bands led by Sitting Bull and Crazy Horse. General Crook was given extra troops and ammunition to deal with the renegades: soon, a large force was put together. By the end of October 1876, many of the Sioux and their allies were eventually forced to return to their reservations. This was because the numbers of buffalo on the northern Plains was decreasing because of the westward spread of white Americans and disruptions caused by the railroads, hunting and mining.

The winter campaign

In the winter of 1876–77, the US army launched a brutal but very effective campaign, under Colonels Mackenzie and Miles. Eventually, in the spring of 1877, Sitting Bull decided to move his people into

Canada – he sent scouts to urge Crazy Horse to join him, but they could not find him.

Meanwhile, Crazy Horse's bands were being pursued by General Crook. Crook sent Mackenzie to attack Dull Knife's group of northern Cheyenne in a dawn raid. Most of these had not fought at the Battle of the Little Bighorn, but had left their reservation when the army had stopped rations. Many were killed in the surprise attack, and the few survivors managed to join Crazy Horse. In December 1876, Crazy Horse decided it was time to make peace, as his band was short of food and ammunition, but Miles rejected this attempt to negotiate.

The blood of our soldiers demands that these Indians shall be pursued. They must submit themselves to the authority of the nation.

An extract from a speech made by Congressman Maginnis in July 1876. Many others felt like this after hearing about Custer's defeat at the Battle of the Little Bighorn.

The end

Small skirmishes continued until April 1877, when Red Cloud told Crazy Horse that Crook had promised that if he surrendered, his people could have a reservation in the Powder River country, and need not go to Missouri. Crazy Horse decided to accept on 6 May, and his band camped outside Fort Robinson, waiting for their new reservation.

However, not all fight had gone out of him. In August 1877, when the US army began to encourage Sioux warriors to scout for it in a war which had broken out against the Nez Perce in Oregon, Crazy Horse tried to persuade them not to help the US army. On 5 September 1877, Crook, fearing Crazy Horse's influence, sent soldiers to take him in to Fort Robinson. Crazy Horse went peacefully but, on seeing that he was to be chained and put in a small cell, struggled as he felt he had been tricked. In the struggle, he was bayoneted in the back by one of the US soldiers, Private William Gentles. He died later that night, aged 35 (see Source B).

GradeStudio

Recall and select knowledge

Briefly describe the final stages of the war for the Black Hills.

Examiner's tip

- Remember – with questions that ask you to *describe* something, always try to identify SEVERAL points/aspects.
- Don't just list these points: try instead to use a few *precise* bits of information to describe or explain your points.

HISTORY DETECTIVE

Find out as much as you can about Crazy Horse.

SOURCE B

A pictograph of the death of Crazy Horse in Fort Robinson, September 1877.

4.11 The final stages of the struggle for the northern Plains

LEARNING OBJECTIVES

In this lesson you will:

- find out about what happened on the reservations after the Sioux surrendered in 1877 and the final phases of the struggles for control of the Great Plains
- get practice in answering a question that asks you to describe one aspect of a topic.

KEY WORDS

Ghost Dance – *the religious dance associated with Wovoka who, following a vision in 1889, said that dancing it would make the whites go away, and all the dead Indians and buffalo come back to life.*

Although the surrender of Crazy Horse on 6 May 1877 ended the Sioux's War for the Black Hills, it was not quite the end of all violence on the northern Plains – or of the sufferings of the Indians still living on them.

The destruction of the buffalo on the northern Plains

One of the reasons the Sioux and their allies had been forced to return to their reservations by 1877 was of the reduced size of the buffalo herds. With hunting proving increasingly difficult, their only chance of regular food – especially in winter – was on the reservations.

The Great Plains' Massacre, which had taken place against the buffalo herds on the southern Plains, was soon put into operation in the north. Already, by the late 1870s, the herds were much smaller than in the past. In 1880, with the Sioux defeated, the destruction of the remaining herds was begun by the authorities. In 1882, over 5000 hunters and skinners were working on the northern Plains; by 1883, the extermination was virtually complete, with only a few hundred left. This meant life on a reservation was now the only option available to the Plains' Indians

The reservations after 1877

As the Sioux had been defeated, all their reservation land was declared by the US government to be lost through right of conquest. The reservations were to be reduced and split up, so more land could be given to the settlers who continued to go West. It also meant the Plains' Indians could be virtually imprisoned or concentrated in camps, isolated from each other.

However, all the problems that had existed earlier on most reservations continued to make life hard for the Plains' Indians. Corrupt traders and government agents frequently cheated them out of money and land. The provision of supplies to the Indians forced to live on reservations, and so dependent for tents, clothing and food, became a big business, and the corrupt traders and agents became known as the 'Indian Ring'. Food rations were often inadequate, as were medical supplies.

Also, although the government decided that the Plains' Indians should be forced to become farmers, the land they were given was often poorly suited to farming. An additional resentment was caused by the increased efforts to educate children in ways approved of by the US authorities, and the missionary work of Christians who tried to persuade Plains' Indians to abandon their traditional religious beliefs and practices. The idea was to turn them into 'proper Americans' (see Source A).

The Dawes (General Allotments) Act, 1887

Life on the reservations was made even worse by the Dawes (General Allotments) Act, 1887. This broke up much of the reservation land to create a private farm of about 80 hectares for each individual Indian family that wanted to farm. Not only was this intended to encourage farming, but it was also seen as a way to reduce the powers of chiefs over their bands or tribes (see Source B).

Although the government decided to hold the land in trust for 25 years, to prevent Indians selling the land to settlers, corrupt agents still defrauded the Indians and sold much of the land to white Americans. By 1900, Indian land had fallen from about 80 million hectares to about 40 million hectares.

SOURCE A

The Indians must conform to the 'white man's ways', peaceably if they will, forcibly if they must. They must adjust themselves to their environment, and conform their mode of living substantially to our civilization.

Comments made by Thomas Jefferson Morgan, commissioner of Indian affairs.

SOURCE B

This looks to the gradual breaking up of the reservations... [and] loosens the fatal tribal bonds by bringing the Indians under our laws, and making the way for their entrance into citizenship.

Comments on the 1887 Dawes Act, by the Indian Rights Association.

The period after 1887 is often referred to as the Assimilation and Allotment period – this approach continued until 1934. As part of this, it was declared that there should be no more inter-tribal trading or celebrations. This was a deliberate attempt to keep each tribe separate from any others, in case they united and resisted what was being done to them.

The Ghost Dance

By 1890, many of the Sioux were in desperation about the conditions they were experiencing on the reservations, and how their traditional way of life was disappearing. Then they heard about a Native American who lived far away in Nevada, who said that if the Plains' Indians practised a new dance, then all the whites would disappear, the dead Indians would return, and the buffalo herds would return to the Plains. The Indian was called Wovoka, and his dance was the **Ghost Dance**. Many Sioux in the South Dakota reservations decided to follow Wovoka's Ghost Dance idea.

The authorities were alarmed as the Ghost Dance spread: by November 1890, it was sweeping across the reservations of Pine Ridge and Rosebud. Some of the dancers wore 'ghost shirts' which they believed would protect them against the army's bullets. The government agent at Pine Ridge, Daniel Royer, decided to call in the army.

Massacre at Wounded Knee

The arrival of the army increased tensions. Sitting Bull – who was not a supporter of the Ghost Dance – was shot dead by a member of the Indian police force. It was claimed that he was trying to resist arrest.

Then, on 29 December 1890, a small band of about 350 Minneconjou Sioux, led by Big Foot, were surrounded by the 7th Cavalry at Wounded Knee Creek. When ordered to disarm – most had no weapons – they did so, but a possible misunderstanding involving a young deaf Sioux called Black Coyote led to a shot being fired accidentally. Although no one was injured, the army opened up with rifles and four Hotchkiss cannons. Some of the Sioux fought back with knives, clubs and pistols. In all, at least 153 Sioux were killed – these included Big Foot, and over 60 women and children. Some estimates put the number of deaths as high as nearly 300 because many of the injured died later. The army's casualties were 25 dead and 39 injured – most of these by friendly fire and their own shrapnel. Historians are divided over whether this was deliberate, or just a tragic misunderstanding.

The wounded soldiers were escorted back to the agency at Pine Ridge. Later, a party of soldiers with wagons was sent to bring in any wounded Sioux still alive; three men and 47 women and children were left lying on the wagons in the bitter cold while the soldiers looked for a place to put them. Eventually, the Episcopal Mission's church floor was used – the banner across the pulpit read: 'Peace on Earth, Good Will to Men.'

This Massacre at Wounded Knee ended the Ghost Dance and, effectively, the Plains Wars, north and south. That same year, the US government officially announced that the frontier was closed, as the USA now stretched from coast to coast, thus completing the aims of Manifest Destiny. The white Americans had finally 'won the West' – and the Native Americans had lost it.

Fact file

By the time of the Dawes Act in 1887, Indian resistance right across the West had come to an end. In 1877, the Nez Perce had surrendered in Oregon and had been moved to Oklahoma; in 1886, the Apache leader, Geronimo, finally surrendered in New Mexico – he died in prison in 1909.

ACTIVITIES

1. Make a timeline of the main events of 1877–90.
2. Explain how the Dawes Act, 1887, made life on the reservations even more difficult for the Sioux.

You have now completed this unit which has focused on why there was increasing conflict between the Plains' Indians and white Americans in the second half of the 19th century, and how the Plains' Indians finally lost the struggle to retain control of their lands. You have also had practice in answering questions designed to prepare you for your exam. Below is an example of one type of exam question, with some hints to help you write a high-scoring answer.

c Study Source A.

Source A

An engraving showing Indians living on a reservation in the late 19th century being given free rations.

Were the Indians glad to be living on reservations like the one shown in Source A? Use the source and your knowledge to explain your answer.

[7 marks]

Examiner's tip

Remember, in order to reach the higher levels in questions that ask you to explain something, the examiners are expecting you to do TWO things:

- use the source and make inferences from it AND
- use your own knowledge to explain several different reasons/ factors, inferred/picked up from the source, giving specific/ precise facts.

If you don't do BOTH things, you will not achieve full marks. You must use the source AND your own knowledge. Don't forget that with the questions which ask you to study/use a source, you can refer to other sources given in the exam paper – provided they are *relevant*.

Fact file

In the exam, you will be asked to answer two questions from Section B, the Depth Study: a source-based question and a structured question. The source-based question is divided into three parts – **a**, **b** and **c**.

Before you write your answer, below are two things to help you start on the right lines.

First, look at the simplified mark scheme on the opposite page. This should help you to write your answer in a way that will allow you to get the full marks available for such questions.

Simplified mark scheme

Level	Skill	Mark
Level 0	No answer or irrelevant answer	0
Level 1	Simple statement (e.g. 'they would have been pleased because they were given free food') BUT no reference to source	1
Level 2	Uses own knowledge to explain ONE reason why they might be pleased BUT no reference to or use of source	2
Level 3	Identifies reasons, using the source, why the Indians disliked reservations OR uses specific own knowledge to explain several reasons why Indians disliked reservations, BUT no reference to the source	3–4
Level 4	*Explains* ONE reason, using the source AND specific own knowledge to explain why Indians disliked reservations	5–6
Level 5	Explains more than one reason, using the source AND specific own knowledge, to explain why Indians disliked reservations	7

Second, look at the sample answer below – noting especially the examiner's comments:

Candidate's answer

The Indians were not pleased to be living on reservations like the one shown in Source A. The source shows them having to accept food from US soldiers, but they look fed up. They don't seem to like being dependent on the US government for food.

This was because their traditional way of life had been that of nomadic hunters, who followed the buffalo across the Great Plains and hunted them. They had been free to roam across the Plains but, from the 1840s, had been increasingly forced to give up their lands to white American settlers and ranchers, and live on reservations instead. These were much smaller, and were often poor hunting grounds. This is why, 50 years later, they were forced to receive free rations from the US government.

Examiner's comment

The first highlighted part of the answer (green) – by itself – gets the candidate into the bottom of Level 3, as ONE reason (not liking to be dependent) is identified/inferred from the source. However, only one reason is identified, and there is no own knowledge added, so the reason is not being *explained*.

The second highlighted part of the answer (red) is providing some useful and precise supporting own knowledge, relating to one relevant reason inferred from the source, and is *explaining* that reason. This gets the candidate into Level 4. However, it only explains ONE reason, and the specific own knowledge is rather limited. Therefore, the candidate does not get to the top of the level.

Look again at the mark scheme above, and you should be able to see what that candidate could have done to push this quite good answer from Level 4 (5–6 marks) into Level 5 and so score the full 7 marks available.

You will see that in order to get into Level 5, and score 7 marks, all the candidate needed to do was identify from the source, and explain, SEVERAL different reasons why Indians did not like living on reservations, using precise own knowledge to support the points being made.

Once you think you have fully understood what is needed to improve this candidate's answer, write your own answer. However, don't use the 'dependent' issue given by the sample answer. Instead, try to explain – using your own precise knowledge – OTHER reasons that can be inferred from the source as to why Indians did not like living on reservations.

Before you start, look back at 4.4 in this Unit. Then try to write your answer without looking at the relevant pages.

ExamCafé

Welcome

Tools and tips

Now you have finished this Depth Study, you will need to make sure that you really learn the skills and the content you have covered in this book – and have a revision programme that is sufficient AND best suited to you. The different sections of this ExamCafe are designed to help you do this, so that by the time of your exam you are able to do your best. It is based on the fact that methods such as simply rewriting your notes, or just reading your textbook several times, are NOT the most effective ways of revising. Also, don't try to revise for an hour or more – your brain will work better if you work for 25–30 minutes at a time, and then have a short break before you start again. This will stop you getting tired – and will allow your brain time to absorb the information.

Finally, it's useful to know that lack of specific knowledge is NOT the main reason why most candidates fail to get the grades of which they are capable – it is not using the correct skills for the different types of questions. It's not so much showing what you know as showing what you can DO with what you know.

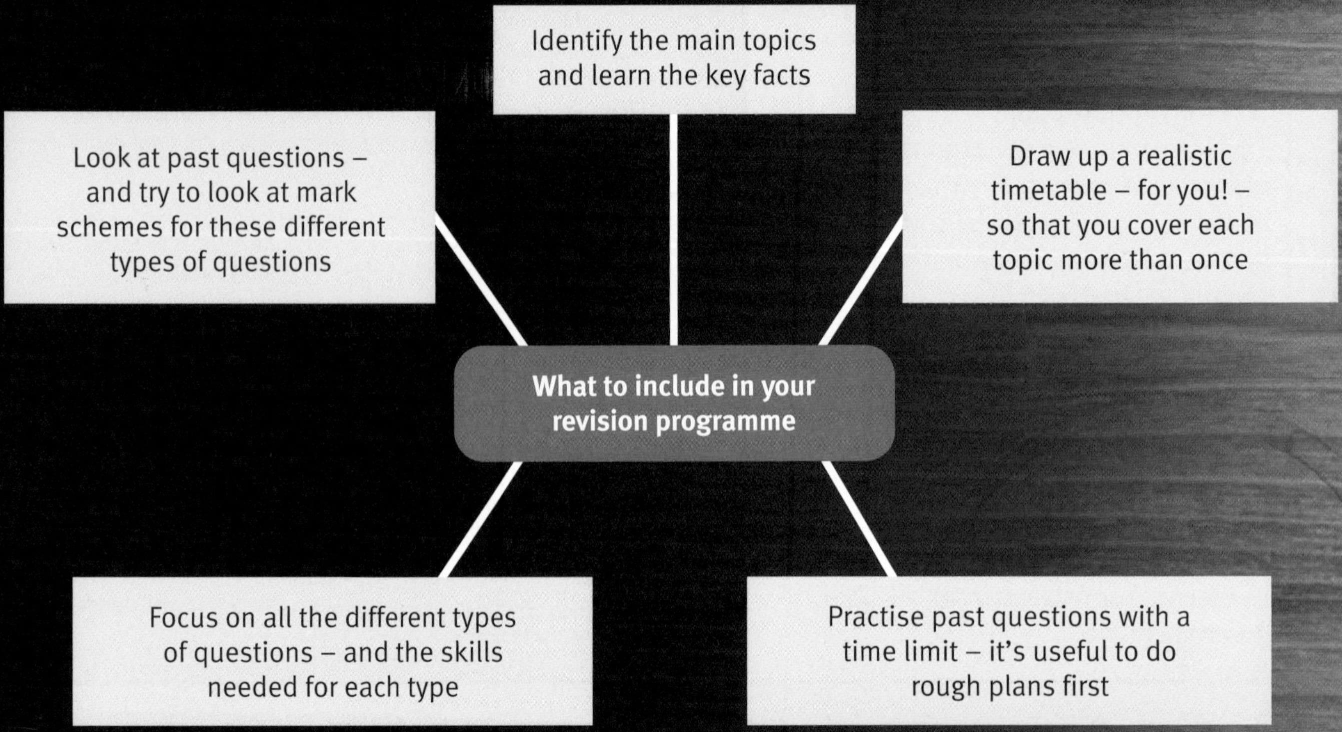

What to include in your revision programme

- Identify the main topics and learn the key facts
- Draw up a realistic timetable – for you! – so that you cover each topic more than once
- Practise past questions with a time limit – it's useful to do rough plans first
- Focus on all the different types of questions – and the skills needed for each type
- Look at past questions – and try to look at mark schemes for these different types of questions

1 Revision tips

Avoid getting get bored or over-stressed during revision, by using a variety of revision methods, for example:

- Use a **highlighter** to pick out the most important concepts and facts in your notes.
- List the most important facts or brief points on **index cards**. You can read them while you're waiting in a queue, or just before you go into a lesson.
- Listen to **recordings** of you (or a friend) going through the main points – many people learn better this way.
- Make colourful **spider diagrams** or **ideas maps** of the main points of the various topics – drawing these will help you remember, while you will then have something you can stick up on your bedroom walls. You can change the display after a few days – again, for some people, this is the most effective way to learn.
- Draw up **revision checklists** for each main topic – and then learn the main points.
- Work with a **friend** – or in a **small group** – and test each other.
- Make up a **word** or **phrase** to help you remember the main points of a topic – some people find making up mnemonics helps them remember key factors.

2 Common mistakes

- In questions asking you to use a source or sources, make sure you DO refer to each one mentioned in the question.
- In questions asking you to comment on the usefulness of a source make sure you DO refer to the source, and try to make inferences about what it shows and doesn't show. Every year, candidates with good knowledge fail to do this – and so fail to get top marks.
- In questions asking you to explain/describe the main points/problems, etc. of a topic, make sure you explain/describe MORE than one – each year, candidates with good knowledge fail to do this, and so fail to get top marks.
- If the question specifies PARTICULAR dates, make sure you stick to these – i.e. don't start giving detailed information about something outside these dates. You won't get any marks for this – and you will be wasting time that you could be spending on other questions.
- In questions asking you to *explain* some aspects of a topic, some candidates just identify or list them, without any attempt to show WHY they were significant/important. While this will get you some marks – about half marks at the most – it will NOT get you top marks. Also – make sure you don't just explain one reason. Top marks are reserved for those who fully explain TWO reasons, using good supporting knowledge for each one.

3 Revision checklists

One way of revising effectively is to draw up revision checklists, either for the whole Depth Study or for the various topics, like the example below:

Revision checklist

Homesteading on the Great Plains in the 1850s and 1860s:

The Homestead Act, 1862 – Aspects of the Act causing problems:

- The prices were sometimes too high for many ordinary people.
- The soil was often poor, so the 160 acres (80 hectares) granted to each family were not enough.
- Consequently, much of the land was bought up by speculators and railroad companies, and many homesteaders were left with poor land.

Natural problems – Practical problems of homesteading on the Plains:

- droughts, harsh winters, lack of water and trees, problems caused by insects such as locusts, etc.
- the conditions in the dug-outs and sod houses
- the isolation of living in remote areas
- lack of proper medical care
- the difficulties of obtaining supplies and selling produce until the coming of the railroads in the 1870s.

Conflicts – Factors causing conflicts:

- The reasons for conflicts between cattle ranchers and homesteaders.
- The attacks by Plains' Indians who resented the growing numbers of settlers on the Plains because they disrupted the buffalo herds.

Check pp. 54–57 of Lesson 2.10 to see if any points have been missed out.

Then, try to make your own revision checklist for another topic area from Chapter 2.

4 Spider diagrams

Another useful way of revising is to produce your own spider diagrams or ideas maps for the different topics – use different colours and highlighters to pick out the really important points. An example of one for **Law and Order in the West in the period 1850–90** is shown below:

Early law enforcement – rapid development of the West after 1840; poor communications until the coming of the railroads in the 1870s; problems of lawlessness in remote and isolated areas; sharing of responsibility between the federal government in Washington DC, and the various states that made up the USA; differences between a US territory and a US state; different types of law officers and the types of people appointed.

The nature of the cow towns – the numbers of saloons, gambling dens and dance halls that appeared in the cow towns, set up by people eager to take the cowboys' money; the kinds of people who often acted as the law officers in the early days – many were corrupt or even outlaws themselves; men far outnumbering women at first; the early lack of families in places such as Abilene and Dodge City.

Law and order in the West 1850–90

The nature of the mining towns – often in remote places; conflicts over 'claim jumping' and race; lack of law officials; vigilante courts and justice; lynchings; Tombstone and Deadwood.

The nature of the cattle drives – hardships experienced on the Long Drive by the cowboys; the often considerable boredom; cowboys reaching the cow towns often looking for exciting ways to have fun and spend their money.

Now check with the relevant Lessons in Chapters 2 and 3, and see if there are other aspects to add to the spider diagram.

Then try to do one for another topic from Chapter 3.

Exam preparation

1 Sample question

CHAPTER 1

Settlement of the Great Plains, 1840–70

Source A

It is almost wholly unfit for cultivation, and of course uninhabitable by people who depend on agriculture. The scarcity of wood and water will prove an impossible obstacle in the way of settling the country.

Major Stephen Long's description of the Plains in 1820.

Source B

An illustration, called 'Across the Continent Westward the Course of Empire Takes Its Way', published in 1868.

EXAM QUESTION

Study Sources A and B. Why do these sources show such different attitudes towards the Plains? Use the sources and your own knowledge to explain your answer. **[7 marks]**

Laura's answer

There are several reasons why these two sources show different attitudes – all of these reasons are closely connected to the dates of these two sources. Source A was written in 1820, while Source B was published in 1868 – during that period, knowledge, attitudes and government policy about the Great Plains changed for several reasons.

One reason is that, in 1820, white Americans knew very little about the Great Plains – and what they knew is shown in Source A. Many believed it was useless, and so were happy to leave this land for the Plains' Indians – it was even called the 'Great American Desert' because of its poor land and harsh climate. This is why in 1832 all land west of the Mississippi River was seen as Indian Territory. At that point, there was enough good land in the east for the population of the USA. However, after the end of the American Civil War in 1865, many people were keen to start a new life. That is why advertisements such as Source B were produced in the 1860s and 1870s, showing would-be settlers how good life was on the Plains.

Another reason for the change in attitudes is to do with the expansion of the USA after it became independent in 1783. By 1820, it had expanded from the east coast to include the area known as Louisiana (the Great Plains). However, in the 1840s, it got new territories through war and agreements and many people, then began to speak of 'Manifest Destiny'. This was the idea of one huge country stretching from the Atlantic coast in the east to the Pacific Ocean in the west. Settling large numbers of people on the Plains was one way of doing this – hence the 1868 poster to encourage it.

Examiner's comment

Laura has made a good start in her first **introductory paragraph**, which shows a clear focus on what the question is asking her to do. She has also wisely noted – and commented – on the fact that the dates of the two sources are different.

Her **second paragraph** identifies and then *explains* one reason – as well as referring to the two dates, she has provided relevant and precise own knowledge to support her point. If she had written no more, she would have got into Level 4 and so scored almost full marks.

Her **final paragraph** identifies and explains a second reason. This is again supported by good own knowledge, and so gets her Level 5 and full marks.

2 Understanding exam language

You will face different types of questions in your exam on the American West, each of which has a different mark scheme for examiners to apply to your answers. Understanding the language of the exam questions will help you make sure you use the right skills for each type of question and so get the top marks. The typical questions below have words/marks written in different colours to help you focus on the clues and understand the language of the exam. Although the real exam paper will NOT have this, you can use different highlighters as you read through the questions to help you focus on the various aspects.

In the first part of your exam, you have to answer **three** compulsory source-based questions – BUT remember that these source-based questions also require you to use your own knowledge in order to interpret and evaluate the sources, and to *explain* your answer.

Types of questions

Sources

Source comparison and explanation

A typical question would be: Study Sources A and B. Why do these sources show such different attitudes to cattle ranching on the Great Plains? Use the sources and your own knowledge to explain your answer. **[7 marks]**

There are three sets of clues/pointers here provided by the principal examiner to help you produce a high-scoring question:

- References to the sources (written in red in the question above) are reminding you to make sure you use BOTH sources AND compare them for content/NOP (Nature/Origin/Purpose).
- The reference to own knowledge (in green) is a reminder to add some specific facts when trying to explain why the attitudes are different.
- The mark (in blue) is a rough indication as to how much to write – with such questions, ALWAYS try to give TWO explained reasons.

Source utility

A typical question would be: Study Source C. How useful is this source for telling you about the warfare practised by the Plains' Indians? Use the source and your own knowledge to explain your answer. **[6 marks]**

The clues here are:

- The words written in red are to make sure you do use the source – AND refer to the correct one.
- The word written in yellow is to remind you that you are supposed to be considering how useful the source is AND is not – so make sure the word 'useful' appears in your answer somewhere.
- The green text is a reminder to use some specific own knowledge.
- The mark (in blue) suggests you need to give SEVERAL reasons why you think the source is and is not useful – one explained/supported reason will not get you the full marks.

Making inferences from a source

A typical question would be: Study Source D. Were homesteaders pleased to be living in houses like the one shown in Source D? Use the source and your own knowledge to explain your answer. **[7 marks]**

The clues here are:

- The words written in red are to make sure you do make inferences from the source – AND refer to the correct one. This ISN'T just an own knowledge question.
- The green text is a reminder to use some specific own knowledge to add to what the source does and doesn't show.
- The mark (in blue) suggests you need to give SEVERAL reasons why you think homesteaders were/were not happy with such houses.

In the second part of your exam, you have to answer one out of two knowledge-based questions – each question has three parts.

Own knowledge

Description

A typical question would be: Describe briefly the main religious beliefs of the Plains Indians. **[5 marks]**

The clues here are:

- The word written in yellow is telling you to do more than just list/identify several religious beliefs – what is needed is some precise own knowledge to describe/explain these beliefs in some detail.
- The green text is telling you what you SHOULD be writing about – so don't write about their attitudes to warfare or hunting.
- The mark (in blue) suggests you need to describe/explain more than one belief.

Explanation

A typical question would be: Explain why the Mormons faced many [illegible] leadership. **[7 marks]**

The clues here are:

- The word highlighted in yellow is telling you to do more than just list/identify several reasons why they faced difficulties – what is needed is some precise own knowledge to explain why they had these difficulties.
- The green text is telling you what you SHOULD be writing about – so don't write about their development of Salt Lake City.
- The mark (in blue) suggests you need to explain more than one specific and supported reason.

Explanation and judgement

A typical question would be: Which was the most important reason for the [illegible] on the Great Plains in the late 1880s: bad weather or the growth of huge [illegible] Explain your answer. **[8 marks]**

The clues here are:

- The words written in yellow are telling you to do more than just add some precise own knowledge about one of these factors – you have to give specific facts and reasons about why BOTH these factors were important, AND make a judgement about whether you think one is MORE important than the other. If you fail to do this last aspect, you will NOT get full marks.
- The green text is telling you what TWO aspects you SHOULD be writing about – so don't write about other factors.
- The mark (in blue) suggests you need to use good own knowledge to explain your views about BOTH these factors.

3 Exam tips

- When dealing with questions that involve sources, make sure you look at – and use – the information provided about the sources by the principal examiner. The dates, details of who wrote it, their position, etc. are all there to help you give a top level answer.
- Don't just rewrite or describe what a source says, and think this is sufficient for an answer. The examiner will be expecting you to use the information as part of your answer, or to make an inference about what the source shows or doesn't show.
- Remember – for all the different types of questions you will answer DON'T just describe something: use your knowledge to explain. Also, add specific/precise information from your own knowledge – general/vague bits of own knowledge will not get you very far.
- Finally, time trouble is not uncommon – so make sure you roughly allocate your time to questions according to the marks available. Working out rough plans in brief BEFORE you attempt ANY writing will help you properly understand what each question is asking you to do, and so help you answer questions correctly – it will also give you something to jot down quickly if you do get into time trouble at the end because examiners may be able to give you a little credit for an incomplete answer.

4 Planning and structuring an answer

Now try to plan and then write an answer to a typical exam question. Before you do this, look through the tips and advice given below:

Source A

An engraving showing buffalo being shot from a train by white Americans. Railroad companies advertised hunting excursions in the late 1860s.

Exam**Café**

CHAPTER 4

The struggle for control of the central and southern Great Plains, 1860–90

EXAM QUESTION

Study Source A. How useful is this source in telling us about the reason why conflict broke out on the southern Plains after 1874? Use the source and your own knowledge to explain your answer.

[6 marks]

Examiner's tips

Skills

- Remember – with questions like this, you MUST use both the source AND your own knowledge if you want to get full marks.
- Also – make sure you show how the source is AND is not useful.
- Don't just identify and explain one reason – the highest level in the mark scheme for this type of question is reserved for those who give SEVERAL different reasons about why the source is and is not useful.

RELEVANT KNOWLEDGE

The Great Plains' Massacre – Wholesale slaughter of the buffalo on the southern Plains: the role of the US government and reasons for this; the growing impact of settlers, the railroads, and hunting buffalo for sport and profit; and the impact on the Plains' Indians.

Problems with the Fort Laramie Treaty after 1851 – Problems in the new reservations: corrupt government agents, lack of food, poor land for crops, pressures to adopt aspects of white American culture and religion; Indian chiefs did not have full control of all the tribes and bands; many younger chiefs objected to the restrictions.

Relevant knowledge

Growing tensions and conflicts in the 1860s – Breaches of the 1851 Treaty: large numbers of miners and settlers began to move into these Native American areas; new Treaty of Fort Lyon (aka Fort Wise) in 1861 (the Cheyenne and Arapaho chiefs agreed to give up their 1851 reservations in return for one at Sand Creek, Colorado); attacks on whites in 1861–64 by Cheyenne warriors leaving the new reservation; the Sand Creek Massacre; the Medicine Lodge Creek Treaty, 1867; the 'winter campaign' of 1868; the 'Battle' of Washita; the Fort Cobb Treaty, 1869.

The Fort Laramie Treaty, 1851 – Main points of this treaty: promised the Plains' Indians reservations for each nation, and said that no whites would be allowed to enter them or settle on them; the Plains' Indian chiefs promised to allow settlers to pass through Kansas and Nebraska, and to give up the previously agreed right of unlimited access to the Great Plains.

Now that you've worked through the tips and advice, look carefully at the answer below and the Examiner's comments:

Jennifer's answer	Examiner's comment
This source is quite useful for telling us why conflict broke out on the southern Plains after 1874. This is because it shows white passengers shooting buffalo from a train. This became a popular sporting trip as the railroads spread across the Plains, as the buffalo were easy to hunt. Railway companies issued special advertisements to encourage this. However, the railways and the hunting for sport had a serious impact on the buffalo herds, which were already in decline for other reasons. As the Plains' Indians depended on the buffalo for their traditional way of life, this disruption and destruction caused growing resentment amongst the various Indian nations living on the central and southern Plains. It was this resentment which led to more fighting, as the Plains' Indians tried to fight a 'war to save the buffalo'.	Jennifer has made a good start in her first introductory paragraph, which shows a clear focus on what the question is asking her to do – i.e. *comment* on the usefulness of a source. She then goes on to *explain* one reason why the source is useful, supporting her comments by making clear references to the source AND using some precise own knowledge. This gets her into Level 4 and she scores 4 marks.

Improve this answer

Look at the relevant Lessons in Chapter 4, and then try to write down what else this candidate should have done in order to get top marks.

And finally...

GOOD LUCK!

Glossary

American Civil War – this was the civil war fought from 1860–65, between the Northern states (Unionists) and the Southern states (Confederates) in large part over the issue of slavery.

Atrocities – events in which large numbers of people are killed, and/or acts such as torture, mutilation and rape are committed – usually on non-combatants – by military/armed forces.

Cattle barons – those cattle ranchers who managed to gain control of huge tracts of land, with great herds of cattle. They sometimes used their wealth and power against smaller ranches.

Cattle rustling – stealing other people's cattle. Rustlers were sometimes known as **jayhawks**.

Chips – the dried dung of buffalo, which is then used as fuel, for cooking and heating.

Claim-jumping – the act of taking over another miner's claim or stake to a gold mine, or someone else's land.

Congress – the governing and law-making body of the USA.

Counting coup – the act where Indian warriors struck an enemy with a coup stick – it usually brought more honour or status than killing him.

Demobilised soldiers – soldiers released from service (and so often made unemployed) once a war is over.

Dog Soldiers – a special hunter/warrior society of the Cheyenne nation. Most Native American nations had these special warrior societies.

Exposure – the Native American practice/custom where elderly/infirm members of a band left their family and village to go off and die, so that they were not a hindrance/burden to the band or tribe.

Forty-Niners – those miners who took part in the Great California Gold Rush of 1849.

Genocide – the destruction, or attempted destruction, of an entire group or race of people, such as the attempt by the Nazis to wipe out all Jewish people in Europe.

Great American Desert – this was what many whites at first called the Great Plains – its hot summers, cold winters and lack of water and trees made them think it was worthless, so they were prepared to let the Plains' Indians keep the land.

Great Plains' Massacre – the deliberate attempt, encouraged by the US government, to hunt the buffalo on the Plains to extinction, so the Indians would be forced to give up hunting, and to live on reservations instead.

Ghost Dance – the religious dance associated with Wovoka who, following a vision in 1889, said that dancing it would make the whites go away, and all the dead Indians and buffalo come back to life.

Homesteaders – those settlers who gained land on the Plains for their homes and farms (homesteads); particularly applied to those who moved onto the Plains after the 1862 Homestead Act.

Indian agents – white people appointed by the US government to run the reservations in which the Plains' Indians were to live. They were mostly unsympathetic to the culture, beliefs and problems faced by the Indians, and were often corrupt.

Indian Territory – the area/areas of land which successive US governments said the Indians could keep – this land was not to be settled on or mined, and sometimes not even crossed, by whites. The size of this land was continually reduced, until Indians were left with much smaller reservations.

Jayhawks – another name for cattle rustlers.

Lasso – the rope used by cowboys to catch cattle for branding etc.

Lynching – the unlawful hanging by a mob of an accused person, usually without a proper trial.

Manifest Destiny – after 1845 used to justify what came to be seen as the USA's 'God-given mission' to settle and control all lands in the west, including those that had previously been promised to the Native Americans.

Migration – the act of moving (migrating) from one area to another to make a new and hopefully better life. A migrant is a person who migrates.

Monogamous – marriage based on having just one husband/wife at a time.

Mormons – members of the Church of Jesus Christ of Latter-Day Saints, founded by Joseph Smith in 1830.

Mountain men – the first European men who hunted in the Plains and beyond, before the great move West. Many of them later helped establish ('blaze') trails for the wagon trains of early pioneers.

Nations and tribes – American Indians lived in bands and tribes, which were subdivisions of separate 'nations' with their own, often quite different, languages, beliefs, customs and ways of life. In the east of America, they included the Hurons, the Mohicans and the Iroquois.

Native Americans – the modern term for American Indians who lived – and still live – in North America. The Native Americans were usually referred to by early Europeans settlers as 'Indians' or 'Red Indians' – this is because Columbus thought he had landed in the Indies in 1492 when, in fact, it was the Americas.

Nomadic – a way of life which, instead of being settled in one place (like a farmer), is based on hunting and therefore the need to move so that herds of animals can be followed.

Open range – cattle ranching took place over huge areas of land: often between 7500 and 250,000 hectares, and sometimes much more. There were no fences, so cattle and people were free to roam.

Permanent Indian Frontier (PIF) – the frontier between the USA and American Indian lands, agreed by the US government with Indian chiefs: all land west of the Mississippi River was to be given to the Indians. This was to be 'permanent', and the government said that non-Indians would not be allowed to settle there.

Pioneers – the name given to the early migrants/settlers who moved West to the Great Plains and beyond.

Polygamy – a system of marriage based on having two or more wives/ husbands at the same time.

Posse – a group of people 'sworn in' by a law officer (e.g. sheriff, marshal) in the West to track down/arrest suspected/actual criminals.

Pull factors – factors that had a positive attraction, leading people to move West.

Push factors – factors that forced people to move away from the East.

Railhead towns – towns where the railways had reached. The most important ones were Sedalia, Missouri, Abilene and Dodge City in Kansas. They grew quickly, and were often notorious for their lawlessness.

Ranchers – people who owned or managed a cattle ranch.

Range wars – the serious fighting/armed conflicts which broke out in the West at times, between big and small cattle ranchers, or between cattle ranchers and homesteaders or sheep farmers.

Refugees – people fleeing/escaping from areas of bad/violent situations to new areas, in search of safety/peace.

Renegades – those Plains' Indians who refused to accept agreements made by their chiefs, or who left the reservations to go hunting.

Reservations – areas of land set aside for Native Americans by the US government. In the 19th century, US governments tried to force Indians to live on these areas, which were much smaller than their traditional hunting grounds on the Great Plains.

Saloon – a place selling alcohol, with added attractions such as music, dancing and gambling.

Scalp – the hair and skin, removed from the head of the dead or dying enemy, as a trophy of war/indication of bravery in warfare. Both Native Americans and Europeans engaged in this practice.

Settlers – people who travelled West to settle on the land of the Great Plains and establish farms.

Shaman – a holy man with special powers, known to the Europeans as a medicine man. Each tribe had a shaman. They also gave advice to chiefs and the councils of elders. They often had strong personalities and great wisdom. The word shaman comes from the fact that they carried herbs.

Shanty towns – settlements/towns of poorly built houses/shacks, normally used as temporary accommodation (e.g. the early mining camps, or for those building the railways).

Stampede – when cattle, terrified by a noise or event, rush off in all directions. Many were lost, killed or so badly injured that they had to be shot.

Sweat lodge – a low hide-covered hut, used by Native Americans in religious/health rituals. Water was thrown onto fires to produce steam – this was meant to 'purify' someone (perhaps so they could receive a 'vision') or to cure an illness.

Texas Longhorns – cattle that resulted from interbreeding between Criollos (the Spanish cattle of Texas) and other breeds, like the English Longhorns. The early cattle trade began in south Texas. At first, cowboys drove millions of cattle across the Great Plains on the Long Drive. Later, cattle ranches were set up, but the cattle boom ended in the late 1880s.

Tipi (also known as tepees or lodges) – large conical tents made from 10 to 20 buffalo hides sewn together in a semicircular cover and spread over about 25 wooden lodge poles, depending on the size of tipi required.

Total war – this did not mean the deliberate killing of women and children but did mean waging war against the whole population. This was to be done by destroying all the animals, food, shelter and clothing of the Indians. They would then be faced with two choices – starvation or surrender and a return to their reservations.

Trailblazers – the first people to find and set up the best routes or trails for the early pioneers/settlers moving West (often in wagon trains) – many of these 'trailblazers' had previously been 'mountain men'.

Transcontinental railroad – the idea of a railway system going across the USA, to link the Atlantic coast in the East to the Pacific coast in the West.

Travois – a Native American transportation sledge, made from tipi poles and hides, used to carry goods/possessions from one camp to the next.

Vacqueros – cowboys (from the Spanish word for cow).

Vigilantes – ordinary people who deal with suspected lawbreakers themselves, without waiting for official law-enforcement officers or agencies to take action. They were quite common in the West, especially in the early days.

Wagon train – a number of pioneer/settler wagons travelling West into and across the Plains together, for added safety/security.

West of the 95th meridian – the PIF was later moved west, along the 95th meridian, the line of longitude running north–south.

Index